GERMAN LITERATURE IN THE SIXTEENTH AND SEVENTEENTH CENTURIES

GERMAN LITERATURE IN THE SIXTEENTH AND SEVENTEENTH CENTURIES

RENAISSANCE— REFORMATION— BAROQUE

By

ROY PASCAL
M.A., Litt.D.

Professor of German,
University of Birmingham

WITH A CHAPTER ON
GERMAN PAINTING
BY
HANNAH PRIEBSCH CLOSS

GREENWOOD PRESS, PUBLISHERS
WESTPORT, CONNECTICUT

Library of Congress Cataloging in Publication Data

Pascal, Roy, 1904-
  German literature in the sixteenth and seventeenth
centuries.

  Reprint of the 1968 ed. published by the Cresset
Press, London, which was issued as v. 2 of Introduc-
tions to German literature.
  Bibliography: p.
  Includes index.
  1. German literature--Early modern, 1500-1700--
History and criticism. 2. German literature--Early
modern, 1500-1700--Bio-bibliography. I. Closs,
Hannah Priebsch, joint author. II. Title.
III. Series: Introductions to German literature ;
v. 2.
[PT238.P3 1979]   830'.9'004   79-9993
ISBN 0-313-21461-1

Reprinted with the permission of Barrie & Jenkins

First published 1968 by The Cresset Press, London

Reprinted in 1979 by Greenwood Press, Inc.
51 Riverside Avenue, Westport, CT 06880

Printed in the United States of America

10 9 8 7 6 5 4 3 2 1

CONTENTS

THE GENERAL EDITOR'S PREFACE

Literature must be seen in relationship to life in general. Any attempt to give a comprehensive account of literature must include at least some discussion and evaluation of such subjects as architecture, painting, sculpture, and music as well as economics, history, sociology, science, and philosophy. It is imperative to see not only the past but also the present in its proper perspective. These are the considerations that underlie the conception of *Introductions to German Literature*.

The history of the past and its literature can be of essential value if (as is particularly the case in German) it reveals characteristic trends of expression, e.g. in his *History of Modern Germany* (London, 1965) Hajo Holborn points to the 'lasting effects' of the High Middle Ages on Germany: (*a*) the creation of a national consciousness, and (*b*) the establishment of the dependence of the princes on the estates (of prelates and nobility) and the rising power of the cities, finally (*c*) the creation of a secular culture. Medieval roots or references can still be traced in literary images of our age.

In his cycle of finely woven poems, *Die Bücher der Hirten- und Preisgedichte, Der Sagen und Sänge und Der Hängenden Gärten* (1895), Stefan George endeavours to recapture the spirit of Greek serenity and the spirit of the Middle Ages: e.g. themes like the vigil, Parzival mood, the young knight, the dawn-song. Yet in moulding his historical and cultural heritage into timeless utterances Stefan George projected into the Middle Ages some meanings which are not to be found there. His poem *Die Gräber in Speier* (*Der Siebente Ring*, 1907) recalls the contests between Pope and Emperor and conjures up amongst the illustrious names of German rulers the memory of 'the greatest of the Fredericks': Emperor Frederick II, the Stupor Mundi:

Zum Karlen- und Ottonen-plan im blick
Des Morgenlandes ungeheuren traum.
Weisheit der Kabbala und Römerwürde
Feste von Agrigent und Selinunt.

... His gaze unites the plans of Ottos, Karls,
With his own boundless dreams of the Levant,
Wisdom of Cabalists and Rome's decorum,
Banquets of Akragas and Selinus.
[tr. by Olga Marx and Ernst Morwitz, 1949,
Univ. of North Carolina Studies]

Another incisive effect on the history, thought and poetry of modern Europe, and particularly Germany, was created by the Crusades. In the eleventh century Pope Gregory VII (Hildebrand) had summoned Christendom to fight the paynim, thereby enabling his successors to weld all the chivalric ideals and ambitions of the West into *one* formidable weapon and place it into the hands of the church where it was soon found useful for purposes other than that of subduing Islam. Ruthless greed for the earthly 'golden' Jerusalem besmirched the Crusaders' cause. The capture and desecration of Constantinople (1204), the Byzantine capital of Christian civilization for centuries and the guardian of priceless ancient Greek art treasures, proved an outward victory which brought dishonour to the spirit of European Christianity. According to Sir Steven Runciman (*The History of the Crusades*, 3 vols, 1954/5, Penguin 1965) the Venetians seem to have been the 'most rapacious ones', but the French and the Flemings, too, destroyed much. 'There was never a greater crime against humanity than the Fourth Crusade.' Although the Crusades in the end led to a vast fiasco from which the Moslem power emerged triumphant, they had brought about the creation of three military orders: the Templars, the Hospitallers of St John, and the Teutonic Knights. In 1235 these Deutschordensritter were directed by Emperor Frederick II to the Baltic regions where they conquered and christianized the pagan Pruzzen (Prussians), but this domination of the

Northern Slavs began to weaken in the fifteenth century and has, in our time, been completely reversed by the events of the two World Wars.

The above examples, quite apart from the impact of the age of Reformation and Humanism, will amply demonstrate how past and present are inextricably interlinked in our contemporary scene. An interpretation of the totality of German literature cannot ignore the changing milieu and the interrelationship between philosophy and economics, etc., of a special period, the religious, intellectual and social events at work in Germany and indeed in Western civilization as a whole: e.g. the effect of the Thirty Years War on German literature, thought and society; nor can it ignore mysticism, Leibniz's monadology, the influence of Baroque art and music, the French Revolution and the Wars of Liberation, Hegel's concept of the State as the embodiment of national spirit which is subject to the laws of absolute universal history, Ludwig Feuerbach's and Karl Marx's materialistic philosophy, National Socialism, Communism, and the many other physical and intellectual forces which are reflected in the mirror of present-day Germany, Austria and German-speaking Switzerland. Not least of these is the influence of World-Literature (a term coined by Goethe in *Art and Antiquity*, 6.1.1827), from the Bible, Homer, Dante, Shakespeare, Cervantes and Racine to Sanscrit, Russian, Chinese and other literatures. From earliest times German literature has been heavily influenced by foreign literatures, indeed, some of the earliest Old High German works were glosses. We trust that all these interrelationships will be highlighted by the extensive bibliographies as well as the discussion.

The arrangement of material in these four volumes has been modelled on that in the *Introductions to English Literature*, edited by Professor Bonamy Dobrée. Apart from vol. I, where more space is allowed to the general introductory section covering seven centuries of early German literature, about one-third of each book is taken up by the Introduction dealing with the literature of the period in all its genres and forms, connecting it with the other arts and with religious, social, philosophical and political movements of the time. The remaining two-thirds of each book provide a 'Student's Guide': a general reading list of recommended books dealing with the period as a whole, and also a critically selected bibliography referring to the various categories of works under discussion: poetry, fiction, drama, chronicles, literary periods, etc., and individual authors and their texts. Historical data, references to leading journals, biography and recent scholarly criticism are also included. In view of the vast amount of research published in Europe and America, only the most important relevant studies can be listed in the bibliographies. Naturally, British research is stressed. Wherever possible, modern translations of German literature into English are mentioned, too. The final choice in the selection of the whole material is left to the discretion and considered judgement of each contributor.

The presentation of the *Introductions to German Literature* in four volumes (instead of five) necessitated a drastic restriction of space allotted to the literary works, genres and movements under discussion: vol. I roughly covers the period 800–1500: Old High German, Middle High German Minnesang, Epics and Romances, the Mystics and movements leading up to the Reformation; vol. II the period: 1500–1700: Reformation, Renaissance, Baroque, and Aufklärung trends; vol. III is dedicated to the two centuries mainly under Goethe's influence: Enlightenment, Storm and Stress, Classicism, Romanticism, Jungdeutschland, Poetischer Realismus, up to Nietzsche; vol. IV deals with German literature from Nietzsche to our day, i.e. fiction from Thomas Mann, Hermann Hesse, F. Kafka, R. Musil, A. Döblin, etc., up to H. Böll and G. Grass; drama from Gerhart Hauptmann, F. Wedekind, F. Bruckner, G. Kaiser, etc., up to B. Brecht, C. Zuckmayer, M. Frisch, F. Dürrenmatt, R. Hochhuth, P. Weiss and contemporary Hörspiel authors; poetry from Arno Holz, R. Dehmel, Chr. Morgenstern, R. M. Rilke,

Stefan George, H. von Hofmannsthal, G. Trakl, to G. Benn, R. Hagelstange, G. Eich, H. M. Enzensberger, and P. Celan, etc. We felt justified in devoting a whole volume to the artistic achievements in German literature of our age.

A work of art, such as *Tristan, Parzival, Faust,* states UNIVERSAL TRUTHS, as does scientific research. But there is a fundamental difference between aesthetic and scientific TRUTHS. If on 4 October 1957 the first Sputnik had not been launched into space, sooner or later it would have been done by the force of technological progress. The same argument would make nonsense in creative art. Without Beethoven we would never have had the *Ninth Symphony* (whatever the human and scientific progress), without Shakespeare no *Hamlet* or *Lear,* without Mozart no *Don Giovanni.* These creations are no Homunculus-productions but aesthetic truths and human self-revelations which vindicate Hölderlin's proud word at the end of his *Empedokles*-tragedy where Empedokles says to Pausanias: 'What are the gods and their spirit if I do not proclaim them?' a phrase which reminds one of the mystic expression by Angelus Silesius (Johann Scheffler): 'God does not live without me: I know that without me God cannot live an instant'.

It is through language that the poet proclaims. Language is the key to literature. Through language we reach the reservoir of man's inmost resources; language preserves the imperishable treasures of the human mind and the human heart; language guarantees the continuity of man's spiritual existence. Ludwig Wittgenstein in his *Tractatus Logico-Philosophicus* remarks: 'The barriers of my language are the barriers of my world'.

In fact, every literary creation is translation, i.e. translation of experience into language. In his *Fragmente* the German Romantic Novalis pointed to the importance of translation. He differentiates between three kinds of translation: grammatical (i.e. literal renderings from one medium into another), interpretative (creative), mythical and symbolical in the highest sense. Novalis saw the whole universe as a symbol: 'Die Welt ist ein Universaltropus des Geistes' (The world is a universal trope of the spirit). To Novalis, Greek mythology is a 'translation' of a national religion into art. In a similar way the modern cult of the Madonna (mother, virgin, and goddess) is seen as the translation of a myth into a symbol.

Much has in the past years been written about the so-called 'willing suspension of disbelief'. In our view, it is not at all necessary to apply this strictly as a condition to art-appreciation. It is quite possible (cf. Bernard G. Heyl in *New Bearings in Esthetics and Art Criticism. A Study in Semantics and Evaluation*, Yale University Press, 1943, 1957 fourth printing) for an atheist to appreciate Rembrandt's *Christ's Supper* (Christus in Emmaus) intuitively. Moreover, we are not asked, as T. S. Eliot has rightly pointed out, to share Dante's theological creed in order to grasp the poetic greatness of the *Divina Commedia*. One could argue similarly about the revolutionary epic *The Twelve* (1918) by the Russian poet Alexander Blok: the twelve soldiers of the Red Army are not heroes; they are bestial, yet guided by a higher destiny. Christ Himself marches with them. Even Nature is symbolical: 'The wind strolls, the snow dances, / A party of twelve men advances.' Likewise, W. B. Yeats's *Sailing to Byzantium* (1927) reveals a vision of a spiritual empire to the reader without necessarily a 'willing suspension of disbelief': 'That is no country for old men . . . caught in that sensual music all neglect / monuments of unageing intellect . . . gather me / into the artifice of eternity'.

H. von Hofmannsthal mocks at the seekers of profundity, whom he contrasts with Goethe: 'The important Germans seem to swim continuously under water; only Goethe, like a lonely dolphin, moves along the shining surface' (*Tagebuch-Aufzeichnungen*). Goethe is, of course, not the only exception. Where surface and depth, the outward and inward worlds merge into an artistic unity, perfection is achieved, e.g. in

Goethe's *Mailied*, Mörike's *Mein Fluss*, Rilke's *Die Flamingos*, George's *Teppich des Lebens*, or Heinrich von Morungen's:

> Ich hôrt ûf der heide
> lûte stimme und süezen sanc.
> Dâ von wart ich beide
> fröiden rîch und trûrens kranc . . .
>
> I heard in the field
> a clear voice, a sweet song,
> whence my sorrow grew light,
> and my joy waxed strong.
> [tr. by Margaret F. Richey in *Medieval German Lyrics*, 1958]

to mention at random just a few examples, which express poetic truths.

W. B. Yeats is right when he states: 'We can create truths, but we cannot scientifically "know" them;' and Saint-Exupéry says: 'We do not discover truth, we create it.'

The poets, however, who are over-anxious to capture the *Zeitgeist* by using up-to-date scientific nomenclature at any price, are far away from poetic truth. The ineffectiveness of mere actuality is obvious. Neon-lights instead of oil-lamps do not make the poem more original! There is no shortage of topical events: the opening of the first railroad from Nürnberg to Fürth in December 1835 and the first railway journey from Leipzig to Dresden a few years later caused sensation and aroused heated controversies about the 'iron beast'. To Jungdeutschland the locomotive became the symbol of a new era which supplanted Romanticism. Heine's attitude to the 'iron beast' (das eiserne Vieh) is expressed in his *Pferd und Esel*: the horse and the donkey look with melancholy at the new monster. The noble horse is obviously the loser, but the poor ass will survive.

A glance at later versifications of technical achievements (mostly by the time of Impressionism and Expressionism) will prove the outdatedness of such literary effusions. Here

are some German examples (apart from many other ones
such as W. Whitman's poem on a locomotive in the winter):
D. v. Liliencron: *Die neue Eisenbahn,* G. Falke: *Im Schnell-
zug,* Gerrit Engelke: *Lokomotive* and *Auf der Strassenbahn,*
H. Lersch: *Die Lokomotive,* Otto zur Linde: *Bau der Untergrund-
bahn,* R. Dehmel: *Drohende Aussicht,* H. Carossa: *Der Eisen-
wagen,* Günter Eich: *D-Zug München-Frankfurt,* A. Petzold:
Der Werkbahnhof and *Bergfahrt,* G. Kölwel: *Bahnfahrt durch den
Vorfrühling,* A. Wolfenstein: *Fahrt,* René Schickele: *Ballade
von unserer Lieben Frau im Coupé,* E. Stadler: *Fahrt über die
Kölner Rheinbrücke bei Nacht,* G. Benn: *D-Zug,* Th. Fontane:
Die Brücke am Tay. With a few exceptions, e.g. Fontane's and
Benn's poems, almost all the above poems are either forgotten
now or live on as specimens of outdatedness. Landscape is
still a dominant factor in many of those poems. In our epoch
of scientific laboratories and engineering triumphs, the
natural order and humanistic scale of Nature have disap-
peared from ultra-modern works in favour of an intellectual
pattern which claims to be impersonal but also anti-historical
and anti-ptolemaic.

It would be misleading to assess twentieth-century literature by measuring it solely with the standards of Goethe's
concept of organic form and universality of outlook. Instead
of totality we now have fragmentation, accompanied by signs
of a temporary retreat from language, cf. *The Retreat from the
Word* (G. Steiner, *Listener,* 1960). The indisputable fact
remains that the 'universal' image is shattered. In his *Second
Coming* W. B. Yeats, surely the most inspired European poet
of our age, expresses the present dilemma:

> The falcon does not hear the falconer,
> things fall apart; the centre cannot hold . . .

Instead of the 'total' view of poetic vision we are offered
pieces of images, like pictures in a kaleidoscope, by rotation
of the metal tube. The self-sufficient artist's ego is dethroned
or absorbed into the web of bewildering patterns of events,
ambitions and manifestations.

Basically, the shattering of the Goethean 'universal' images signifies not only the loss of a once generally accepted world-order, but it also triumphantly declares the supremacy of linguistic artistry over an apparently chaotic fragmentation of the universe. Yet, we should remember that in the creative literature of a nation the resources for renewal are inexhaustible. It is therefore unrealistic to speak of a complete 'tabula rasa', however strongly such a mood must have been felt under the stress of Germany's apocalyptic downfall in and after the last War. But we heartily welcome bold experiments which emerged on the German literary scene since 1945.

To *this* present our thoughts and efforts are directed. In *this* present lie the seeds of our future. Allowing for some variation of the theme, Gottfried's words (which actually refer to the community of the noble hearts, the 'edele herzen') in his 'Prologue' to *Tristan und Isolt* may lend expression to what is our deepest concern:

> ... dem lebene sî mîn leben ergeben,
> der werlt will ich gewerldet wesen,
> mit ir verderben oder genesen ...

> ... To this life my life be dedicated,
> To this world let me belong,
> With it to perish or be saved ...

In vol. I there was no room for the planned additional chapter on art or music, as the Introduction to Medieval German literature had to cover the vast material from Old High German to Middle High German and up to late medieval and transitional literature. But the Appendix to vol. II brings an essay on German Painting (up to the time of Baroque).

The crisis created by the breakdown of the medieval order of society and the struggle between Humanism and Reformation led to a recasting of man's attitude to life, which is reflected in the intellectual and artistic landscape of the new age.   A. CLOSS

I

THE POLITICAL SOCIETY

In decisive contrast to the emergence in France, England, and Spain of unified national states, Germany failed in this period to develop a central power and a political identity. The name and forms of the empire persisted, but the emperors, always the heads of the Habsburg dynasty, had like other German princes no more power than their hereditary dominions provided.

The Golden Bull of 1356 had undermined the emperor's authority without providing, in the council of the Electors or the Imperial Diet, a viable alternative. Despite various attempts at strengthening the central executive, the great feudal lords were strong enough to resist the growth of a central power; individually or through alliances, lands and cities could defend their privileges or assert their claims only by force; classes with weaker financial or military resources, like the Imperial Knights or the peasantry, steadily lost their rights. The larger states promoted and profited by this anarchy, but it favoured too, for a long period, the cities. Increasing greatly in size during the fourteenth and fifteenth centuries, and developing rapidly through technical crafts and trade, many cities were able to purchase charters of freedom from weak emperors and princes, and to enlarge their power through mercantile and military alliances the greatest of which was the Hansa. A vigorous and independent municipal life developed in Lübeck and Hamburg and other maritime cities, and in those on the great overland trade routes like Frankfurt, Leipzig, Nürnberg, Strassburg, Augsburg, and Basel. Great advances took place in commerce and banking, in mining, the metallurgical industries, and printing. In the sixteenth century, merchant houses like the

Fuggers and Welsers of Augsburg financed not only large industrial and commercial enterprises, but also the military campaigns of emperors and princes. But the German cities never grew into territorial states like the Italian, and in the struggles of the sixteenth and seventeenth centuries they increasingly succumbed to neighbouring princes, and lacked the political strength to maintain themselves against the foreign maritime states in the West and round the Baltic.

The reigns of the emperors Maximilian I (1495–1519) and Charles V (1519–56) form a decisive turning point. The sense of political crisis was widespread round 1500. Local warfare was making a mockery of law. The Swiss Confederacy broke away from the empire in 1499. Numerous risings occurred in many cities, where merchants and craftsmen asserted their right to share the privileges of government with the old patriciate, and there was continual unrest among the journeymen and labourers. The rapid development of a money economy, added to the rapacity of feudal lords, produced great distress among the peasantry, and a series of local risings culminated in the great Peasants' War of 1524–5 in which, along with the demand to restore traditional rights, there flamed up the revolutionary idea of an egalitarian peasant society directed against the supremacy of the cities as well as ecclesiastical and secular lords. In 1523 Sickingen led a revolt of Imperial Knights in a vain attempt to stem their economic and political decline.

In these circumstances, spasmodic efforts were made to guarantee internal peace and law, to create a representative imperial authority and army, supported by a common tax. Churchmen and humanists, representatives of the cities, religious reformers, spokesmen for the Imperial Knights and the peasantry, looked to the emperor to defend the common weal. But Maximilian was too concerned with establishing his precarious hold over his Habsburg inheritance, too much of an adventurer, to become the leader of the nation; and Charles, who ruled also over Spain, the Low Countries, and Naples, was continually distracted from inner-German affairs by conflicts with the French and the Turks. Above all, the larger German princes demonstrated on many occasions that they were determined to prevent the growth of a strong central authority. When Charles, at last asserting his power in the Schmalkaldic War (1546–50), was at the point of success, he was abandoned by Catholic as well as Protestant allies and forced to renounce the struggle.

The religious Reformation, which became a political issue when Luther's doctrines were condemned at the Diet of Worms in 1521, only intensified the political conflict between emperor and princes. Once Luther had placed the secular prince at the head of his reformed Church, Protestantism became an instrument of separatism; Catholicism likewise became a political interest. When in 1555 the Religious Peace of Augsburg sealed the right of the secular authorities to decide the religious observance of their subjects (*cujus regio ejus religio*), it asserted with it the political independence of the princes and established the principle of separatism for three centuries.

The separate states were of great variety, ranging from small estates to large states like Austria, Bavaria, Saxony, and Brandenburg, and including ecclesiastical principalities and free cities; the north, and many of the great cities, became predominantly Lutheran, the south remained Catholic, while some of the central states (Hessen, the Palatinate) adopted after 1555 the Reformed Church of Calvin. Despite all differences, however, one decisive trend took place. All these states were still feudal in structure, i.e. the power of the prince was hedged in by the traditional rights of their subjects, defended by provincial diets ('Landtage') and town councils. But by 1500 some of the stronger princes were turning the provincial diets into instruments for collecting taxes, and after 1555 centralized administrations were gradually established. Privy councils were set up, customary law and legal procedures gradually replaced by Roman law, schools and universities founded to provide the administrators, lawyers, doctors, clergy, and teachers required by the state.

Economic regulations were devised to strengthen the exchequer, and trade was controlled through excise and customs barriers. Some of the powerful cities like Nürnberg, Frankfurt, and Hamburg continued to expand, but even before the outbreak of the Thirty Years' War (1618) in many German cities the spirit of independence and enterprise was, with their prosperity, declining. As the Counter-Reformation gained strength, the expulsion of religious dissidents caused not only great misery and impoverishment, but also the destruction of local rights and institutions.

The terrible war that brought devastation to many parts of Germany and the destruction, largely through starvation and plague, of at least a third of the population, was from the beginning as much a political as a religious conflict. It began as a Habsburg war against Bohemian religious separatism which, through the election of the Protestant Frederick of the Palatinate to the throne of Bohemia, had taken a pronounced political form. For the Habsburgs, the positive result of the whole war was the strengthening of the central power in the hereditary dominions, of which the Counter-Reformation, which continued vigorously in Habsburg territories after the war, was an important instrument. Mixed religious-political motives dominated throughout, and interstate rivalries were such that at no time was there a simple alignment of Protestants versus Catholics. In the first phase, the imperial armies advanced successfully to the Baltic. The second phase opened with the participation of Gustavus Adolphus of Sweden, who sought to make himself the champion of Protestantism; but his intervention, which resulted in the Swedish acquisition of large German territories, left Brandenburg and Saxony suspicious and hesitant. With Gustavus Adolphus' death in 1632, Catholic France came to play a dominant part in the anti-Habsburg struggle, in alliance with Swedish and German Protestants, and the war became unambiguously a political struggle for territory, fought largely with foreign troops, Spanish, French, Swedish, not to speak of Croats, Poles, Italians. By the Treaty of Westphalia in 1648 large areas of the empire were annexed to France, Sweden became a German power, and Poland secured her claims over West Prussia. The German princes were now in fact independent, and the empire reduced to a name and a formality.

The violent oscillations of power during the war, the devastation, the creation of standing armies, greatly increased the power of the princes over their subjects and removed many of the hindrances to the development of the absolutist state. After the war, each prince could exert his power much more freely, managing his state as if it were his private property. The lesser nobility was weaned from its local independence and granted assured privileges as a class; it became the chief support of the princes, entrusted with the high offices of state. The educated middle class fulfilled the functions of an officialdom. A new courtly culture arose modelled on the absolutisms of France and Spain; and even the free cities reflected this trend. Some princes used their power and wealth for pomp and display, but many, like Karl Ludwig of the Palatinate and Ernst der Fromme of Gotha, pursued an energetic paternalistic policy, fostering new industries and trade, reforming education, offering asylum to Huguenots and Jews in order to promote prosperity. In principle the ruler was absolute and held power by 'divine right'; in practice the most successful recognized that their welfare was intimately dependent on the welfare of their subjects.

The Treaty of Westphalia did not put an end to the war in Germany, but changed its character. In the west, the latter part of the century is dominated by the conflict between France and Austria during which France conquered Loraine and Alsace and ravaged far into Germany. In the north-east, the Great Elector pursued, in alliance with France, the interests of Brandenburg, and succeeded in extending his dominions at the expense of Sweden. He more clearly than any other German ruler grasped the meaning of the collapse of the empire and the opportunities of his position; with the rise of Prussia a new era dawns in Germany.

In this period, German political theory reflects the confusions of rights and powers, the discrepancy between the emperor's titular and actual power, the differences between different regions and religions, the rival claims of traditional local rights and princely power, the differing attitudes and situation of the Churches. Lutherans denied any right of resistance to the secular ruler, appointed, as Luther affirmed, by God, but were puzzled by the problem of the authority of Catholic princes, especially of the Catholic emperor. Hippolitus a Lapide, a Protestant in Swedish service, the author of a violent attack on Habsburg pretensions, tried to restore in theory the authority of the effete Imperial Diet. On the other hand Althusius, reflecting the situation of the North German Protestant city-republics, could claim that government is the instrument of, and dependent on, city and provincial corporations. Catholic political thought was equally confused. There was little echo in Germany of that Jesuit doctrine, later condemned as heretical, that a misgoverning monarch might be deposed by the people, and German Catholics found it as difficult as Protestants to reconcile the authority of the emperor with that of the princes. In general, the growing independence of the absolutist princes was accompanied by the widespread acceptance of the doctrine of divine right, though, because of the rivalry of different authorities and the still lingering rights of cities and provincial diets, with no such consequence and ruthlessness as with Hobbes. Only towards the end of the seventeenth century were the confusions cleared up in the system of Pufendorf, whose thought, nurtured by his experience in Sweden and Brandenburg, built on that of Bodin, Grotius, and Locke. He recognized that the empire, in its present form a 'monster', was evolving into a federation of independent states, and, asserting the divine right of the separate rulers, yet demonstrated that the prince is the embodiment of a commonwealth and must observe the natural rights of man, that include security of life and property and within certain limits freedom of religious worship. Pufendorf's system, in its rationalistic method and its conclusions, inaugurates the Aufklärung.

The literary culture of the period moves within this political framework. Throughout it lacked a national centre, a cultural focus and hot-house, comparable with London or Paris. In the sixteenth century it remained a local and burgher culture, remarkably homogeneous in spite of differences between court and city, nobles and commoners, learned and craftsmen. Only the peasantry remains apart, and it is noticeable that the symbolic figure of the 'common man', traditionally a peasant, after the Peasants' War becomes an artisan. The Latin literature occasionally, in the poetry of a Celtis or a Johannes Secundus, shows a high degree of differentiated personal feeling and thought. The German writing is embedded in communal burgher life, public rather than private in character, lacking differentiation of personal psychology and subtlety of expression, often based on traditional popular forms. In the seventeenth century, social stratifications become much more marked. At many courts an aristocratic culture separates out, Italian, French, or Spanish in its forms and often in its language. At the other end of the scale, the culture of the craftsmen becomes deprived and coarse. The development of German culture is the work of the new class of university-trained officials and professional men, with wider intellectual horizons and broader responsibilities than tradesmen, and linked by their studies and interests in a network that transcends local and state frontiers. They are, as officials, clergymen, teachers, and academics, often closely connected with courts and dependent on princely patronage and favour, and much of their work is courtly in form and character; in it they pay homage to the 'Erden-Götter' who control the fortunes of states and live by other standards than the common man. It is remarkable that this feature is as marked in the cultural leaders of Free Cities like Nürnberg and Hamburg as it is among those in the service of princes, just as the incredulous horror at the execution of Charles I was shared by all writers, under whatever constitution they lived. But they are also conscious of their own dignity as an 'estate', as members of professions with social and moral responsibilities, and their work also establishes the dignity of their own way of life. Thus their literature displays a courtly artificiality and a rhetoric of utterance that is often painfully at variance with any reality of experience, but also demonstrates their consciousness of the dignity of their social class and a search for a greater individuality and wider range of personal experience than we find in the sixteenth century. This culture is called the Baroque. It begins to break up at the end of the seventeenth century when this middle class begins to free itself from the exaggerated deference towards courts and aristocracy, from the spurious self-exaltation of rhetoric, and slowly gains confidence in the values of its own way of life.

II

INTELLECTUAL AND RELIGIOUS LIFE

THE culture of the sixteenth century is centred in the cities
and reflects in its intellectual and spiritual range the strong
communal spirit, the enterprise and independence of the
burghers. There is no distinctive court culture and no sharp
division between men of learning and the practical professions, between art and craftsmanship. Artists like Grünewald, Riemenschneider, Dürer, Cranach, Peter Vischer, remained burgher artists even when they worked for princes,
churches, or monasteries; the musicians of the imperial court,
Heinrich Isaak, Heinrich Finck, Ludwig Senfl often used
popular melodies for their new polyphonic settings, and
through publication addressed their work to the burghers.
Just as Dürer, Vischer, and Holbein gained an enduring
European reputation, not paralleled by other German artists
till the twentieth century, so also with German writers. They
produced a remarkable series of works that gained immense
popularity in Europe for many generations, and that created
symbolic figures of universal appeal—Brant's *Ship of Fools*,
Reynard the Fox, Till Eulenspiegel, Fortunatus, Grobianus,
Dr Faustus, the *Lalebuch*. Works of such wide and lasting
significance are utterly lacking in seventeenth-century Germany, indeed until the Goethe period.

Numerous documents testify to the growth of burgher self-
confidence. Many chronicles of cities, like those of Augsburg
and Nürnberg, were written in a spirit of local pride. The
table-talk of private life was published, of Erasmus, Peutinger
in Augsburg, above all Luther in Wittenberg, fascinating
records of the range of their interests and their personalities.
Comparable with the self-portraits of Dürer are Hutten's
Epistola vitae of 1518 and Pirckheimer's sketch of his life, and

the remarkable series of autobiographies that distinguish this century. They are still rather like chronicles, listing events rather than recording personal thoughts and feelings; but in the accounts of the priest Johann Butzbach, the knight Götz von Berlichingen, the craftsman Thomas Platter and the surgeon Felix Platter, the Stralsund burgomaster Bartholomäus Sastrow, as in Hans Sachs's *Summa all meiner gedicht* (1567), there is expressed the dignity and inner security of life in this burgher world, despite all suffering and hardships. This self-consciousness and security are lost in the seventeenth century.

The Printing Press

The consolidation of burgher culture was vastly stimulated by Gutenberg's invention of printing in Mainz in the 1440s. Presses were soon set up in other German cities and German craftsmen took the invention to Italy and France—Caxton learnt his trade in Cologne. At first older books were printed, but rapidly the press became used for new writings, for theological, philosophical and scientific works, for translations, pamphlets, broadsheets, for entertainment literature. As the process became fully mechanized, even to the mechanization of illustrations through the woodcut and later the engraving, the books became cheaper and available to a large number of readers. The book or pamphlet became the means to speak to a vast public.

In the early stages, the language used in German publications reflected the local dialect of the press and printer. As time passed, the printers saw the advantage of attracting the largest readership possible and contributed greatly towards the evolution of a common 'Schriftsprache'.

Within the space of two generations, a totally new and modern intellectual situation came into being. The scholar, instead of being dependent on rare libraries scattered over Europe, now had close at hand, often in his own possession, great resources which, with the aid of printers, he could rapidly enlarge. The Bible, the works of the Fathers of the Church, the Greek and Roman classics, the works of contemporaries, all lay before him; time and distance had suddenly shrunk. Opinions, so often enshrined hitherto in unassailable ecclesiastical decretals and dogmas, could now be tested by examination: hence came editions of the Greek New Testament, of Roman Law, of the sacred books of the Hebrews. The publication of Tacitus awoke a patriotic interest in the German past, and the news of the discovery of the New World by Columbus penetrated everywhere. It was possible to attempt to write the history of the world, to describe the world, as Sebastian Franck and Sebastian Münster did in works that were re-printed again and again. From the close cooperation of author, artist, and printer, magnificent works like Agricola's mineralogy or Bock's herbarium could extend knowledge in an unprecedented way. Books rapidly became indeed valuable objects to collect, and collections like those of Johann Jakob and Ulrich Fugger became later the basis of famous libraries. In the Thirty Years War, book collections were a prized booty.

Without the printed pamphlet and book, Luther's reform could scarcely have become a national movement; through books, schooling, especially higher education, received a new, solid, and extensive foundation. Martin Opitz's reform of literature was promoted through the accessibility of foreign literatures, and through the printed word his principles spread into all regions of Germany. Though the pamphlet and broadsheet were extensively used from early on, it was not until the late sixteenth century that newspapers began to appear as periodical publications to inform the public of recent events, and the first daily newspaper was published by Ritsch in Leipzig from 1660 to 1672. The troubled state of the country and the strict censorship held this development back. Thomasius's *Monatsgespräche* (1688–9) was the first periodical to attempt to form educated opinion, and the 'Moralische Wochenschriften' of the eighteenth century were its successors, through which the tastes and values of the middle class asserted themselves with a self-confidence that marks the emergence of a new cultural era.

Humanism

By 1500 the Church had become a mighty organization, the owner of vast territories and administrator of large revenues which were needed to support a great hierarchy centred in Rome, as well as to maintain its religious orders, monasteries and parish churches, its schools and charitable work. Just as it governed all universities and higher learning, so it controlled all thought and moral doctrine. But the practical objective of maintaining the Church was more and more taking precedence over its spiritual function. Obedience to ecclesiastical authority, superstitious practices, the all-too-frequent observance of Saints' Days, pilgrimages, the cult of shrines, money penances such as the purchase of indulgences as a substitute for contrition, all were encouraged since they increased the prestige, power and wealth of the Church. All over Europe, parish priests and members of religious orders, town councils and princes, sought for moral and practical reasons to check this abuse of religion. It was felt most acutely in Germany where there was no strong central power capable of checking the Church in the public interest and stemming the outflow of wealth. The movement known as Humanism, like the Reformation, was an attempt to restore a purer Christianity from within.

Humanism was by no means a purely German movement. It began in Italy and from Italy spread throughout Christendom. The German humanists nearly all studied or travelled in Italy and established close contact with colleagues in France, England and the Low Countries; Erasmus, the acknowledged leader of the Germans, was a Dutchman educated in the Low Countries, Paris and Italy, who lived in England before settling finally in Basel. Through the Italian humanists the Germans came into contact with the thought of the Ancients, of Aristotle, Plato, Cicero and Seneca, and were encouraged towards new ideals of moral and philosophical independence as well as towards criticism of traditional Church dogmas.

Humanism was a movement of scholars concerned primarily with the quality of personal life. Profoundly Christian, they saw Christ as the ideal moral personality and blended this ideal with the ideal of self-reliance they found in the Roman stoics. They found in classical Latin the best medium for the discussion and expression of this new philosophy, in contrast to the dog-latin of the Church and the as yet crude concreteness of German, and thus the study of Latin, the achievement of a Ciceronian eloquence, became a prime concern—men like Conrad Celtis and Sebastian Brant won fame as teachers of Latin, and Erasmus dazzled his contemporaries with his linguistic skill. Later, skill in Latin was to become an end in itself, a pedantry against which Opitz had to rebel, but in this early period it was a condition of clear thinking and rational discussion.

But Humanism, though a movement of a small élite, was not divorced from the main concerns of public life. All those beliefs and practices that were hostile to a truly religious and moral life were sharply attacked. Thus the humanists attacked the religious superstitions of the day, the greed of the Church, the ignorant arrogance of theologians, the malpractices of lawyers and usurers, etc. A noble series of works by Erasmus, Beatus Rhenanus, Agrippa von Nettesheim, Sebastian Franck, sharply condemned the warfare of the secular and ecclesiastical lords, the employment of mercenaries, and called for peace and tolerance. Reuchlin, a scholar and lawyer, boldly attacked the ignorance and prejudice of theological faculties in the course of a protracted struggle against a new wave of persecution of the Jews, and was supported by other humanists not only in the *Epistolae clarorum virorum* (1514), but also in the exuberant satirical work by Crotus Rubianus and Ulrich von Hutten, the *Epistolae obscurorum virorum* (1515), a parody of the smug arrogance of the theological faculties.

Though most of these works were in Latin, some of the

humanists wrote at times in German, when they needed to address a wider audience. The most famous works of Brant and Thomas Murner are in German, and Hutten turned to German in his last phase. A broad concern for Germany appears also in the new spirit of patriotism. Celtis edited the *Germania* of Tacitus, and appended a plan for a history of Germany, himself writing a well-documented history of Nürnberg. Wimpfeling's *Germania* actually betrays a nationalistic anti-French prejudice. Rhenanus fulfilled Celtis's plan of a history of Germany, and Aventinus wrote a history of Bavaria, both showing a remarkable knowledge of ancient sources. A German patriotism was founded that, frustrated in the political field, prospered and sometimes luxuriated in the world of learning and literature. It led to the great collection of ancient German documents and literature published by M. Goldast in 1606, that was an inspiration to Opitz and his successors, and to the comprehensive history of ancient German literature in D. G. Morhof's *Unterricht von der Teutschen Sprache und Poesie* of 1682.

The humanists did not challenge the basic beliefs of Christianity or the basic authority of the Church, but they sought to establish their authoritative foundations. Instead of contenting themselves with accepted formulations, they re-examined the original documents. Thus Reuchlin published his Hebrew grammar and dictionary, and Erasmus edited the Fathers of the Church and the Greek New Testament. Their questioning of accepted opinion was still restrained by the weight of authority; the study of Augustine or Jerome, of Aristotle or Plato, liberated their thought but also often imposed a new authority. Thus it was that the attempts to reconcile Aristotle or Plato with Christian tenets led to a speculative and often obscure theosophy, that runs riot in Beatus Rhenanus, Paracelsus, and many others. Unscientific and irrational as much of this thought is, it yet bears witness to a genuinely philosophical urge to comprehend the unity of the universe, to find a rational understanding of Christian truth. Their boldest thought is often expressed only in their private correspondence. Thus Erasmus could write: 'Hell is that fear and anxiety of the soul which constantly besets the sinner', and Mutianus sketches a synthesis of Christian and ancient philosophy, going so far as to suggest that Christ, Moses, and Prometheus are all symbols of the same divine essence. So Sebastian Franck could consider theology and the Church itself to be hindrances to the true inward reception of the spirit of Christ.

Together with these religious-philosophical probings, and justified by them, there ran a new attention to the world of nature, to natural science, and mathematics. Regiomontanus, the inventor of trigonometry, compiled a table of the planets, built the first German astronomical observatory, and set up a mechanical workshop. Paracelsus ridiculed traditional medical dogma, and sought to base a new therapeutics on observation, though he had, typically, to construct a strange theosophical system to justify the study of nature. Another doctor, Hieronymus Bock, showed in descriptions and woodcuts of his *Kreuterbuch* a more exact devotion to nature, and the geological knowledge and mechanical skill of German miners were such that they were brought to England to establish their practical science here.

The world in which the humanists moved was crude and violent, cradled in traditional prejudices from which few were free. Thus many of them shared the anti-Semitism of the period that was nursed by theologians, broke out in cruel pogroms and expulsions, and found expression in popular literature, Passion plays and Fastnachtspiele, folksongs and broadsheets. But Reuchlin, and with him a large band of associates, defended the purity of Jewish religion and condemned forcible conversions, and even pointed out that the hated practice of usury was imposed on Jews by Christian laws. Brant and Murner attacked Christian usurers as sharply as Jewish. Luther was to foment a violent hatred of the Jews, and religious and intellectual leaders were to encourage for the next two centuries the belief that the desecration of the

Host or the shedding of infant Christian blood were ritual practices of the Jews; but a humanist tradition of understanding and tolerance tempers such prejudices in writers like Ayrer, or Grimmelshausen, or Schupp, to set against the virulent *Endinger Judenspiel*, or the harsh mockery of Folz, Sachs, Fischart, the malicious hostility of Moscherosch, Buchholtz, or Abraham a Santa Clara.

Humanism was not a secularist movement. It set up an ideal of the Christian life, of goodness, truth, peace, and criticized all in Church and state, in dogma and custom, that frustrated this ideal. Its strength and weakness lay in its belief in and appeal to men's reasonableness. It prepared the way for the Reformation, but was submerged in the violent religious and social passions that erupted with it. From the advent of the Reformation, German intellectual life was dominated by theological conflict; until the times of Leibniz and Thomasius the voice of philosophical enquiry remained timid and hesitant.

The Reformation

When Martin Luther nailed up his Ninety-Five Theses on the church door in Wittenberg in 1517, he was acting, in one sense, in harmony with the spirit of Humanism. But his protest against the indulgence—a practice that meant that remission of sin could be bought—struck directly at the princes of the Church and the papacy for whom it was an important source of revenue, and arose from a profoundly religious conviction, a harrowing sense of sin and a consuming longing for grace. As ecclesiastical champions like Eck opposed him, and once the papal interdiction was pronounced in 1518, he proceeded with impassioned radicalism to examine the whole basis of religious belief. By 1520 the programme of a reform was drawn up. Asserting that canon law, the popes, even a Council of the Church might err, he fell back on the ultimate authority of Holy Scripture; he not only challenged the right of the Church to secular power, but also the religious authority of the clergy, claiming that the

Church is the community of all believers. Indicting manifold abuses and finding in Holy Scripture the justification for only two sacraments, those of baptism and the Eucharist, he went still further than any contemporary in calling on the secular authorities, emperor, princes, and town councils, to take in hand the reform of the Church; the idea of a nationally based Church was already taking shape.

When the imperial ban was pronounced on Luther at the Diet of Worms in 1521, Luther was sheltered by his prince, the Elector of Saxony, one of the chief opponents of imperial power. The actual reform of religious life and observance began now in Luther's enforced retirement. At the instigation of Wittenberg associates like Andreas Carlstadt, monks and nuns disowned their vows of celibacy, monasteries were disbanded, the Mass was abolished. Enthusiasts (*Schwärmer*) reshaped religious worship and preached their own gospel. Long oppressed Hüssite communities, humble craftsmen, carried the religious reform over into the social sphere, and revolutionaries like Thomas Münzer were soon to seek to reform social life on Christian principles of equality, opposing secular as well as ecclesiastical authorities, and in some cases trying in their communities to re-establish a sort of primitive communism. The leaders of the Peasants' War of 1524-5 justified their social demands on evangelical principles and called on Luther for support. Religious enthusiasm swept through the lower classes in the cities, a fanatical belief in the imminence of the Last Judgement mingled with the religious and social reform movement; out of this enthusiasm arose, in the ensuing period, sects like the Anabaptists, Hutterites, Mennonites, Moravian Brethren, which have survived in spite of persecution to the present day.

Luther was appalled at the religious and social anarchy his work had provoked and, returning to Wittenberg in 1522, set about defining his own new order. He insisted that the secular authority was instituted by God and that all social wrongs and abuses of power (many of which he himself forcibly criticized) could be righted only by the ruler: the subject had only to obey. Thus he condemned the peasants' rising, and in horror and fear called on the princes to exterminate the rebels 'like mad dogs'; he was equally ruthless in regard to the social reforms of the sects. In religious affairs he rapidly, with the aid of able collaborators like Melanchthon, built a new orthodoxy. He condemned sectarian groups and took steps to ensure that they were suppressed or banished; he hounded even so mild and tolerant a man as Sebastian Franck from place to place. He defined his theology more strictly, instituted an authoritative form of church service, established ecclesiastical authorities to regularize observance and belief, and placed the secular lord at the head of the new Lutheran Church; with Melanchthon he reorganized schools and universities. Several principalities and many cities adopted the new teaching, and by the end of the 1520s the new Church was in essence completed. The spread of Luther's doctrine was hastened by the material benefits accruing to the secular lords from the confiscation of ecclesiastical property, and by the 1540s most of Germany was Protestant. Further expansion was checked by the Schmalkaldic War, and the division of Germany into Lutheran and Catholic states was stabilized by the Religious Peace of Augsburg, 1555.

Luther's profound conviction of the significance of faith as opposed to 'works', that alienated the more rationalist of the humanists like Erasmus, gave a new depth to personal and communal religious life. The Bible became the centre of the religious service and private devotion, and through his translation (the New Testament was completed in 1522, the whole Bible in 1534, though it was continually revised until his death in 1546) became directly accessible to all. In place of the Latin liturgy, the sermon and hymn engaged the congregations in the act of worship. Through the use of German, religious experience enriched, and was enriched by, the whole world in which Germans moved, and daily life, family life were deepened by religious dedication. Religious writing, in prose and verse, gained a new expressiveness, and religious themes gave fresh life to the literary forms of the dialogue, lyric, and drama. But the authoritarian structure of the Lutheran Church, exacerbated by doctrinal dissensions and religious wars, its submission to secular lords, brought about a rapid ossification of religious and social thought. After the middle of the sixteenth century, Calvinism with its more republican forms and spirit replaced Lutheranism as the aggressive leader of Protestantism, and gained a strong hold in the south-west; but even Calvinism did not develop in German conditions the intellectual and social energy that characterized it elsewhere in Europe. Throughout Protestant Germany, theology became dogmatic, an oppressive orthodoxy was supported by state power, and virulent interdenominational polemics took the place of the bold enquiry of the earlier period.

The Counter-Reformation

Faced by the challenge of the Reformation, which rapidly spread throughout northern Europe, the papacy called the Council of Trent (1545–63) which gradually established a stricter discipline in the clergy. Of still greater importance was the renewal of religious life from within, led by Ignatius Loyola, who founded the Society of Jesus in 1534. Inspired by a fanatical faith, Loyola re-created a personal discipline of faith, secured through devotional exercises, an exterior discipline of service, and an intellectual reform. Other Orders were reformed on similar lines, but the Jesuits became the leading force in the recapturing of lost ground. Their grammar schools became the best of the time, providing a wider and more practical curriculum than others, an excellent training for officials and administrators as well as clergy; practice in eloquence and argument soon included the acting of plays, following a principle encouraged by Luther in his schools, and the Jesuit religious drama established a dominant tradition of the seventeenth century. From the first Jesuit church in Rome sprang the new Baroque architecture of which St Michael's in Munich was the earliest German representative, a church that was a single hall dominated by the high altar and directly accessible to the preacher, enriched by sculpture and frescoes engaging the senses in adoration and wonder.

Several Jesuit communities and schools were established in Germany by the middle of the sixteenth century, and Jesuits were soon entrusted with responsible positions throughout the country, as indeed they were throughout the Catholic world. They brought with them a wider intellectual range than the orthodox Protestants. Their allegiance to a powerful Order encouraged them to criticize more boldly than others abuses of secular and ecclesiastical authorities. In the sixteenth and the early seventeenth centuries an epidemic fear of witchcraft seized Germany, as it raged through many parts of Europe, and thousands of victims were sentenced in mixed ecclesiastical and secular courts. Only a rare humanist like Agrippa von Nettesheim had dared to oppose this belief in witchcraft: most Protestants and Catholics shared in the superstition, and enlightened men like Opitz, Gryphius and Grimmelshausen deferred to the frenzy when they used the supernatural in their works. Only Jesuits openly condemned both the sentences and the methods of the courts. The *Cautio criminalis* (1631) of the Jesuit Friedrich von Spee, who was chaplain to the condemned in Paderborn (Würzburg?), is one of the noblest and most enlightened writings of the century, in which he proposes a thorough reform of court-procedure and prisons. Not able to deny the existence of witchcraft, Spee yet asserts that those victims he examined were not guilty, and that the cruel methods of examination would have created the same confessions and incriminations had there been no substance at all in the charges. There must have been many Germans who doubted, for Spee's book was reprinted and translated into German; but it was only in 1701 that a Protestant, Thomasius, was bold enough to denounce witchcraft as an unfounded superstition (*De crimine magiae*).

Equally, the Jesuits found room within the Catholic

religion for profound personal experience. They systematically encouraged the achievement of mystical union with Christ or the Saints such as characterized St Theresa or St John of the Cross. The personal emotions were enlisted in the service of God, and religious raptures were expressed in the vocabulary of intense human love. A new mystical religious poetry spread throughout Germany, a spiritual love-poetry of which the lyrics of Spee and the convertite Angelus Silesius are the finest examples. It is characteristic of the Baroque that this religious feeling spread into Protestant circles too. Catholic books of devotion and Catholic poetry were translated from Spanish, Italian and French by Protestants such as Opitz, Harsdörffer, Zesen and many others, and their imagery was universally adopted. Particularly in Silesia, a territory of many small principalities where Catholics, Lutherans, Reformed, and numerous sectarian groups existed side by side, closely mingled in spite of bitter conflict, there was an interpenetration of the various streams of thought; to this interpenetration may be ascribed the dominant part played by Silesian writers in the literature of the seventeenth century—Opitz, Gryphius, Czepko, Logau, Hofmannswaldau, and Lohenstein.

Mysticism and Pietism

Amongst the humanists there had been much theosophical speculation, interpretations of the world as a revelation of the Divine Spirit, influenced by neo-Platonic, cabbalistic and alchemistic thought such as we find in the works of Agrippa von Nettesheim and Paracelsus. Later, the speculations of the astronomer Johannes Kepler illustrate the continued influence of this search for a metaphysical framework to existence. In some cases, as with Sebastian Franck, this type of thinking merged with the older mystical tradition of an inward-turned devotion repudiating all theological definitions as distortions of the truth of religious experience.

This mystical thought continued under the surface, cultivated by small groups here and there, reformulated in various ways by men like Valentin Weigel and Kaspar Schwenkfeld. It found many adherents in Silesia. Jakob Böhme, a cobbler, fused in his works the theosophical and alchemistic trends with the mystical longing for personal union with God. He conceived of the world as the 'signature' of God, spiritual in origin and meaning yet estranged from its source, and sought in mystical contemplation to restore the lost unity. A loose community formed round him, linked by the energy of Abraham von Franckenberg, a Silesian nobleman who renounced his estate in order to live for the spirit, and who published Böhme's works and wrote his first biography. The thought of this group, transcending confessional barriers, links up with that of Catholic mysticism, and discovers a paradoxical identity between God and man, the divine and the natural. Johann Scheffler belonged to the group, and his *Der Cherubinische Wandersmann* is its most succinct expression. Scheffler himself was converted to Catholicism, and, as Angelus Silesius, eagerly promoted the Counter-Reformation in Silesia.

The mystical thought of Silesius is highly personal and private; Protestant mysticism tended always to be more associated with group practices, group devotions, and to a large extent for this reason was continually harried by the orthodox. Persecuted communities were forced into exile, to the tolerant city of Danzig, to Holland, to the New World. It was in Holland that Quirinus Kuhlmann, also a Silesian, abandoned all worldly learning and hatched out his exalted plans for the reform of the world according to the principles of true Christianity, a strange and obscure doctrine. Here he founded his first communities, and here he found refuge before his last apostolic mission to Russia, where he met a martyr's death.

In many other groups this apocalyptic enthusiasm took the more quietistic form of pietism. Turning from the aridity of dogmatic theology and the worldliness of the clergy, they sought the renewal of personal faith, the personal feeling of grace, through private and group devotions, practised in the intimacy of the home. A number of the clergy, like the Dresden court-preacher Philipp Spener, were able to combine these private pietistic practices with orthodox observance, but sharp dissensions often occurred. The conflict of conscience involved led Gottfried Arnold, a Lutheran professor and clergyman, to study from a new angle the whole history of Christian belief. In his *Unpartheyische Kirchen- und Ketzer-Historien* of 1699-1700 Arnold demonstrated with moderation and learning that it was the heretics and sectarians who had preserved the purity of Christ's teaching, and the Churches that had distorted and suppressed it. This book, indeed, became not only a handbook for sectarians, but also, as a defence of the rights of personal conviction, a work of great significance for the Aufklärung. In *Dichtung und Wahrheit* Goethe testifies to its profound importance in his own development.

That Arnold, later in his life, was reconciled with his Church indicates a development characteristic of the eighteenth century. The turning point is even more sharply evident in the history of August Hermann Francke (1663-1727). In 1687 Francke renounced worldly learning in order to practise and preach the personal renewal of religious devotion. The hostility of the orthodox drove him from Leipzig, and with the help of Spener, now at Berlin, he was given refuge at Halle. Here, though often attacked, he promoted the study of the Gospels and a heart-felt devotion, and led a puritanical movement against worldliness in all its forms. At the same time he established a complex of charitable educational institutions, at the core of which were pietistic devotional exercises, that became famous all over Germany. Here the characteristics of Pietism were established: an inward-turned piety and scrupulous self-examination, reinforced by strict control through the group and combined with energetic charitable activities. The psychological, social, and intellectual effects and tensions that resulted belong peculiarly to the eighteenth century.

Literature and Intellectual Life

Authoritarianism, exacerbated by violent religious and political dissensions, dominates the thought of the seventeenth century. The universities, much despoiled and ravaged by the wars, remained the homes of dogmatic scholasticism, and Humanism became little more than classical learning and a status symbol. Study was not specialized, and a university education meant an indiscriminate combination of theology, the classics, law, mathematics, and medicine. There were advances in mathematics and the sciences, and there were efforts to reform school education to turn it towards more practical purposes. But in general one studied in order to learn the authorities in each subject, usually spending a brief period at several universities, and often travelling abroad. A remarkably large number of Germans studied at Leyden, and there is evidence that many of the writers were here infected by the high standard of scholarship, the more independent spirit of enquiry, the broader tolerance, that distinguished this great university. But the acquisition of a vast amount of knowledge still was the dominant purpose—Gryphius, who lectured as well as studied at Leyden, gave lectures there on a startling variety of topics. The most celebrated German scholar of the period, D. G. Morhof, gave in his much celebrated compilation, *Polyhistor* (1688), an example of accumulated learning that leads nowhere. What was absent was the spirit of philosophic and critical enquiry that inspired, in this same period, the work of Francis Bacon or Descartes; Germany, rich in religious martyrs, shows no philosophical challenge until Leibniz, Pufendorf, and Thomasius, all concerned to overcome confessional barriers, found the Aufklärung.

The consuming issue of the literature of the period is religious in character. By far the greatest amount of the poetry written is religious, much of it explicitly confessional, Protestant or Catholic. The deepest preoccupation of the Poetics is how the practice of literature can be reconciled

with religion. Yet, in various ways, the cultivation of literature constituted an implicit revolt against the theological
orthodoxies, just as it meant participation in a German
cultural community transcending state frontiers. In their
attempt to give dignity to personal life, even in their concern
with so secular an activity as literature, the poets from Opitz
onwards raised a serious theological problem which was only
evaded, not settled, by the argument that poetry was justified
provided its themes were religious or moral. If the practice
of secular poetry, above all love poetry, never found an
utterly confident theoretical champion, it still was a challenge to ecclesiastical authority. More deliberate is the blur-
ring, in this literature, of confessional differences. We might
ascribe the fact that the Calvinist Opitz adopted the forms
and style of Catholic poets and translated a work of Catholic
propaganda to a personal indifferentism on his part, or to
careerism—for he served at different times Catholic, Lutheran, and Calvinist lords. But many other Protestants
followed suit. Gryphius, the convinced Lutheran, translated
a Jesuit play and borrowed much from the Jesuit dramatic
tradition. Zesen, a citizen of Hamburg and honorary citizen
of Amsterdam, and Harsdörffer, a Nürnberg patrician, translated Catholic devotional literature. In Zesen's *Die Adriatische
Rosemund* and Opitz's *Trostgedichte* confessional conflict is
deplored, while it is arraigned in Grimmelshausen's *Simplicissimus*. The Lutheran clergyman Rist rebukes the intolerance
of the clergy in *Das Friedejauchtzende Deutschland*. This movement beyond the Confessions is usually subdued and hesitant,
except in the thought of theosophists and mystics like Böhme
and Czepko; it finds frank expression only in the bitter
epigrams of Logau, who asks, where, in this world of warring
churches, is Christianity.

There was in this new cultural community also a certain
distancing from particularist and political interests, but its
social criticism is even more subdued than the religious. The
purposelessness and brutality of war are deplored by Opitz
in his *Trostgedichte*, by Rist in his *Irenaromachia*, and frequently

with great pathos by Gryphius. Moscherosch unmasks the banditry in the armies, and Grimmelshausen denounces the disastrous impact of the war upon the common people. But no writer, not even Grimmelshausen, dares to arraign the authors of the war, the powers. The Peace of Westphalia evoked a large number of works in which the blessings of peace are effusively attributed to the princes. Social criticism, so bold in the sixteenth century, is now timid and trivial, aimed in general at manners rather than morals, at those imitating in dress and manners their betters, not at these betters themselves, at the malice and pedantry of the clergy, rather than at doctrine, at the uncouth peasant rather than at the bourgeois or the lord. Only in Logau's polished epigrams do we find caustic resentment of the hypocrisy, self-seeking, and pretensions of the mighty, and a reminder of the sufferings of the peasantry.

Helpless in the face of the political power of the princes and the might of armies against which even the free cities could not prevail, the middle class found their ultimate consolation in a Christian stoicism, mystical withdrawal, and the hope of Eternity. The greatest poetry is rooted here, and the tragedy of the period centres on the dramatic contrast between worldly glory and its impermanence. The figure of Fortuna rules the imagination, raising and overthrowing men according to a mysterious and uncontrollable will, the favourite emblem in a period in which books of allegorical emblems, creating a fixed framework of religious and moral commonplaces, were amongst the most popular reading matter. Only very rarely do we come across an energetic and unorthodox sentiment like Paul Fleming's 'Was du noch hoffen kannst, das wird noch stets geboren'. But even the most energetic imaginative figure of the period, Grimmelshausen's Simplex, is brought by bitter experience in the end to withdraw to a hermitage.

III

LANGUAGE

THE phonological and morphological changes that distinguish New High German reach back to the thirteenth
century and proceeded at different rates in different parts of
Germany. Standardization through a common 'Schriftsprache' was promoted by the Imperial Chancery, to which
the various state chanceries approximated, and powerfully
stimulated by the printing press. But, since Germany lacked
a central court and administration, the creation of a unified
'Schriftsprache' was slower than in England or France.

The most influential unifying element was Luther's Bible,
a book on which generation after generation of Protestants
were schooled. Luther's translation was based on the local
Saxon idiom and adapted to the conventions established by
the Saxon Chancery at Meissen, though he also made an
attempt to accommodate Upper German forms used by the
Imperial Chancery. His Bible did not remain static. Printers
in other cities, e.g. Frankfurt, adapted his forms and orthography to their own practice, and indeed the Lutheran Bible
of the seventeenth century was considerably different from
his final revised version of 1545. He influenced not only
Protestants, for Catholic German Bibles used many of his
forms as well as his stylistic principles. Since his aim in translating was to make Holy Script accessible to all, he con-
solidated the actual trends of the spoken German of his day.

During the sixteenth century, this High German of
Luther's, based on the East-Middle dialect, was adopted
more and more widely by the state chanceries; the pre-
dominance of Saxons and Silesians in the literature of the
seventeenth century further extended its authority. Chanceries and printers in the Low German and Swiss areas also

adopted it—the last Bible to be printed in Low German was published in 1621.

Luther's sentence-structure and grammar, based on common usage and directed towards clarity and expressiveness, are very flexible. With the growth of grammar schools, both Protestant and Catholic, however, the principles of Latin style and grammar began to be applied to German. In the seventeenth century, through the authority of such grammarians as J. G. Schottel, the grammatical forms of a correct German were established, particularly as regards conjugations and inflexions and the position of the verb and verbal prefixes in the sentence, and a turgid Latinized academic German dominated until the reforms of Lessing and the 'Sturm und Drang', and still dominates in the language of science and learning. Luther was careless and much at the mercy of his printers in the matter of spelling, and here again the seventeenth-century grammarians strove to establish a general convention for vowels and consonants, for the use of capitals, etc. Since local diversity ruled in speech, there was still much argument on orthography, and Zesen invented a system of his own. The 'Sprachgesellschaften', pre-eminently the 'Fruchtbringende Gesellschaft', spent much energy on these problems and performed a useful service in establishing agreement on grammatical and orthographical conventions.

The ideal of style altered greatly too. In Luther's pamphlets, the style is remarkably racy, lively with turns of speech and images from common life; his Bible has the same robust earthiness enhanced by the rhythms and imagery of Hebrew poetry. In his *Sendbrief vom Dolmetschen* he brilliantly defined his stylistic principles. But the learned writers of the seventeenth century, despising the crudities of common speech, followed the principles of Latin rhetoric and created a flowery, ornate style. Opitz saw in the epithet and metaphor the chief beauty of language, and his successors strained to form far-fetched composite nouns, a practice for which Zesen invented the term 'Füge-Kunst'. In some writers like Moscherosch, Grimmelshausen, and Schupp, we can see the

Lutheran tradition still operative, but in general the literary language became divorced from the language of common usage; towards the end of the seventeenth century the revolt against 'Schwulst', against ornate bombast, the return to a plainer language in the works of Weise, Thomasius, or Rachel, begins to close an epoch, though the admiration of the far-fetched and piled-up metaphor is still evident in Haller, even in the early Schiller.

Luther's language was greatly enriched by loans of terms, images, even structures, from Hebrew, Greek, and Latin, for which there was no actual German equivalent. Foreign loans became a serious problem in the seventeenth century with the growing prestige of Italian, Spanish, and French literature, the adoption by the German courts of foreign culture and manners and languages, and the presence on German soil of foreign armies. The language of administration and diplomacy, of ordinary communication, became bespattered with foreign words, partly for convenience of understanding, partly for prestige; for many of these terms, e.g. military or diplomatic, there was no German equivalent. It was a chief concern of the 'Sprachgesellschaften' to stem this debasement of German, to find or invent German equivalents—we find for instance that Gryphius, revising his poems after his election to the 'Fruchtbringende Gesellschaft', systematically replaced foreign words by German: 'Phantasie' by 'Bild', 'Port' by 'Ufer', etc. This principle led then, as in later times, to absurd pedantry, as when Zesen replaced 'Fenster' by 'Tage-Leuchter' or 'Natur' by 'Zeugemutter', or invented a whole series of German terms for the Latin Gods ('Venus' becomes 'die Liebinne', etc.).

Despite pedantry and preciosity, however, this patriotic endeavour enriched German with a wealth of terms, often compound formations, and discovered anew the creative potentialities in the German prefixes.

IV

LITERATURE—THE METHOD
OF STUDY

THE political and social, religious, intellectual, and linguistic features of this period have been summarized with a view to their significance for the imaginative literature of the time. How should we proceed to examine the literature itself? It might well be studied as a factor in these other developments, as evidence of political, intellectual, or linguistic attitudes; but if this were done, the specific quality of a literary work would be ignored. The artistically important works might be taken in the chronological order in which they occurred, a method that properly brings out the intimate connections between contemporaries. In a period as politically, socially and ideologically complex as this, this method is likely to lead to confusion, and above all to a failure to distinguish the meanings that different forms of utterance, e.g. dramatic, lyrical, narrative, have. All works of art are both rooted in their times and linked in a tradition, a tradition of a genre that imposes its own rules on the writer. The specific quality of a work, that is the supreme concern of the literary critic, can only be grasped if both factors are present in the mind.

Instead, therefore, we shall follow up the genres individually. This method has the disadvantage that it breaks up the sense of continuity, separating what is being done in one literary field from what is going on elsewhere. But in every case we shall be faced by a historical development, and therefore shall not lose sight of the historical situation; and this common basis should enable the reader to relate the separate chapters to one another. Since there was, at the end of the sixteenth century, in almost every respect a profound change in literary forms, accompanied by a change in the concept of literature itself, the account is divided into two main sections, the sixteenth and the seventeenth centuries, reflecting in this way the political, social, intellectual changes already summarized.

This method of study is more than a mere convenience to the understanding. The literary genres have remained remarkably constant over a long period of human history, mutually influencing one another, yet retaining their distinctiveness till today. They seem to constitute the essential forms through which the human situation can be imaginatively depicted; they correspond both to the character of the human situation, the relationships of man to man and of man to the universe, and to the mode in which we understand it. As Paul Böckmann has put it, the genres are 'die Auffassungsformen, in denen sich die Dichtung aller Gehalte vergewissert und durch die sie allen Erlebnissen und Erfahrungen erst Bedeutung gibt' (*Formgeschichte der deutschen Dichtung*, p. 2). The genres, both the general form the writer adopts, and his own specific adaptation of it, are the means for man 'to reach understanding about himself'. Thus, in following their history, we follow one of the most vital human themes; and we identify as great, as truly poetic, those works from which we ourselves gain an accession of understanding, of ourselves, of man.

'Literature' is a very capacious term, and includes a great variety of genres such as the sermon and homily, the polemical pamphlet, the philosophical, scholarly, and scientific treatise, historical writing etc. A complete study of this period would demand the study of all these. But we confine ourselves to imaginative literature, 'Dichtung', to that literature that does not investigate facts and is only indirectly concerned with philosophical, religious, or moral enquiry and instruction; that is, with the genres of the lyric, the drama, and the fictional narrative. Satire is included since it too is an imaginative form.

The Literature of
the Sixteenth Century

V

SATIRE

SATIRE, the depiction of behaviour and attitudes with the object of provoking ridicule, occurs as an element in many forms of literature. It is a traditional instrument of moralists, and many medieval and Renaissance preachers (Geiler von Kaisersberg) made their sermons lively with satirical anecdotes and descriptions. Many of the polemical writers of the time, above all Luther, make incidental use of satire, and it is a major instrument of comedy and Fastnachtspiel. In 1494, however, with the publication of Sebastian Brant's *Das Narrenschiff*, satire acquired a form of its own, and this book, re-issued in innumerable editions and translations, remained influential throughout the sixteenth century.

Brant's purpose was to cure men of their vices, to recall them to a Christian way of life, to get men to accept the social responsibilities of their station and to respect order and authority. Thus he criticizes abuses at all levels, pluralism in Church dignitaries, sloth and greed in priests and monks, self-seeking in princes and anarchy in the Reich, rapacity in lawyers, merchants and monopolists, the usury of Christian financiers ('Mit dem Judenspiesz rennen'), the unruliness of journeymen and peasants; together with a whole host of traditional failings, gluttony, lewdness, coarseness of manners, extravagance and display, etc. The book owed its immense success to the comprehensiveness and pungency of its social criticism, but also to the form Brant invented.

Adopting the image of the Ship of Fools, Brant linked up with a popular feature of Carnival processions, in which masked figures were trundled along provoking laughter and ridicule; thus gaiety had a place in his satire. By depicting vices as 'follies'—again a traditional custom—Brant was able to lighten the severity of his criticism. The 'Knittelvers' in which he wrote, the popular medium of folk wisdom, heightened the pungency of style. Numerous woodcuts added to the vividness and humour of presentation. Each chapter is introduced and closed by general reflections of the author, often with learned references, and this moralizing is narrowly puritanical and conservative; the great impact of the work was due above all to the vividness of description and style, to the humour and verbal dexterity (e.g. Kap. 71 'Zancken und zu gericht gon' or Kap. 73 'Von geistlich werden').

In a series of satires, the Franciscan monk Thomas Murner imitated and developed Brant's method. He was a more passionate and engaged character than Brant, and his satire is more biting; it gains an added dimension when he allows the Fool himself to propound or enact his folly. While Brant's positive principles are rather vaguely expressed, Murner's attack on the self-seeking of priests (brilliantly described in *Die Narrenbeschwörung*, 1512, No. 38, 'Eier uf dem altar finden') his outspoken attack on the political ambitions of the Church (No. 11), on the abuse of excommunication (No. 20), is crowned by his criticism of the belief in the efficacy of works and his appeal to the Pauline doctrine of faith (No. 77). Murner's composition and writing is less tidy, less urbane than Brant's; his descriptions are even more concrete and vivid, and his language is racy with popular idiom, a great storehouse of popular saws.

In this pre-Reformation period, there is also a great deal of satire written in Latin that indicts the same sort of follies, e.g. the dialogues *Stylpho* (1486) of Wimpfeling and *Sergius* (1496) of Reuchlin. Latin was however a much more supple medium than German, and Erasmus's *Praise of Folly* (1515) or his *Colloquies* (1519) employ a subtle irony that is without parallel in the blunter German satires—though at the same time it is less direct and urgent. While Brant and Murner exhort directly, Erasmus's cutting satire provokes the free play of intelligence. This subtlety is evident too in the brilliantly aggressive *Epistolae obscurorum virorum* (1515), ascribed to Crotus Rubianus and Hutten, in which the parodied theologians condemn themselves out of their own mouths.

As the storm of the Reformation gathered, there was little room for ironical satire. Ulrich von Hutten, participating as a humanist in the Reuchlin controversy but soon engaging himself as an Imperial Knight in the Reformation struggle, wrote five dialogues in Latin, 1518–20, biting attacks on the pretensions of the Church. He then translated them into German verse, as the *Gespräch büchlin* of 1521, in which the Roman ecclesiastics display cynically their lust for power and wealth. But in this work, still more in the *Clag und Vermanung* of 1520, satire runs over into challenge, and becomes invective. Generally, in the bitter struggles of the Reformation period, polemics and caricature take the place of satire. Thus Murner's attack on Luther, *Von dem grossen lutherischen Narren* (1522), though effective in places, descends often to distorted parody and caricature, and the many dialogues for and against Luther, like the *Karsthans* (1521, probably by Vadian), or those of Hans Sachs or the Catholic Cochlaeus, however effective, are polemics rather than satire. The pamphlets of Luther or Eberlin von Günzburg have brilliant satirical traits, but only incidentally. As the Reformation proceeded, virulent polemics ousted satire, except in imaginative literature, in plays and anecdotes.

Throughout the Middle Ages, satire had created its own medium of fable and anecdote, popular among the common people as its criticism of the mighty and its imaginative revenge. Particularly the animal fables, that circulated in many forms, especially in France, made of Reynard the Fox the admired rebel against secular and moral authority. In the Low German version, *Reinke de Vos*, published in Lübeck in 1498, the anecdotes are composed into an epic whose hero is the wily fox, making his way by his sheer wits, arraigned for his crimes against the simple and the stupid, the sacred and the mighty, and befooling at the end the king and the law. In each episode, humour and satire are brilliantly fused, the narrative is terse and vivid, and pointed by pithy turns of speech; the author fuses the behaviour of the animals with the human attitude they symbolize, and satirizes the latter from within; practical mother-wit is evident everywhere, for instance in the scene where the fox makes a hypocritical confession of sin. The unknown author sought to lessen the impact by adding moralizing glosses, but the fox remained for centuries a symbol through which the common people took an imaginative revenge on authority. In the Rostock edition of 1539, the anti-clerical tendency of the work was developed into a direct and violent attack on the Catholic Church, but its homogeneity and its humorous and witty quality were thus impaired. It was translated into High German in 1544, and remained immensely popular; Gottsched and Goethe wrote versions.

In a somewhat similar way, popular anecdotes celebrating the success of the common man in outwitting his betters were united in *Ein kurtzweilig lesen von Dyl Ulenspiegel* of 1515, based on a Low German original. This work, in prose, is far less polished than *Reinke de Vos*, both in composition and in style. Numerous anecdotes are collected, but they do not form a narrative whole, and they end abruptly with Till Eulenspiegel's death. But here again we see how the social outsider maintains himself against all those with a stake in society, against peasants, artisans, innkeepers, merchants, lawyers, doctors, clerics, princes, the pope himself. Eulenspiegel is a tramp, ready to take any odd job, but always out to befool, often using the ambiguities of language in order to discomfit the solid world of settled practices and values. The clumsy prose is not descriptive; its great quality is the terse narrative, enlivened by the speech of the characters, practical and unreflective people bewildered, amazed, and often in the end delighted by Till's roguish inventiveness. It is not a work of social criticism, but its great and enduring popularity is due to the fact that Till embodies the unease that men feel among the social forms and moral taboos that they know

SATIRE 39

they have to accept (hence the obscenities in which it is rich). Eulenspiegel is a sort of safety-valve for repressions.

There is no satire in the post-Reformation period comparable in scope with the satire of the earlier period. The anecdote ('Schwank') in verse or prose becomes more polished, but the satirical intention is blurred, and it is of chief significance in relation to the development of narrative forms. The best satires limit themselves to more specific, less controversial matters. Hans Sachs's tolerant humour rarely has the sharp edge of satire. The author of *Das Lalebuch* of 1597, the original of *Schiltbürger*, enjoys the stupid simplicity of his burghers too much to be called a satirist. Satire proper tends to confine itself to particular, limited themes and to avoid the controversial.

The most successful of the later satires was Friedrich Dedekind's *Grobianus*, published in Latin in 1549, and translated into German by Kaspar Scheidt in 1551, many editions following until the last in 1640. It belongs to the old genre of 'Tischzuchten', but Dedekind, instead of merely giving admonishment on table manners, puts his satire indirectly. The Grobian himself describes and defends his coarse behaviour, with the exuberance of self-approval, and thus both behaviour and attitude are satirized with great gaiety; Jonathan Swift found the book 'diverting' and may have learnt from its method.

The general trend of satire under the stress of the religious struggles of the later sixteenth century can be seen in the work of Johann Fischart. A citizen of Strassburg, a lawyer and administrator, a Calvinist engaged in the struggle against the Counter-Reformation, he was a prolific writer, often adapting other men's work to his purposes. Much of his work was didactic, but in *Floeh Hatz* (1573) he writes with gay and exuberant inventiveness of the war of women with fleas. His famous adaptation of Rabelais's *Gargantua*, *Die Geschichtklitterung* (1575), shows likewise his delight in grotesque anecdote and linguistic inventions, and ridicules extravagantly every sort of human folly, but the satire is somewhat uneasily married to stolid moralizing and religious exhortation. Fischart also engaged, in several works, the most important of which is *Vierhörniges Jesuiterhütlein* (1580), in religious polemics, and here his satire, as exuberant as ever, is virulent and slanderous. The distance, the urbanity required of satire was no longer possible, except in respect to the less significant vices like gluttony, bad manners, or cleanliness, etc. Satire was to revive in the seventeenth century in a new form.

VI

THE LYRIC

THE German lyric of the sixteenth century is song, verse to be sung. Only in Latin was a lyric poetry composed that sustained itself entirely on words, a tradition common to the European humanists that drew heavily on the Roman lyric poets, Horace, Propertius, Catullus, and others. Until the end of the century this neo-Latin poetry remains curiously separate from the German lyric, which began to absorb its characteristics only with the Baroque. Much of this Latin verse was a mere exercise in metre, practised in schools and universities, the status-symbol of the scholar. But it was also the only medium through which poets were able to reflect on intimate personal life, to celebrate love and friendship, to explore the personality. In the reflective verse, the panegyrics on friends and on Germany itself, the eclogues, and above all the love-poems of Conrad Celtis a true poetic personality takes shape, and in the elegies and songs of the Dutchman Johannes Secundus there is a liberation of feeling and sense, an attentiveness to personal experience, that find no parallel in German. The German poetry of the time is not only rougher and cruder in style and form; it is not intended primarily as a personal statement, it is meant to be sung to and with others, it is communal in character.

Folksong

Folksong is of ancient origin and many of the songs sung in this period go back far into the past. Many new songs, too, were composed in the fifteenth and sixteenth centuries, and their types can be distinguished—worksongs, dance-songs, historical ballads, love-songs, songs accompanying popular festivals and religious rituals, etc. Some have come to light only in modern times, through the investigations of folk-lorists, but the texts and tunes of a great number were recorded at the time. We know them through manuscript collections made by private persons for their own pleasure, through printed broadsheets hawked by itinerant singers, through published collections, often with new settings. In this period the songs are divorced from their original source (in ritual or work, for instance), and are appropriated to the burgher culture. They merge with the newer 'Gesellschafts-lied', songs to be sung by the burghers at home or at the inn, of which Georg Forster's popular collections provide many examples.

We can only guess at the authorship of the oldest songs, but many of the new songs of the fifteenth and sixteenth centuries indicate their authors—'ein lanzknecht gut', 'reiters-mann', 'ein gut gesell', 'von adel ist er geborn'—sometimes giving their names. They are properly folksongs, partly because they were widely popular over many generations, partly because they were continuously adapted through oral transmission. Because of oral transmission many of the older songs were mutilated in several ways: verses were dropped, words distorted, texts amalgamated, so that coherence was often damaged. But for this very reason the songs also were made more striking and poetic. The highlights of a ballad would be remembered, and the omission of links made the whole more dramatic (*Tanhauser*); the popular imagination deepened poetic symbols ('Es ist ein Reis entsprungen' becomes 'Es ist ein Ros entsprungen'; 'die König von finis terrae' becomes 'die König vom finstern stern'). The less ancient of the songs are less affected by such changes, and many show an individual and artistic composition.

The most common metrical form is the four-lined stanza with four stresses in each line, rhyming in pairs (*Ulinger*); frequently the lines have alternately four and three stresses, the rhyme linking only the second and fourth (*Tanhauser*). Both these are derived from ancient German forms. There is an irregular filling of unaccented syllables, but a noticeable tendency towards a fairly regular alternation of unaccented and accented syllables. But there are also stanza forms of more complex structure, often of five or seven lines, which allow for a greater variety of tone—sometimes enhanced by the music, which repeated lines or parts of lines (*Linden-schmid*). Some of these stanza forms go back to the Minne-sang form of two 'Stollen' of identical structure and melody, followed by an 'Abgesang' with a variant melody. *Moringer* actually contains two stanzas of a poem of Walther von der Vogelweide, and is composed on this pattern. In Georg Forster's collections we find a great variety of stanza forms, corresponding to the desire for variety in the sociable enter-tainment they were intended to provide.

The themes of folksongs range widely from the lusty humour and mockery of drinking and hunting songs to love and religious worship. The highest literary quality is found in the ballads, the love-songs, and the religious songs. Some ballads go back to ancient heroic lays (*Hildebrandslied*) and to medieval legends (*Tanhauser*), to classical legends like Hero and Leander (*Elslein*), to half-legendary tales of knights re-turning from long pilgrimages (*Moringer*) and of sinister killers like *Ulinger*. The more recent ones are often in the nature of news sheets, telling of great events (*Pavia*), or of the exploits of bandits (*Schüttensam* or *Lindenschmid*), whose ex-ploits captivated the popular imagination; in some cases we can thus date the poem's origin. Outstanding is the vigour of the narrative, which singles out the main stages in the action, and which is made lively by dialogue. Some of these ballads lived on for long. *Lindenschmid* was included in *Venus-Gärtlein*, a 'Liederbuch' of 1656, and was among the folksongs that Goethe collected in Alsace.

Many ballads are tales of unhappy love, and there is a great number of love-songs, many betraying their origin in work-songs. Travelling journeymen take a sad farewell of their loves, the miller's or reaper's song is a love-song. The situations are simple, and there is little description; dialogue is frequently used, and is often remarkably fresh and delicate.

Like all ancient poetry, these songs develop a group of fixed symbols: harvest and the end of love; the mill wheel and departure; certain birds or flowers are fixed symbols (nightingale, owl, forget-me-not, honeysuckle—'je länger je lieber'). In some, e.g. *Keuzlein* or *Es ist ein schnee gefallen*, the symbol is extended most skilfully into a lament for loneliness; in the most famous of all, *Innsbruck ich muss dich lassen*, the physical and spiritual parting intertwine. With great art this simple situation is developed into a subtle and tender dialogue between the parting lovers (*Ich stund an einem morgen*).

Nearly all the religious songs derive from some particular situation in the religious year. There is a great group known as 'Leisen', which arose within the Church service from the response of the congregation, the 'Kyrie eleison'— the greatest of all is *Christ ist erstanden*, sung on Easter day; amongst them is the mockery of *Ach du armer Judas*. There are pilgrimage songs, often like ballads, and full of salty and humorous comment, like *St Jakob*. There are songs for festivals like epiphany, which reflect the gaiety of folk-festivals (*Die heiligen drei Könige*); Christmas songs of the greatest delicacy, like *Es ist ein ros entsprungen* or the cradle song, *Joseph liebster Joseph mein*, which captures the rhythm of rocking. All aspects of popular faith are mirrored in these songs, at its deepest and most moving in Easter songs such as *Da Jesus in den garten ging*. A number of the religious songs are translations of medieval Latin hymns, some are macaronic, i.e. with German verses mingled with Latin. In general, style and form is the same as for the secular folksongs, indeed many religious songs were pious parodies ('Kontrafakturen') of secular songs, and used the secular melodies.

Meistersang

As contrasted with folksong, Meistersang is an art-form of many rules, practised in small groups of initiates, and not intended for public singing—it was forbidden to publish Meisterlieder. It arose in the fourteenth century among lay fraternities of the Church, under clerical guidance ('Magister'—hence the name 'Meistersang'), who met in the church, to practise congregational singing. This connexion with the church remained after the groups released themselves from clerical guidance, and the 'Hauptsingen' continued to be held in church, after the morning service, though at the instigation of Hans Folz, the barber-surgeon of Nürnberg, serious secular themes were added to the religious. A second meeting was held in an inn, which often took a jovial and even riotous character. Meistersang spread in the sixteenth century to many cities in South-West, South, and East Germany; its members were predominantly master-craftsmen, but included teachers and town officials. Through the energy and ability of Folz and Hans Sachs, Nürnberg became the leading centre, and manuscript collections of their Meisterlieder and their rules spread its influence everywhere.

The Meistersinger claimed to be the heirs of the Minnesänger, and kept at first to twelve melodies that had come down from them. Folz however invented new melodies, and in the sixteenth century a member became a Master only by inventing a new melody. The structure of a Meisterlied also was based on that of Minnesang; each poem ('Bar') consisted of a number of stanzas ('Gesätze'); each 'Gesätz' of two 'Stollen', identical in form, in length and number of lines and melody, followed by an 'Abgesang' of a variant structure and melody (though a bipartite form is also found). The music was based on plainsong, the words sung in unison as a sort of recitative with much melismatic ornamentation. The length of line was reckoned by the number of syllables, without any reference to stresses, and was not allowed to be longer than could be sung in one breath. The pattern of rhyme was often very intricate, and much attention was paid to purity of rhyme and to correctness of inflections—in this respect the Meistersinger contributed to the creation of a German Schriftsprache. The rules were codified in several 'Tabulaturen', the most influential of which was Hans Sachs's, which formed the basis of Adam Puschman's published *Gründtlicher Bericht* of 1571.

The groups ('Schulen') were composed, like guilds, of learners, members, and masters, and rules laid down how mastery was to be achieved. The 'Schulordnung' laid down the procedure to be followed at the meetings in church and 'in der Zeche'. The high point of the latter was competition among the masters for prizes, and 'Merker' were appointed who marked down the faults (faults of doctrine as well as of melody, language, and metre).

Meistersang is extremely prosaic and pedantic. Hans Sachs, the master cobbler, enlivened it in many ways. He wrote new melodies, some of which, like the 'Rosenton', are tuneful. He introduced new material, especially from medieval legend, fables, from Renaissance and contemporary anecdote, which he handled with humour and narrative skill. Here and there a folksong motif gives uplift to his imagery and verse. But there is no lyrical movement, no music in his verse. He used many of his Meisterlieder as the basis for anecdotal poems, 'Schwänke', written in a simpler form, which he could publish, and these, though still prosaic in expression, are more lively than his Meisterlieder proper.

Even in its heyday, Meistersang was despised by the learned and unknown among the common people. It lingered on, in small groups of craftsmen, into the nineteenth century. It is interesting as a first attempt in Germany to formulate an art of poetry, but its pedantic rules and the prohibition of the expression of personal feeling (love-poetry was forbidden) made it sterile. Thus the cultural leaders of the seventeenth century almost entirely ignored it, though Schottel used some of its technical terms and Harsdörfer praised its technical skill, while deploring its lack of metre. In *Herr Peter Squentz* Gryphius amusingly satirized its moralistic provincialism, quaint rules, and rough verse, even including a parody of its melodies. Christian Wagenseil's account of Meistersang in his history of Nürnberg (1697), upon which Wagner's *Die Meistersinger* was based, is patriotically sympathetic, but unmistakably patronizing.

The Hymn

The last great type of lyric in this period is again of communal character, the hymn. Both Latin and German hymns were sung through the Middle Ages, but Luther's Reformation created and fulfilled a new need. One of the most fundamental principles of the Protestant Churches was the direct participation of the congregation in the Church service, and this was realized above all through the hymn. Luther himself composed many hymns, often based on older melodies, for congregational singing; the earliest were published as broadsheets (1523) and then collected with others in hymnals from 1524 onwards, the first authoritative one being the *Klugsches Gesangbuch* of 1529.

Luther's hymns show a variety of forms. There are translations of Latin hymns ('Mitten wyr ym leben sind'), which is a 'Leise', versifications of the Psalms and other passages of the Bible, adaptations of folksong ('Vom himel hoch') with the use of folksong idioms. In several he uses Meistersang form ('Ein feste burg'); *Ein neu Lied von den zween Martyrern Christi* adopts the form of the ballad. They are mighty expressions of a confident faith that gives them sweep, rhythmical movement and firm structure; not personal or questing, several of them have remained eminently fitted for communal worship.

With this example, many Lutherans, mainly clergymen and teachers, wrote hymns; no less than 187 hymn-books were published by 1571. Many of these hymns were wooden and didactic but some have remained in the Lutheran hymnal. Sects such as the Moravian Brethren created their own hymnals, and the versifications of the Psalms by Calvinists were later to have a peculiar importance. Even Catholics followed suit, the first Catholic hymns being composed by M. Vehe in 1537; Luther's hymns were imitated and adapted and the resources of religious folksong utilized.

Towards the end of the century the character of the Protestant hymn begins to change. The expression of personal piety and of family worship begins to supplant the great congregational hymn, a change we find consummated in the seventeenth century. The Catholic hymn of the Counter-Reformation, particularly cultivated by the Capucins and Jesuits, begins to draw on a Spanish and Italian tradition, and to establish a new imagery and piety. It is in this same period that the tradition of the secular folksong begins to fade and to be replaced by a new music, new verse-forms, a new stock of images, coming pre-eminently from Italy. These changes constitute so great a rupture of tradition that they are best considered as the dawn of the Baroque.

VII

THE NARRATIVE

As with folksong, there must have been an abundance of narrative in this period—folktale, fable, anecdote—that was passed on by word of mouth in the home, the inn, the coach; preachers like Geiler von Kaisersberg or Thomas Murner drew on this oral stock as well as on printed material. We are concerned here with what was published. Publication, the detachment of the tale from the speaker, from voice and gesture, makes new demands on the artistry of the narrator, as regards both the use of words and the composition of the whole. It is not surprising, therefore, that the technically most skilful narratives derive from medieval or classical sources, while the art of narrative develops more slowly with newer, more original material. Stories are told for a variety of usually mixed purposes—to enthral, to amuse, to ridicule, to teach practical wisdom, to drive home a moral. There is no theoretical discussion of the form of narrative, and when put to it, writers justify their stories, which were often attacked by theologians as being idle and pernicious, on the grounds of their moral usefulness.

Fable and Anecdote

Printing made available a great stock of material from classical and romance literature to add to the stories transmitted orally. Aesop became known directly through the *Esopus* (c. 1476) of Heinrich Steinhöwel, whose simple, idiomatic translation made the book popular for two centuries. The Lutheran clergyman, Erasmus Alberus, made the fable the vehicle of a more explicit social and religious satire, directed at Catholics and sectarians, princes and peasants. At the same time he enlarged its scale, placed the incidents in German settings, enlivened them with dialogue, and used many local references (*Das Buch von der Tugent*, 1550). Another Lutheran, Burkard Waldis, also used the fable for polemical purposes, and he also, in his *Esopus* of 1548, uses traditional as well as Aesopian fables. With him, the fable loses its dry and abstract character, it becomes a short verse-narrative, seemingly derived from the German life of the times, lively in movement and pithily idiomatic. This fable tradition, like the anecdote, remained popular as a sort of cultural substratum; for the Baroque poets it was too deeply rooted in common life to rank as literature. It was again given literary status in the eighteenth century.

As narrative, the Low German *Reinke de Vos* is outstanding, for here numerous incidents are combined in an epic tale of the fox's adventures that comes to a climax in the scenes at the lion's court. Here, alone in the fable literature, do vividness of characterization, wit and humour, combine in a large narrative structure. There is as yet, as in all the anecdotal and fable literature, no development of personality, but there is a development of incident.

The verse fable is noticeably more vivid, neater in structure, more pithy in expression, than the prose fable. The same is true at first of the anecdote. Early prose anecdotes are clumsy in sentence-structure and expression, and often in narrative construction. On the other hand, the Latin *Facetiae* (1508-12) of Heinrich Bebel, drawing on the humanist tradition, are skilful in composition and precise, terse, in expression. A comparable collection of German anecdotes and exemplary tales made by the Franciscan monk Johannes Pauli, *Schimpff und Ernst* (1522), is crude in style and clogged by the didactic intention. Later in the century many such collections were made, and there is a great improvement in German prose style. The best of them is Jörg Wickram's *Das Rollwagen büchlin* (1555), put together for the entertainment of travellers. Though many of the tales make fun of Catholic clergy, lawyers, peasants, bandit knights, and so forth, a good-tempered spirit prevails; Wickram's style is rich in colloquial terms and has the liveliness of speech, and each story takes us close to the world of which he writes. They are nearly all humorous tales, some indeed in the manner of the times drastic, though Wickram's avowed aim was to provide more 'decent' entertainment than was normal. Many similar collections of 'Schwänke' followed.

A more artistic impact is made by collections centred on a single person, like the *Dyl Ulenspiegel* of 1515. The character of Eulenspiegel remains constant, the sly rogue living on his wits who repeatedly befools his betters by his feigned misunderstandings. Of the others of this type, *Hans Clawerts Werckliche Historien* (1587) is the best. It is by Bartholomäus Krüger, the town clerk of Trebbin, and is based on the real exploits of a local practical joker. The stories are told with considerable skill, and testify to the constant, even if reluctant, admiration for shrewdness and wit. The same effect, in reverse, is achieved by *Das Lalebuch* of 1597. The burghers of Lale are so burdened by their reputation for wisdom that they determine to be foolish, and the book consists of exploits like the famous one in which they forget to put windows in their new town-hall, and try to remedy the defect by filling sacks with sunlight. As in *Hans Clawert* we find a much more fluent style, much more actual description of circumstance and behaviour, than in the earlier part of the century. The book was copied in *Die Schiltbürger* (1598) and *Grillenvertreiber* (1603); it became famous all over Europe as good-humoured satire of faulty reasoning and naïve self-importance.

All these books borrow and adapt freely from one another and from the great popular store of anecdotes. The same is true of Hans Sachs. He used such material in his Meisterlieder, his plays, and his verse 'Schwänke', which were widely known. These are amongst the best verse tales of the time, lively and pointed. Sachs did not however try to combine separate Schwänke in any more complicated form.

In general, prose came to take the place of verse in the anecdotal literature, particularly in those with a central character. But even in these, the whole is not composed in a mounting epic narrative. The technique of the novel was acquired from a different source.

Romance

An immense flood of prose romances, mostly translated from the medieval French epic, swept over Germany in the fifteenth century, and remained popular for long. They are tales of heroism and love, and the earliest were translated by noble ladies, Elizabeth von Nassau-Saarbrücken, who died in 1456 (*Hug Schapler*) and Eleonore von Vorderösterreich, who died in 1480 (*Pontus und Sidonia*). Some appeared in magnificent editions, with splendid woodcuts and bindings, some in cheap paperbacks; they were read by all classes, princes and burghers. Nothing bears clearer witness to the collapse of medieval courtly culture than these tales. Love has become mere physical desire, heroism becomes brute strength, supernatural powers appear as elves and fairies. The style is usually very crude, though later adaptors often improved the earlier versions (compare the later versions of *Hug Schapler* and *Pontus und Sidonia*). They show the continuing prestige of the prowess of legendary figures, like the *Kaiser Oktavianus* or *Die Heymonskinder*, both printed in 1535, but unwittingly debase it. *Die schöne Magelone*, translated in 1535, is an exception, for here a firm grasp of story is evident, the language is much more skilful and eloquent, and there is delicacy of feeling; Spalatin, the clergyman, could recommend it for the reading of ladies. Nearly all these romances of chivalry are in prose; the translator of *Tristrant* explained in his preface that he had chosen prose because people no longer liked or understood verse.

Along with these chivalrous romances came many other tales from medieval sources, *Die hystori Troyana* (1498), Marco Polo's travels, moralizing tales like *Der Ritter vom Turn*, humorous dialogues like *Salomon und Marcolph*, tales of the Wandering Jew etc. From Germanic legend came the *Lied vom hürnen Seyfrid*, a much coarsened version of the

Nibelungenlied, that probably goes back beyond the medieval epic; the earliest prose version extant is of 1727.

All these Volksbücher show a conflict of cultures; an ideal of chivalry and heroism that is naïvely debased and coarsened, sometimes parodied. They remained popular for centuries, but were derided after the middle of the sixteenth century by the learned as vulgar and immoral ('pestiferi libri'), and they lived on only among the lower classes, ultimately as children's reading. Yet, strangely enough, it was from a Spanish romance of this type, the *Amadis*, that the German courtly novel of the seventeenth century arose. And Goethe and the Romantics were later to pay tribute to their naïve charm.

The Novel

Within the tradition of romance and anecdote two works stand out as precursors of a more complex narrative form, the novel—*Fortunatus* (1509) and *Historia von Dr Johann Fausten* (1587).

The first contains many of the elements of the romance, even the fairy-tale, for the hero undergoes many adventures in different lands, and is given by the goddess Fortuna a magic wallet, always filled with gold currency, and a cap of invisibility. But the hero is a merchant, and we follow his business career till he dies prosperous and ennobled, while his sons, lacking wisdom, cannot live up to their social position, and die in misery. Thus the book presents a coherent story, and the story itself has a moral meaning; the central character learns from experience, and the misfortunes of his children illustrate his fault in seeking gold rather than wisdom. The style is still very clumsy, the secondary characters are only shadows, but the work has a unity and purpose that look forward to the novel—not least in that the author is dealing with burgher concerns in more real circumstances than the normal romance provided.

The Volksbuch of Dr Faustus arose from anecdotes associated with, or attached to a historical figure, a learned quack reputed to possess magical powers. But the anonymous author, probably a Lutheran cleric, composed these anecdotes into a story that should teach a moral lesson—the evil of intellectual pride. To intensify the lesson he describes Faust's impatient ambition, the pact with the devil, his enquiries and his pangs of conscience and links up his moral rebellion—the union with the shade of Helen—with the intellectual. Against the author's will something of the grandeur of a hero attaches to Faust, and his last farewell before the devil takes his soul is not lacking in eloquent pathos. Thus, in spite of some scrappy incident, there is a real unity of story composed significantly round an important moral theme which involves reflection and moral struggle. The language, with a greater range of expression than was common at the time, conveys movingly the despair and resolution of Faust, the anguish of soul. The Faustbuch is not unworthy of its great successors, the stage versions of Marlowe and Goethe, and both Busoni and Thomas Mann went back to it. But the various narrative versions that won popularity in the seventeenth and eighteenth centuries only weakened its force; the dramatic intensity concentrated in its single character could not be incorporated into the novel till much later.

Fortunatus and *Faustus* are on the border-line of the old epic and anecdote and the modern form of the novel. A more deliberate step towards the novel was taken by Jörg Wickram. He wrote romances of the traditional type like *Ritter Galmien* (1540), and his *Goldtfaden* (1554) was half courtly romance, half fairy-tale. But his *Der jungen Knaben Spiegel* (1554) can be considered the first German novel. It is a didactic tale intended to show how moral living leads to prosperity and happiness and evil living to disaster. He follows the interwoven lives of three main characters, and for the first time we can observe different milieux and different attitudes related and composed into a whole; the scenes of low life particularly are described with realistic vigour, and there is precise and consistent characterization. The style is still rather clumsy, the psychology typical rather than individual
,

but this novel is a worthy anticipation of the eighteenth-century bourgeois novel; and the theme of hard work, self-control and obedience, of the superior worth of inward qualities over rank, anticipates later developments.

Thus in the sixteenth century the lineaments of the novel begin to appear. But the Baroque largely disregarded these trends. *Reinecke Fuchs*, *Eulenspiegel*, *Fortunatus*, and *Faust* remained popular reading, but the writers of the seventeenth century looked elsewhere for their models; as in the lyric and the drama, there is an abrupt breach.

VIII

THE DRAMA

THERE were no theatres, no professional actors in the six-teenth century. Dramatic performances were all occasional, at schools and universities, at local festivals, above all at Shrovetide, and were held in schools or public rooms, in inns and churches, in courtyards, tennis courts, or market squares. The stage was a bare platform without scenery, back-cloth or curtain; the words alone indicated place and time. Typical costumes and accessories would indicate different ranks—an emperor or pope, a cleric, a burgher or peasant, etc. Despite the meagreness of productions, all records testify to the immense popularity and power of the drama in this period.

The medieval Mystery play, stretching shapelessly through many 'stations', continued sporadically in Catholic lands and reaches over to modern times in the Oberammergau Passion Play of the seventeenth century. The Morality and the Shrovetide plays with their more condensed form were more suited to the needs of the times. These traditional forms were supplemented and modified by the new knowledge of Roman and Greek drama, especially through the editions of Seneca, Terence, and Plautus, though ideas about the ancient theatre remained confused. From the Romans the humanists learned the art of pointed repartee, and such dialogues as Wimp-feling's *Stylpho* and Reuchlin's *Sergius* are playlets near to the Fastnachtspiel; Reuchlin actually made a five-act Latin play (*Henno*, 1497) out of the French farce of *Maître Pathelin*. The anonymous *Eccius Dedolatus* (1520), a scathing attack on Luther's antagonist Eck, uses various devices of the Fast-nachtspiel in the classical framework of five acts. The Ger-mans learned from the Roman dramatists how to compose an extended play, divided into acts that represent stages in the action, and they frequently used prologue and epilogue and choruses between the acts as a means for moralizing comment. There was much give and take in theme and form between plays written in Latin and in German, and many Latin plays written for production at schools and universities were translated into German.

The Fastnachtspiel

The origins of the Shrovetide play lie in the Spring fertility rites from which mysterious figures like Meister Eckart, ritual forms like beatings and dance remain. Carnival still was a time when taboos were lifted, hence the frequent obscenities in fifteenth century farces, hence too the satirical function they came to serve. In the uproarious gaiety of Carnival the typical failings of all classes were ridiculed, of priests, lawyers, nobles, burghers, and peasants. The plays are usually introduced by a Herald, and figures like Meister Eckart or the Fool may intervene with satirical, humorous, or moralizing comment. A rough 'Knittelvers' is used and there is little action, the characters usually entering one by one and speaking their piece to the audience. Hans Folz in Nürnberg showed some dramatic skill in satirical playlets, and Hans Rosenplüt widened the scope by taking a large contemporary theme for his *Des Türcken Vastnachtspiel*. Similarly the Swiss, celebrating the achievement of the independence of the Confederacy, performed patriotic plays like the *Ürner Tellenspiel* (c. 1511).

The issues of the Reformation period brought a remarkable development. Pamphilus Gengenbach, a Basel printer who wrote several poems and ballads on popular themes, produced a series of Fastnachtspiele between 1513 and 1521. In *Die zehn Alter* figures representing the various ages of man come on the stage, speak a piece and leave; there is no action, and the satire is very general. *Die Gouchmat* (1516) is similar in form; representatives of different social classes visit Venus, dance with one of her handmaidens, and are despoiled; it finishes with a traditional quarrel between a peasant and his wife and a homily against adultery. *Der Nollhart* is a more ambitious review of the state of Christendom and introduces a great number of figures, the emperor and the pope, St Brigit and the Cumaean Sybil, mercenary soldiers and a Jew, but it is hardly composed. Of the greatest interest is *Die Todtenfresser* (1521?) which seems not to have been played, perhaps because of the inflammatory content. The pope and other Church dignitaries are devouring a corpse, a drastic symbol of the profits of funeral rites, Death plays his fiddle beside them, as in medieval Dances of Death, and representatives of the secular orders lament the corruption in the Church. The play is still without action; but here indignation has created a drastic image more concentratedly developed than hitherto.

A bolder spirit, Niklaus Manuel (Deutsch) of Bern, soldier, painter, and administrator, grasped the polemical potentialities of the Fastnachtspiel. *Von Papsts und Christi Gegensatz* (1522) is little more than a dialogue demonstrating the contrast between the pope and Christ who pass in procession before the speakers. But *Vom Papst und seiner Priesterschafft*, also played in Bern at Shrovetide, 1522, is a work of great dramatic power. The *Todtenfresser* theme is developed, a group of scenes depicts the pope neglecting his religious duties and preparing to attack the evangelists; a nobleman, an official, and peasants make their drastic criticisms, a preacher expounds the true doctrine, Peter and Paul vent their indignation over the papacy; it closes with the pope's preparations for war, and a resolute confession of faith by an evangelist. While the action is diffuse, and more epic than dramatic, there is great movement in the play and great vigour of expression. In Manuel's *Der Ablasskrämer* (1525) an indulgence pedlar comes to a village and is forced to reveal his tricks by the peasants who ridicule and torture him. Here there is real interplay between the characters, concentrated dramatic action.

It is the greatness of the issues that makes the power of

these plays, and they were dangerous firebrands to throw among the people. Perhaps for this reason *Der Ablasskrämer* was not performed; we know that elsewhere, at Nürnberg for instance, the authorities suppressed works of inflammatory character. Burkard Waldis of Riga found a different way to use the Fastnachtspiel for polemical purposes. In 1527 he wrote a play on a Biblical subject, *De parabell vam vorlorn Szohn*, in which the story of the Prodigal is turned into an illustration of the Lutheran doctrine of grace. A man of learning, Waldis divides the play into two acts representing the rise and fall of the Prodigal, and uses prologue and epilogue to drive his doctrine home. The play shows a new sense of dramatic form, and the scene in the inn where the Prodigal is despoiled, is psychologically realistic in a new way and betrays the influence of Terence. Though still nominally a Fastnachtspiel, it leans rather in the direction of the school play both in its theme and its method.

Such themes tend to disappear from the Fastnachtspiel after the early stormy years of the Reformation. The work of the greatest writer, Hans Sachs, illustrates the general tendency. His pre-Reformation Fastnachtspiele are in the old tradition, in revue style with folklore figures like Der getreue Eckart and the Fool. With the advent of the Reformation he engaged to great effect in evangelical polemics in his poems and dialogues, writing no more plays until after 1527, when the prudent Nürnberg town council forbade him to publish any more inflammatory material. The vast number of plays, Schwänke, and Meisterlieder that he wrote during the rest of his long life, satirical as they often are, do not take take up any great issues.

Sachs was not only a writer. He played a leading part in producing the Fastnachtspiele, using a secularized church or a public room, and negotiating for permission with the town council which was always suspicious of the effect of plays on the populace. His stage was still a bare platform and the costumes meagre; entrances and exits of characters are clumsily engineered. But Sachs surpasses all contemporaries in the neat contrivance of plot, in terse and sometimes pointed dialogue, and in characterization; the usual direct address to the spectators is less prominent, the characters speak to and with one another.

Sachs took his themes from a vast stock of legendary and Biblical lore, from romance and anecdote, from contemporary life; he often adapted the plays of learned contemporaries. But he turns all the characters, whether God or Adam, Alexander or Caesar, Oedipus or Aristotle, king or nobleman, into the simple man or woman of his own times. Where he excels is in the portrayal of the common man, the burgher or peasant. His work is all satirical-moral, true to the tradition of Shrovetide; but it is also good-humoured, tolerant, gay, and provokes laughter over human foibles—folly, short-sightedness, simplicity, hypocrisy, credulity, etc. —not indignation or anger. Great issues of state or of feeling are beyond Sachs's range, but as satire of the manners of everyday life his plays are most skilful works of art. His characters have a warm individuality that is missing from the work of his disciples, Peter Probst and Jakob Ayrer.

The limitations of Hans Sachs's imagination and dramatic power are only too evident in his more ambitious lengthier plays. These are mostly dramatized versions of romances, such as *Griselde* or *Herzog Wilhelm* or *Der huernen Seyfrid*. But Sachs utterly fails to understand or express nobility, heroism, passion, or grief. Nor does he understand composition. The plays are divided into anything from five to eight acts, but the act has no dramatic function. These plays are symptomatic of a longing for high tragedy for which Sachs himself, and no doubt his artisan players, were unfitted. They help to explain why it was that the arrival of the Elizabethan players in Germany conquered all audiences and put an end to the Sachs tradition.

There are many other Fastnachtspiele in this century, some like those of Martin Hayneccius, Tobias Stimmer, and Johann Stricker, being skilful playlets. But with the seventeenth century, the Shrovetide ceremonies lost their lustre and with them the Shrovetide play declined into a coarse amusement of the lower classes. The plays and their artisan players could not measure up to the splendours and skill of the professional troupes from England.

The School Drama

The term School Drama is given to plays acted by students or schoolboys and written by their teachers. It was customary to honour a special occasion, a princely visitor, with such performances, and throughout the sixteenth and seventeenth centuries such plays, in Latin or in German, were written to provide instruction in the art of speaking and deportment. But they were not merely instruments of education. In a time when there was no theatre, such school performances were great occasions for a community, all the notabilities and many of the burghers would be present, and the plays became an important feature of civic cultural life and remained such throughout the seventeenth century. In Protestant lands they replaced the public Mystery plays and in Catholic they rapidly surpassed the latter in importance.

A number of factors combined to shape the form of these plays. The writers were acquainted with the ancient drama and strove to create a dramatic plot; they borrowed from Latin an expressive and pointed language and learned from Terence in particular how to fit language to personality and social status; their pupils could be taught how to speak and act appropriately. The stage in a public hall imposed a unity of action as contrasted with the numerous, separate stations of the Mystery play. At the same time, they sought to provide a large number of parts so that many pupils could take part, and above all to provide a theme that should be of religious and moral value.

In their dialogues, written for university production, Wimpfeling and Reuchlin had shown the effectiveness of dramatizing subjects of contemporary significance. Waldis, in his Fastnachtspiel on the Prodigal Son, found a way to marry religious and moral instruction with entertainment. Luther quickly recognized the opportunity, and in 1534 recommended the use of Biblical themes in school plays. An enormous number of such plays, on the Prodigal, Judith, Susanna, Joseph, etc., were now written—over 400 authors are known in the sixteenth century, a quarter of whom wrote in Latin. In addition, the Morality was also eminently suited to school production, and there were several versions of *Everyman* adapted from the Dutch or English originals. There were lively centres of dramatic life in Saxony and Switzerland, but every schoolmaster worthy of the name wrote or adapted such plays. If written in Latin, they might also be performed in German (like the *Pammachius* of Naogeorgus), if in German, they might be translated into Latin (like Sixt Birck's *Judith*). Hans Sachs adapted many of these plays to his purposes.

The *Acolastus* (1529) of Gnaphaeus set the definitive example. The stages of the Prodigal's career are divided into five acts. While, in the first and last, the religious issues come to the fore, the middle acts compose a psychological action with unusual artistry, and the characters of the whore, the bawd, the inn servants, stand out sharply; something of the delight of extravagance and love, as well as its disillusionment, are skilfully portrayed. Likewise, in the last act, the meeting of the Prodigal with his forgiving father is delicate and moving. In the German translation the delicacy and poise of the Latin verse are lost, but unity of plot, dramatic movement, and psychological realism are maintained. This work was of immense influence, and 39 editions appeared by 1581.

Macropedius wrote in Latin several Biblical plays, among them *Asotus* (1537), also on the Prodigal Son, and *Joseph*. His most successful play was *Hecastus* (1539), a new and Protestant version of *Everyman*. As with Gnaphaeus, the chief figure is less of an allegorical type, more individual and human, than in the original, and around him are grouped a number of characters in their personal relationship to him, wife, sons, servants, etc. In Johannes Stricker's *De Düdesche Schlömer* (1584) the theme is used as a means to criticize the

Holstein Junkers. In Switzerland Sixt Birck wrote, in German, among other plays a *Susanna* (1532) and a *Judith* (1534?), both showing a great liveliness of dramatic incident, while the Catholic Hans Salat, who produced the Luzern Easter Play in 1538, also wrote a *Judith* (1534?) and a *Prodigal Son* (1537?). The Judith theme, with the miraculous power of God at its centre, was to become very popular on the Catholic stage, while the more moralistic themes of the Prodigal or Susanna were more popular among the Protestants.

Formally the most remarkable of all these Biblical dramas is the *Susanna* (1535) of Paul Rebhun, an Austrian who had migrated to Saxony. He builds out the domestic feeling by introducing Susanna's children, and adds a sub-plot to darken still further the character of the evil elders. It is a drama without intensity and the character-drawing is faint. What is remarkable about the play is the versification. Sixt Birck was the first to introduce choruses to be sung between the acts (in *Judith*); Rebhun introduces here a considerable variety, using forms close to folksong and hymn. But he goes further and uses various metres in the dramatic text itself, pentameters and hexameters, carefully scanned iambs and trochees, as variations from the predominant Knittelvers. In themselves, these variations are a remarkable anticipation of the metrical forms of the seventeenth century, but they are even more remarkable in that they interpret a situation, the gravity of Susanna's position and the frivolity of the court bailiffs, etc. Through the metre, an unusual depth of feeling and some subtlety of mood is given to characters and situations. Rebhun's achievement seems to have been too subtle for his audiences, for later editions of his play remodelled it in Knittelvers.

The aggressiveness of the early Reformation continues in the work of the Lutheran, Thomas Naogeorgus. His *Mercator* (1540), an adaptation of the *Everyman* theme, contains a sharp attack on the Catholic priesthood, but his greatest and most famous work, *Pammachius* (1538), is altogether a virulent and brilliant onslaught on the papacy. Its form is near to that of the Morality. In the opening scene, Christ delivers the world to the rule of Satan until such time as He will send a deliverer. The play itself shows how Pammachius, the embodiment of the papacy, schemes to win power over the world, forcing the emperor to do his will, and bit by bit, with the help of Satan, asserting his supremacy until, in Act 4, Christ sends Paul and Truth down to Wittenberg to rescue humanity. The play ends with a Council of the Church (Trent), presided over by Pammachius, plotting bloody devices against Truth. The bitter and eloquent passion of its language is preserved even in the German Knittelvers into which it was immediately translated.

It is a powerful drama, lurid in the depiction of evil, full of bitter irony. It is not surprising that, when produced in Cambridge in 1545, it caused a riot. But, as with Manuel's plays, it was only religious passion that provoked this great imaginative sweep; nothing later is comparable with it. Bartholomäus Krüger tried to do something similar in his *Von Anfang und Ende der Welt* (1580), a play half Mystery, half Morality, but its diffuseness betrays the decline of conviction.

Something of the vigour of the early part of the century flares up again in the work of Nicodemus Frischlin, a Swabian scholar whose scathing tongue aroused the ire of colleagues and authorities and brought him to his death in prison. He wrote a number of Biblical plays in Latin, *Rebecca* (1576) and *Susanna* (1577), but more important are his plays on classical subjects following the lead given by Heinrich Knaust with his *Dido* of 1566. Frischlin's *Dido* (1581) and *Venus* (1584) are dramatized versions of parts of the Aeneid divided into five acts, linked by a narrative chorus, and their dramatic structure is very weak. He was more at ease with the loose form of *Priscianus vapulans* (1578), a capricious and witty satire of his academic colleagues, and in *Julius redivivus* (1585), in which Caesar and Cicero visit the Germany of the sixteenth century, admire its achievements and comment on its vices. Two of Frischlin's plays, *Hildegardis magna* (1579) and *Frau Wendel-*

gart (1579)—the latter the only one of his extant plays written in German—are dramatizations of romances. Here, as elsewhere, his strength is shown in the incidental comic scenes and sub-plots. Frischlin translated Aristophanes into Latin, and his own satire has something of Aristophanes's fantastic and reckless wit, but it always remains spasmodic and is never artistically controlled in a composed dramatic form.

In the varied drama of the sixteenth century there seem to lie potentialities such as were fulfilled in England on the Elizabethan stage. But in Germany they were not realized. From the religious-Biblical drama, especially the form the Jesuits gave it, there emerged a new classicistic drama that, in the interests of moral concentration, of composition, reduced the medley of event and with it the imaginative range that here and there authors were seeking to express. But there was a sort of fulfilment of the groping popular imagination in the plays that the English Players brought over with them, that gripped audiences of all classes, and though this story belongs in the main to the seventeenth century, it can most properly be treated in the framework of the sixteenth.

The Englische Komödianten

The first English players, called 'Instrumentisten' and 'Springer', accompanied the Earl of Leicester on an embassy to Electoral Saxony in 1585; the first company to act plays arrived in 1592, and thereafter various troupes made more and more extended visits until the 1630s. They were accredited to various courts such as Braunschweig, Hessen or Saxony and called themselves after their German patrons, but they also more and more toured the cities far and wide, playing at fair-times and charging for entrance.

At first they played in English and must have relied greatly on mime. The clowning scenes seem to have been the earliest to be acted in German and the clown, Pickelhering or Stockfisch, soon became most popular. The earliest translations are in a rough prose, but they improved as German actors were enlisted in the troupes. After the Thirty Years

War, companies calling themselves 'Englische Komödianten' were all German, the first German strolling players, but still in possession of the texts from the old repertoire. The 'Haupt-und Staatsaktionen', the Hanswurst of the eighteenth century, derive from the English players; Tieck reports that he saw strolling players act what was evidently Dekker's *The Shoemaker's Holiday*, and in the form of a puppet-play *Dr Faustus* was performed well into the nineteenth century. Thus the English players founded the professional theatre in Germany even though they had to rig up temporary stages in public rooms, fencing and tennis courts, etc.

They played on a bare stage without scenery or front curtain, but often with a rear gallery and sometimes (later) an inner stage which could be closed by curtains. The rear of the stage was draped with arras behind which actors could be hidden—thus the Prodigal Son could move round the stage knocking at various 'doors' to be rejected by voices from 'within'. They carried with them many properties, a throne and other symbols of majesty, fountains and rocks, trees, grave-stones, and with these could create an illusion that dazzled and delighted their audiences. Their productions abounded in 'theatre', violent action, murder and hangings, disguises, ceremonies of coronation, feasts and weddings. Above all these professionals were versatile actors, practised speakers and dancers, masters of gesture, acquainted with all the tricks to enthral and amuse, always capable of extemporization. The texts have an abundance of stage-directions, hitherto scarcely known in Germany. The Clown was ubiquitous, always ready to jump in to revive interest if it flagged.

We know of the repertoire from civic archives and private documents, printed programmes and texts in manuscript, and from a publication of 1620 (second edition 1624) *Englische Comedien und Tragedien*. Later collections of 1630 and 1670 are connected with the English repertoire by little more than their titles. Many of the texts are lost; some of those extant are particularly interesting in that they go back to unknown English plays, or to lost versions of known plays (e.g. *Hamlet*). The variety is great. There are Biblical and Morality plays like *Esther*, *The Prodigal Son*, and *Von Niemand und Jemand*. There are short farces and jigs, playlets to be sung. And then a great number of famous plays like Marlowe's *Jew of Malta* and *Dr. Faustus*, Shakespeare's *Romeo and Juliet*, *Merchant of Venice*, *Hamlet*, *Julius Caesar*, *Lear*, *Twelfth Night*, '*Thisbe und Pyramus*'.

All these plays were, however, reduced to the bare skeleton of crude action; all depth of reflection, all subtlety of human feeling and human relationships are lost. The characters have become wooden, the plots are reduced to a series of violent blood-curling actions; crude and obscene farcical interludes proliferate, even in late versions like those of *Der Jude von Venetien* (c. 1670) or *Der bestraffte Brudermord—Hamlet* (1710). The language is crude prose, sometimes stiffly ceremonious or inflatedly bombastic in court scenes. Yet they captivated the Germans with a vision of a world of great happenings, of heroism and passion, gaiety and fancy, and the prose, poor as it was, was less inhibiting than the traditional wooden rhyming Knittelvers of the German stage.

The first impact of the Englische Komödianten provoked imitations. Duke Heinrich Julius of Braunschweig, a host and patron of the players, followed their style in a bloodthirsty and crude tragedy, *Von einem ungeratenen Sohn* (1594). His *Vincentius Ladislaus* (1594) is an exuberant satire of a braggart, the 'miles gloriosus', perhaps reflecting Shakespeare's Armado, and was incorporated into the repertoire of the players. In this play, as in a series of little peasant comedies, in which local dialect was used, there is a clown Jan Bouset, the figure the English player-manager Sackville created. Throughout Heimich Julius writes in prose. Jakob Ayrer was more ambitious but much less skilful. A citizen of Nürnberg, who returned there as a notary in 1593, Ayrer saw many of the English plays, as the players visited Nürnberg almost every year between 1593 and 1605, the year of Ayrer's death.

His earlier work is entirely in the tradition of Hans Sachs, Fastnachtspiele and formless, crude historical plays. But several of his plays betray in theme and style the influence of the English plays, and he prescribes that 'Agiren und Spilen' should be in the 'neue Englische manier'. Unfortunately he only takes over the crudest externals, the blood and thunder, the shapeless chronicle, the farcical and obscene interludes, and he still uses a wooden and inexpressive Knittelvers. His *Comedia von der schönen Sidea* has some affinities with Shakespeare's *Tempest*, though it pre-dates the latter and probably indicates some common source that the English Players acted. Ayrer also wrote several 'singende Possenspiele' in the style of the English jigs, little comedies to be sung—one is entitled after 'der engellendische Jan Posset'. There is some naïve charm about these comedies, the plot of which is usually taken from the Fastnachtspiel; but here again Ayrer is clumsy, using throughout each playlet only one simple ballad tune, where the English players used several, and spoiling the dramatic liveliness by allowing his characters to sing too many verses at a stretch.

Later, the popularity of the Englische Komödianten was confined to the uneducated. The learned and decorous leaders of middle-class culture turned their faces from the riotous imagination and vulgarities of the English plays, from their flat and unedifying prose, and there are surprisingly few references to them in their writings. But, largely under their influence, prose became established for comedy, and the most charming comedy of the century, Gryphius's *Herr Peter Squenz*, derives indirectly from them, while Weise's *Die böse Catharina* and *Der Niederländisch Bauer* pick up themes from *The Taming of the Shrew*. High Baroque drama followed other paths, and it was only in new circumstances, as a result of the intellectual revolution led by Lessing, Herder, and Goethe, that Shakespeare entered into the mainstream of German culture.

The Literature of
the Seventeenth Century

IX

LITERARY THEORY AND PROBLEMS

In the sixteenth century there is no clear conception of imaginative literature or of the poet; even among the humanists 'poeta' meant primarily a man of classical learning capable of turning out Latin verses. Except in the narrow field of Meistersang, questions of form and metre were discussed only in connection with classical literature. The new taste for Italian and French song, for new metrical forms, for a new type of novel and play (with which later chapters deal) asserted itself at first imperceptibly, but it constituted such a break with traditional practice and set such difficult problems that, as earlier in Italy and France, adherents of the new cultural forms began to formulate the rules of the new literature, to prescribe them, and to join together in seeking to establish them. The old was not utterly disregarded. Luther's metrical practice was recommended when convenient, older folksongs and hymns still appear in new anthologies and hymnals, a few writers still draw on the narrative method and style of the sixteenth century, and a Schupp defends himself against the charge of scurrility by an appeal to Luther's example. But on the whole, the rupture of tradition was remarkably sharp, and the new Baroque writing required the justification and guidance of theory.

The Sprachgesellschaften

The formation of societies for the improvement of taste and language was symptomatic. By far the most important was the 'Fruchtbringende Gesellschaft', founded in 1617 and presided over after 1629 by Duke Ludwig of Anhalt-Köthen. The others were local groupings. In 1633 the 'Aufrichtige Gesellschaft von der Tannen' was founded in Strassburg; in

1643 Zesen's 'Teutschgesinnte Genossenschaft' in Hamburg; in 1644 the 'Hirten- und Blumenorden an der Pegnitz' in Nürnberg; in 1656 Rist's 'Elbschwanenorden'. Of these, only the Nürnberg group survived the death of the founders. The less pretentious circle in Königsberg, known as 'Die Kürbishütte', ceased to meet when its leading spirit Roberthin died in 1648. The others followed the pattern of the Fruchtbringende Gesellschaft in giving every member a name and symbol and motto; Ludwig, 'Der Nährende', had a loaf as his symbol, Opitz was 'Der Gekrönte', Queintz the grammarian 'Der Ordnende', etc. The Nürnbergers chose flowers as their symbol and names from pastoral poetry, hence they were called the 'Pegnitzschäfer'. This playful solemnity they took over from Italian academies of which some of them, like Ludwig of Anhalt and Harsdörffer, were members.

The Fruchtbringende was from the beginning an academy of noblemen—at first, only its secretary Tobias Hübner, was a bourgeois—and remained predominantly so throughout; courteous deference was always required of its bourgeois members. Opitz, although acknowledged to be the leader of the new poetry, was admitted only in 1629 after he had been ennobled by the emperor. Afterwards, more and more of the middle-class writers were admitted, professors, lawyers, officials, who proudly placed the Palm Tree, the Society's symbol, on the title-page of their books; among them were Buchner, Schottel, Harsdörffer, Moscherosch, Gryphius, and the idiosyncratic Zesen, who was by no means so submissive to Duke Ludwig as custom required. It was a loose association held together by personal contact and correspondence with Ludwig. Significantly, only two clergymen were members (Andreae and Rist), and though it was predominantly Protestant, a few Catholics were admitted; in a time of religious war, Ludwig was determined to keep confessional conflict out of cultural discussion.

Its avowed object was to cleanse German of superfluous foreign words and to cultivate 'die reinste art im schreiben und Reimedichten'; it therefore concerned itself with such matters as pronunciation, orthography and grammar as well as with literary forms. At first it promoted translations of Italian and French poetical works as examples of style. Later, especially after 1635, when the Peace of Prague left Ludwig freer to devote himself to cultural affairs, he urged Buchner, Queintz, and Schottel to write their grammars of German, and took an active part in the establishment of a 'correct' German, as well as in arguments over poetic forms and metre.

The Fruchtbringende Gesellschaft survived Ludwig's death in 1650 for a few decades, but its prestige rapidly waned in spite of the ardour of its new secretary Georg Neumarck, who was its first chronicler. Doubt has been cast on its importance altogether, since Opitz and Buchner established the new metrical and stylistic principles independently, and often in conflict with Ludwig. But it had importance: it brought writers together, made them feel that they belonged to a patriotic movement in which the nobility also were involved, and thus increased their self-confidence. In their correspondence with Ludwig, they learned to argue with moderation and deference, but the freedom with which they write is a tribute to Ludwig's generosity and tolerance of mind.

The other, locally based Sprachgesellschaften were essentially meetings of the educated middle-class at which the new poetry was practised and its principles discussed. The Königsberg circle, including the composer Heinrich Albert, spent unassuming sociable evenings in singing and reading. The most ambitious were the 'Pegnitzschäfer' led by the patrician Harsdörffer. He was a widely travelled and learned man, a translator of numerous French and Italian works, and a productive author. He gives an idealized model of the Society's gatherings in his *Frauenzimmer-Gesprechspiele* (1641-9). Women join with men; all of them—though burghers—have noble titles, and the conversation is conducted with polite decorum. Harsdörffer brings all possible subjects into the discussion, including travels, mathematics and philosophy, but all adapted to the drawing-room.

Through translations and discussion the company is introduced to the forms and principles of foreign literatures, to
pastorals, allegorical plays, operettas, etc. They play elegant
parlour games, set one another riddles. An ideal is sketched
of elegant society, of graceful learning, of cultured leisure. In
the same spirit Harsdörffer wrote with his friends Klaj and
Birken a group of pastorals in which, disguised as shepherds,
they compose virtuose poems and converse with elegant
gravity. Artifice and preciosity arise when the gulf is so great
between the actual world and the cultural ideal. Yet one can
respect the attempt to break through the narrow confines of
practical life, to get beyond confessional strife, to make
learning a subject of courteous conversation; to extend
words beyond their practical use, to adorn life with art,
music, and poetry.

The Poetics

The Sprachgesellschaften enable us to glimpse the cultural
ideal embracing the new poetry. In the numerous Poetics of
the seventeenth century we find definitions of the forms of
this poetry and discussion of some of the problems it raised.
These Poetics serve a variety of purposes. In some part they
give the most elementary instruction on how to write metrical
verse, a sonnet or an ode, as primers on Latin verse did; they
sometimes include practical aids like lists of rhyming words
or poetic metaphors ('poetische Schatzkammern'). One of
the most important features is the definition of poetical forms
and genres, the sonnet, elegy, ode, epic, and tragedy, etc.
The definitions, taken from Renaissance Poetics, are meagre
and confused, sometimes based on the content or mood of
different types (elegy and tragedy are 'sad', lyrics are 'gay'),
sometimes on the form (sonnet, or echo-song). The confusions
demonstrate how difficult was the task of mastering these
forms new to Germany. But the practice of metrical expression and the definition of genres, however crude, opened up a
variety of forms, each expressive of an attitude and a human
relationship, which therefore, in being considered worthy of

literary expression, were enhanced in dignity. However rigid and wooden the formal prescriptions of the Poetics are, behind them lies a new appreciation of the possibilities of personal experience.

In all these Poetics there is a pronounced and in some cases extravagant patriotic ambition to raise German poetry to the level of the Ancients, of the French and Italians. Often this is accompanied by adulation of the ancient Germans. But in spite of this, the traditional forms of German literature are all derided or ignored and the patriotic endeavour turns, paradoxically enough, to rivalry through imitation. The models are foreign, the admired arbiters, Scaliger, Heinsius, Du Bellay, etc., are foreign.

Opitz

How much the new ideals were addressed to the learned can be judged from the first manifesto, Martin Opitz's *Aristarchus* (1617) which, written in Latin, appealed to scholars to write in German and imitate the example of foreign poets like Petrarch, Tasso, Ronsard, and Sidney. His *Buch von der Deutschen Poeterey* (1624), though hastily written, outlined with examples the main arguments for the new poetry and became authoritative for a century. An outline of his themes will serve as a basis for the discussion of the problems and arguments issuing from it.

He first seeks to justify the practice of poetry and the morality of poets; poetry was originally 'eine verborgene Theologie' and remains a means of teaching wisdom. With abundance of classical references Opitz insists that poets have been good practical citizens and that their art demands skill, invention, and a great spirit. Poetry is a practical and philosophic discipline for it consists of 'Nachäffen der Natur' and describes things not so much as they are as 'wie sie etwan sein köndten oder solten'. It serves therefore to persuade, instruct and please. The use of the names of pagan gods is not irreligious since they only stand for abstract qualities. Some poets, Opitz admits, have been immoral, but their 'epicurean' works do not mean that all love-poetry is unchaste; love is in any case justifiable as a theme since it is for the poets 'der Wetzstein, an dem sie ihren subtilen Verstand scherffen'. This defence of poetry against narrow Christian moralists remained a chief concern of the century.

After praising the poetry of the ancient Germans, Opitz proceeds to his main task, the definition of poetical forms. Following Scaliger, he divides his subject into 'erfindung und eintheilung der dinge' and 'zuebereitung und ziehr der worte'. He defines the subject matter and to some extent the form of the genres, epic, tragedy, comedy, lyric, elegy, ode, etc. Of words he demands 'elegantz', by which he means purity and clarity, avoidance of dialect and foreign loans. Metaphor and epithet, he believes, constitute the particular 'dignitet' of poetic speech, and he considers composite words ('arbeittrösterinn' for 'Nacht') to be 'eine sonderliche anmutigkeit'; he shows appreciation of the expressive value of sounds, of euphony. He insists that poets should observe the natural order of the sentence (no inversions such as 'mündlein roth', etc.). There is no one poetic language, for it must vary according to the theme. The last part deals with rhyme and metre, with verse-types like the Alexandrine, with forms like sonnet, ode, and epigram. Of greatest historical significance is the recognition that stress in verse must correspond to the natural accentuation of speech, and that the regular alternation of accented and unaccented syllables, the sequence of metrical 'feet'—iambs and trochees—constitutes verse. Opitz admits that he himself had not always recognized this law, and we see that he is concerned to oppose not only the roughness of older German verseforms, but also the belief that German accentuation is based, like Latin, on quantity (a view still to be maintained for some time by a few scholars and poets like Schottel and Weckherlin).

In his first chapter Opitz warns his readers that the observance of rules and laws does not make a poet, that inspiration is necessary, a warning his successors often did not take to heart; his sincerity is confirmed in his closing remarks by a moving personal confession of the 'unvergleichliche ergetzung', exaltation, and spiritual comfort that converse with the great poets brings.

The great prestige of this little book owed much to Opitz's poetical achievement. He gave examples of all the new types of poetry and verse in his *Teutsche Poemata* (1624), his epic *Trost Gedichte in Widerwertigkeit des Krieges* (written 1621, not published till 1633), the pastoral (*Schaefferey von der Nimpen Hercinie*, 1630), and through translation of operatic texts (*Dafne* 1627), tragedy (Seneca's *Trojan Women*, 1625, *Judith* 1635, from the Italian, and an adaptation of Sophocles's *Antigone*, 1636) and the novel (Barclay's *Argenis*, 1626–31). The prestige of Opitz was still further enhanced by the wide range of his intellectual connections abroad and in Germany, and certainly too by his successful career as a secretary and counsellor to lords and princes. But above all he displays, in his work and his life, the proud self-confidence of a poet; even his panegyrics to the great assert this dignity of his calling. There is in all his work a certain coldness of feeling, a formal virtuosity, that is paralleled by the indifferentism and expediency with which he served both sides, religious and political, in the war. But the positive aspect of this is his high conception of the sovereign poet, indeed of a cultural community that creates its own forms and values in rivalry to the practical pressures of life, that is above the strife of states and religions. More detached from any particular interest, profession, or local allegiance than any other seventeenth-century poet, Opitz created in his work and his person a new ideal of the poet.

Variants and Developments

Opitz's principles of poetic language and metre were extended in various ways in the Poetics of his successors. The principle of regular scansion, based on the natural stress of words, was universally adopted, but Buchner added to the iamb and trochee the dactyl, anapaest and spondee—Opitz himself adopted the dactyl in his verse-rendering of the Psalms (1638). Zesen and the Nürnberger advocated and practised, like Buchner in opposition to Duke Ludwig, the mixing of metre in the same poem, what Zesen and Birken call 'mängtrittige Verse', and allowed in the Alexandrine a shifting caesura and enjambment. Opitz's restrained use of onomatopoeia and other euphonic devices was lavishly developed. Metaphor became an end in itself, and Zesen saw in the creation of composites—to which he gave the name of 'Füge-Kunst'—a supreme poetic device; Klaj similarly saw in metaphor, 'Machtwörter', the heart of poetry. Emblem and allegory were established as genres (Harsdörffer). Opitz's commendation of verbal dexterity (in such forms as the anagram) became a cult of verbal ingeniousness, invention, for its own sake. We find indeed that critics of the later part of the century (Rachel, Sacer, Stieler, Omeis), satiated with the lavish decoration of the middle period, call for a return to the sobriety of Opitz's principles.

While the same rather perfunctory rules continue to be enunciated on the epic, it is surprising that, since Opitz called tragedy 'die fürnehmste Art der Poeterey', little of significance is written on it in the Poetics of the century. Opitz had written in the *Buch von der deutschen Poeterey* that tragedy deals with highly placed persons, with murder, incest, war and rebellion, and that the sphere of comedy is common life, and this distinction of class is always reiterated. The critics are chiefly concerned with the moral effect of tragedy. Birken insists that it is blasphemy if goodness is not rewarded, and like Harsdörffer requires the hero of tragedy to be a perfect example of morality. Kindermann is more subtle in adding that we can bear with tragic disasters partly because we enjoy being pitiful, partly because we know the work of art is only an artifice, an imitation, and therefore enjoy the realization that we ourselves, the spectators, remain unscathed. The most significant remarks on tragedy are expressed in the prefaces to plays. Opitz, in the preface to his translation of the *Trojan Women*, again strikes the decisive note. Tragedy, he writes, presents the disasters of Fortune common to man, and through the heroic fortitude of the hero prepares us to meet our own misfortunes. This is the view of Gryphius as he puts it in the preface to his first published play *Leo Armenius* (1646) and of Lohenstein in his dedication of *Ibrahim Bassa* (1653). The moral purpose of tragedy was so deeply felt by Gryphius that it justified, he claimed, the choice of a middle-class theme (preface to his 'bürgerliches Trauerspiel' *Cardenio und Celinde*, c. 1650). There is no uniformity in the Poetics on the form of tragedy, though usually the classical form of five acts connected by choruses was prescribed or assumed; the choruses were to be a medium for moralizing comment, as Lohenstein explained in the notes to *Ibrahim Bassa*. Gryphius justified the use of the supernatural on the grounds of Christian morality, but his argument betrays his consciousness that he is going against an authoritative body of opinion. The severity of classical form was rarely insisted on before Gottsched. Birken allows comic interludes, and Harsdörffer permits more than a single action and changes of scene.

There is great unclarity too in the discussions of comedy except that all critics insist it must be moral: Birken indeed calls it 'Tugendspiel'. It is further recommended since it should teach men how to behave in normal bourgeois life, and hence to observe the decencies of behaviour and language (Kindermann). Rist, bolder than the others in admitting a satirical purpose, requires the satire to be general not personal, and in particular commends satire of the peasantry (preface to *Das Friedejauchtzende Deutschland*); the coarseness of his own peasant scenes he defends on the grounds partly that it is true to life, partly that it follows the example of Cervantes and Sorel. There was a strong tendency to replace satirical comedy by the so-called 'Freudenspiel', a courtly allegorical form celebrating some nobleman or festival, enlivened perhaps by comic-satirical interludes, or by the Pastoral, both forms of very loose dramatic structure. Only at the end of the century does Christian Weise, in prefaces to his plays of common life, sketch the beginnings of a theory of didactic, realistic satirical comedy.

The novel is rarely discussed, largely because it does not figure in ancient Poetics. Those critics who do discuss it are always chiefly concerned with its morality, an acute problem in a genre that was so much concerned with love. Gottard Heidegger in his *Discours von den so benannten Romans* of 1698 expresses a widely held view when he condemns novels out of hand as depraving love-stories. But others defended them as offering models of courteous behaviour and language, of heroism and virtue rewarded, and also as an agreeable means of giving instruction (much indiscriminate learning was packed into the Baroque novel). Omeis cannot do more than apply the traditional views on the epic to the novel: it must be about the high-born, it must start in the middle of the story, its characters must be representative psychological types; Omeis particularly admires the roman-à-clef. The plebeian novel disregarded these principles, it is true, but even Grimmelshausen justified the entertaining parts of his *Simplicissimus* as 'gilding the pill' of edification.

While the critical and poetic authorities for the Poetics are all foreign, the later writers take Opitz's modest defence of the antiquity and dignity of German to extravagant lengths. Their insubstantial patriotism claimed that ancient German literature was estimable because it was courtly, and they derided and ignored the burgher tradition of the preceding century. In this respect it is interesting to compare the attitude of Joachim von Sandrart, a distinguished painter (1606–88) who, in his *Academie der Bau-, Bild- und Mahlerey-Künste* (1675), did for the visual arts what the Poetics did for literature. Sandrart collaborated with Harsdörffer and Klaj, and Birken wrote poems on a group of paintings he did at Schleissheim; he was a member of the Fruchtbringende Gesellschaft and shared its ideals of virtue, courtly elegance, and decoration. He prescribes the forms of art in the same way, accepts the same aesthetic authorities, and makes the same perfunctory remarks about nature, imitation, idealization, etc. But Sandrart rescued the fifteenth- and sixteenth-century painters and sculptors from the oblivion into which they were falling—Wolgemut, Dürer, Grünewald, Peter Vischer, Cranach, and many others—and praised not only the 'hohe Fürtrefflichkeit' of their virtue and art, but also their skill in 'Ausbildung von Affecten'. He recognizes that modern art, though it must be different, can learn from them. This recognition of a living German tradition is totally different from the exalted patriotism of the literary legislators.

Theoretical Problems

The Baroque Poetics bear witness to a great uniformity of literary taste, and what developments are to be observed issue coherently from Opitz's first manifesto. The new forms are defended consistently upon the authority of classical writers like Aristotle and Horace, of Renaissance critics like Scaliger and Heinsius. Such authority weighed heavily in a time when thinkers in every field appealed to the prestige of authority and dogma. But the literary critics, as we have already seen with Opitz, sought also to find a philosophical justification of the new taste, and the main issues of discussion are revealing.

The largest problem is one with which their foreign models were far less engrossingly concerned: how can poetry be reconciled with Christian belief? This religious concern was genuine, and the objections of Fathers of the Church to the secular practice of poetry were taken seriously. The critics proclaim with relief that King David was a poet, but can never free themselves from unease. Masen, the Jesuit, insists that the only poetry permissible is religious; Birken states that 'Gottesfurcht' is the purpose of poetry and instructs writers to take their themes from the Bible. Herdegen ('Amarantes') justifies pastorals on the grounds that Christ is the Good Shepherd. All the writers wrote religious poetry, and many regretted publicly the secular poetry to which in their youth they had been tempted (Rist, Zesen). A sharp conflict of conscience arose over the use of the names of pagan gods and goddesses. Harsdörffer was one of the few who supported Opitz's rather easy-going attitude, and Buchner justified their use as an attractive disguise for religious and moral instruction—in his own words, such devices 'gild the pill'. Zesen rendered the gods harmless by using abstract equivalents, 'Liebinne' for 'Venus', etc. But Rist and Omeis call it sinful to write odes to gods, Birken forbids themes from classical antiquity, and Hadewig is completely intolerant of the practice.

Similarly, all the critics demand that poetry should serve morality in the direct sense that it utters moral sentiments, and as we have seen in respect to drama and novel, gives examples of good behaviour and shows virtue rewarded and evil punished. All in principle condemn the licentious poets of antiquity and stoutly assert that good poetry is morally good. The greatest controversy arose here over love-poetry. Opitz and others defend love-poetry where it is chaste, and indeed recommend that poets should 'von Liebes-Sachen melden' as love is a great sharpener of wits. Zesen however, like many others, could not reconcile love-poetry with his religious and moral convictions and publicly repudiated his early love-poems as the excesses of youth. In spite of such scruples, much love-poetry in German as well as Latin continued to be written and was defended with a characteristic and frequently met argument. The poems, it is stated, do not refer to any real experience, the emotions are only simulated for the sake of a poetic exercise. Kindermann announces that his loves were invented and Birken wrote the lines:

> Das Hertz ist weit von dem, was eine Feder schreibet,
> Wir dichten ein Gedicht, dass man die Zeit vertreibet.
> In uns flammt keine Brunst, ob schon die Blätter brennen
> Von liebender Begier. Es ist ein blosses Nennen.

Purely aesthetic problems, in contrast to the moral, are discussed most perfunctorily. Art, says Opitz, repeating what Scaliger and others had said, is imitation of nature, and in the same breath, imitation of 'what could or should be'. The

glib phrase combines two contrary tendencies, the realistic
and the idealistic, the conflict between which had led to protracted controversies in Italy on the nature of reality and to
bitter arguments between Aristotelians and Platonists.
Scaliger himself, following a great tradition, asserted that
universals are real and things and facts only phenomena, and
he therefore required of the artist the depiction of ideal forms
of which perceived reality is the imperfect reflection. But
there is scarcely an echo in the German critics of these problems. When they speak of drama and epic, they pay lip-
service to the imitation-theory by asserting that the characters must be true to life and use the type of speech appropriate to their station, while they justify the idealization of
the hero on moral not aesthetic grounds. Art, says Buchner,
is preferable to nature because it is not 'gemein'. The German critics never show an inkling of the idea that Sir Philip
Sidney and some of the Italians had grasped: that poetic
utterance is different in principle from a historical or philosophical statement in that it does not claim to be a statement
about actuality. Buchner only claims that the poet differs
from the historian in the ordering of his material and his
style, and Neumark asserts that they are the same, except
that the poet uses a more elevated style and adds 'verblümte
Bilder'. When Harsdörffer distinguishes orator and poet, he
is content to say that, while the orator speaks about the truth,
the poet distorts truth in the interests of decoration. Thus the
Germans maintain that the poet is a liar, but a liar in a good
cause—to improve morals and religion or to give dignity to
life through decoration, etc. (Buchner, Harsdörffer, Titz).

The views are however confused. The ancient aphorism,
'ut pictura poesis' is always reiterated and it means two con-
tradictory things. On the one hand, it means that poetry is
as illusionistically natural as the realistic 'counterfeits' of art;
on the other hand it is fantastic and decorative like painting
—the two qualities that are wonderfully combined in Baroque painting (in the same way, in dramatic theory, verisimilitude is always required within a framework of the ideal

and exemplary—Masen, Gryphius). Words are uncritically equated with colours and serve to enrich and embellish, not simply to portray. This decorative function of poetry is particularly stressed in the middle of the century with Rist, Zesen, and especially the Nürnberg school. Harsdörffer thus asserts that the poet must 'das natürliche Wesenbild verstellen', and Stieler makes the typical claim: 'Die Wahrheit will verbildet und ümgekleidet seyn, verzuckert und vergüldet'. Imitation of nature comes to be valued chiefly as an intellectual exercise. Buchner asserts that pleasure in artistic imitation arises from the recognition of likeness, and the later writers intensify this pleasure by making it a harder exercise, veiling and disguising nature in figures of speech, emblems, riddles and such. As Neumark wrote, the chief objective of poetry is 'Aus-Schmücken'. Decoration, rich imagery, rhetoric always tended towards courtly pomp and led to much pseudo-elegance as in the preciosity of Zesen ('Hand-Schleyer' instead of 'Handschuh'). Vulgarity and ugliness were ruled out on the grounds that it is a law of nature that men are repelled by them. Thus Klaj could proudly write that 'unsere Helden Sprach wird Hofgemäss bereit' and could hope that the princes would now 'adopt and love it'.

This urge to decorate and enrich led to a proliferation of metaphor and epithet, to a stilted bombast that later critics began to turn from. Morhof, Sacer and Schupp call for more restraint, and Rachel, Wernicke and Canitz begin to deride the bombast, the piling on of images, and seek to return to common sense, to the sobriety of Opitz. But delight in high-flown style and far-fetched imagery remained long after Weise, Thomasius, and Leibniz had championed prose as against verse and established the principles of a sober prosaic style.

Gottsched, also appealing to the authority of Opitz, inaugurates a new era not merely in that he attacked the rhetoric of the Baroque and many of its literary principles. He called his Poetics 'Critische Dichtkunst', in distinction to the Baroque Poetics which were not 'critical'. That is, he did not satisfy himself with a set of rules, but tried to establish the rational grounds of the literary forms. Lessing, in criticizing Gottsched, fully introduced Germans to true critical thought. The Baroque writers, though they required poetry to be an 'imitation of nature', never asked such questions as: 'Of what is a lyric poem an imitation?' They repeated the Aristotelian view that tragedy arouses pity and terror (Harsdörffer prefers 'Erstaunen und Mitleiden', a typical variant), but never enquired more deeply, though their Italian predecessors, not to speak of their French contemporaries, discussed such questions at length. Only in the eighteenth century, largely as a result of a direct engagement with Aristotle, were such matters critically investigated.

The Baroque Poetics assert rather than critically justify new cultural tastes. Their grasp of drama and epic is feeble and reflects an uncertain wavering between a middle-class religious tradition and an unsubstantial alien courtly culture. The thought and poetical practice of the critics were hampered by the supremacy of a rigid religious doctrine enforced by the secular power, to which they paid tribute though the practice of poetry was implicitly a protest against its rigidity; they submitted to the prestige of a nobility that valued precedence higher than achievement and from which they were separated by mode of life and rank. But, with all their confusions and trivialities, the Poetics are a considerable cultural achievement. They are richest in the field of lyric poetry where they reveal a remarkable feeling for the musical and evocative resources of words and the expressive potentialities of verse. This pre-occupation with words, even though it led them to bombast, to preciosity, to sheer virtuosity, is also a pre-occupation with human potentialities, with possibilities of feeling and attitude that could not be imagined in the preceding century. Similarly, the critics' concern to define the genres and types of poetry was an enquiry into the variety of attitudes available to a man in regard to God, to life, to disaster and good fortune, to friends, to the beloved. There is much that is artificial and pedantic in the Poetics, and their prescriptive form makes it often seem as if the different types of poetry and the different attitudes involved in them may be adopted at will without any corresponding experience. For all these drawbacks the Poetics mark a pronounced development in the consciousness of the dignity of the individual personality, of the richness of human relationships, to which the new literature and above all the lyric poetry bears witness.

X

THE BAROQUE LYRIC

Sources

The lyrical forms proclaimed and defined by Opitz have three sources: the new song taken primarily from Italy; the neo-Latin verse of the learned; and the Renaissance lyric of Italy and France. The influence of Petrarch permeates all these forms.

After the publication at Nürnberg of Scandello's *Canzone* in 1566, Italian song-forms, villanelles, madrigals, etc. replaced the older 'Gesellschaftslied' in the cities and courts. The court musician Jakob Regnart from the Netherlands provided German translations of the texts in his collections of villanelles (1567, 1577, 1579), and German composers, notably Hassler, Haussmann and Hermann Schein, followed his example. Since singing was a chief recreation of the whole period, the influence of these and later song-texts was deep, and there is abundant evidence of the close association of music and poetry, composer and poet, throughout the seventeenth century.

Most of the early song-texts are translations and adaptations of Italian texts and often, like the comparable Elizabethan madrigal, they are of great charm. They constitute a new departure in German verse in the following respects.

1. They introduced new stanza forms with varied rhyming schemes and, especially with the madrigal, a freer form capable of a more varied expressiveness than any older German form.

2. The verse borne by the music acquired cadence and tended towards a smooth alternation of stressed and unstressed syllables.

3. Describing feelings rather than events or situations, the texts often reach true reflective lyrical utterance.

4. They introduced a new world of imagery and style, deriving from Petrarch, that dominated the love-poem for over a century. Through the typical formulae of Venus and Cupid and the conventions of the pastoral artifice, love could be surveyed in its subtle variations, distanced, and reflected upon. The dialectics of feeling are expounded: joy that is pain, love that is bitter-sweet, that gives life and death. Though there is much in these texts that is sheer formula— the perfection of the beloved, the fire of love, the lover drowning in tears, the weeping of fountains etc.—they express, and perhaps promoted, an unprecedented delicacy and richness in the love relationship.

There are still themes and turns of speech from folksong, metrical and grammatical naïveties in these texts, that the Baroque legislators had to censure. But they demonstrate that Baroque forms were founded on a widespread movement of popular taste.

By contrast, the Latin lyric cultivated by the humanists was a poetry of the learned and was not sustained by music. From Celtis onwards there is a great stream of Latin verse, panegyric, ode, elegy, love-lyric. Latin verse was the only poetical medium of the sixteenth century in which men could reflect on life and death, on patriotism, on personality, though most of this verse is rhetorical, a learned exercise. From Latin models such as Catullus and Propertius, however, a tradition of love-poetry remained alive, sensuous and passionate, the secret delight of the scholar. In this Latin tradition, the greatest attention was paid to metrical form and rhetorical devices. It was a chief object of the Baroque poets to reproduce in German verse the themes, the metrical and stylistic principles, the pomp of this Latin verse, and many of them, Opitz and Fleming as well as professors and theologians, continued to compose in Latin. The idea of the metrical foot and of verse as an arrangement of metrical feet came from Latin, though it was not till Opitz that the principle of German accentuation was clearly grasped. Theobald Hock's verse stumbles along in spite of his assertion that German verse can and must scan; as he puts it in 'Von Art der Deutschen Poeterey' (in *Schoenes Blumenfeld*, 1601):

> Man muss die Pedes gleich so wol scandiren,
> Den Dactilum und auch Spondeum rieren . . .

Many of the learned (e.g. Weckherlin) held that German should scan by quantity like Latin instead of by natural stress, and Schottel still held that usage, 'die blinde wanckelnde Gewohnheit', was an untrustworthy authority.

The third source of the new poetry was the work of the Renaissance poets of Italy and France and Spain. Here already a literature had been established to rival the ancient, inspired by the patriotic pride displayed in the manifestos of the Pléiade. New and varied verse-forms had been created, an elevated poetic idiom invented and vernacular equivalents to the metrical forms of the Ancients established—notably the Alexandrine and the *vers commun* of Ronsard. This achievement was a constant inspiration to the German poets, a proof that a German vernacular literature could be created to rival that of the Ancients and their neighbours.

The Secular Lyric

Opitz defines 'lyrica' as poems suited 'sonderlich zur Musik', but we take the term here much more broadly as poems in which personal emotion and thought not sustained by narrative are directly expressed.

As a teacher, Opitz is here again of supreme importance. In his *Teutsche Poemata* of 1624, that was often reprinted, he gave examples of most of the new types of lyric, of metre, stanza forms, and imagery. Some poems are written to the new Baroque melodies, many are translations from the approved models—the Greek Anthology, Roman authors like Propertius, neo-Latin poets like Scaliger and Heinsius, Renaissance poets like Petrarch and Veronica Gambara. The collection includes love-songs, odes, epigrams, elegies, epithalamia, epicedia, philosophical meditations, odes religious and secular, epitaphs serious and humorous, etc. With this collection and his numerous later poems Opitz established the image of the new sovereign poetic personality able to adopt a wide range of attitudes. But virtuosity rules at the expense of intensity of feeling. The conventional forms hide whatever personal experience lies behind the poem, the thought is superficial and often hardly developed, without force or pressure of feeling or belief.

Opitz's Alexandrine, the proud medium of elevated thought and feeling, is clumsy, rigidly divided by the caesura and without cadence. He is far more successful with rhythms nearer song, no doubt under the influence of song-texts. Such songs have conventional themes; *carpe diem*, the beloved's eyes are stars, a pastoral motif, etc.; but in 'Itzund kommt die nacht herbey', and the most famous, 'Ach Liebste lass uns eilen', Opitz gives more than examples of imagery and metre. There is expressive rhythm in the lines, movement in the composition; in the second, the alternation of long and short line interprets the swaying argument between time and love. It is a major achievement that the music of words asserts itself in its own right.

Of all Opitz's immediate followers, Paul Fleming, his ardent disciple, is the only one to bring the new conventions to life; he is the greatest lyrical poet of the century. His love-poems, Latin and German, move within the accepted framework and illustrate the whole Petrarchian love-dialectic. The beloved is beautiful and virtuous, she outdoes the sun, her eyes are like stars, lips like rubies, etc. She gives and takes away life, her glances delight and wound; he finds himself and loses himself in his love, he adores his slavery, etc. From the Roman poets comes a more sensuous note too, as in his poem on kissing—'Nirgends hin als auf den Mund'. But with Fleming there is often an unmistakable note of personal experience, of joy and anguish, parting and hope, questioning and comfort. In a broad sweep of rhythm he can give the Alexandrine the unity of a felt experience:

Ach, Schwester, fühlst du nicht, dass du zwo Seelen hast?

The lines combine in a mounting movement:

> Ich irrte hin und her, und suchte mich in mir,
> und wusste dieses nicht, dass ich gantz war in dir.
> Ach! thu dich mir doch auff, du Wohnhaus meiner Seelen . . .

His love-poems mirror a specific relationship and have a unique delicacy and tenderness. In the complex stanzas of 'Es ist umsonst das Klagen', the alternation of long and short lines, the use of enjambment express the conflict in his feeling between the joy of love and the grief of parting, between desolation and comfort, and make it a true lyrical meditation.

Equally in his reflective poems, those for instance to his mother, there is a grasp of a whole poetic mode. His philosophy is based on the conventional combination of trust in God and Stoic self-reliance, but in the sonnet 'An Sich' ('Sey dennoch unverzagt. Gieb dennoch unverlohren') there is a personal note that is rarely heard, and a vigour of movement that expresses an enterprising self-reliance very rare in the German Baroque:

> Thu, was gethan muss sein, und eh man dirs gebeut.
> Was du noch hoffen kanst, das wird noch stets gebohren.
>   Was klagt, was lobt man doch? Sein Unglück und sein Glücke
> ist ihm ein jeder selbst. Schau alle Sachen an.
> Diss alles ist in dir, lass deinen eitlen Wahn,
>   und eh' du förder gehst, so geh' in dich zurücke.
> Wer sein selbst Meister ist, und sich beherrschen kan,
>   dem ist die weite Welt und alles untertan.

Contemporaries could criticize Fleming for impurities, but in his work the new stanza and verse forms, the new rhetoric, are thoroughly mastered and become the means to express and communicate a new depth of experience.

The poetry of the Königsberg group, of Simon Dach and Robert Roberthin, has a character of its own. Moving within the same general conventions, it is rarely grandiloquent, reflecting the social gatherings of a group of unassuming burghers in the remote province; the metres are simple, sometimes close to folksong and hymn, and many of the poems were published as texts of Heinrich Albert's *Arien*. There is little adventure of spirit or imagination in these poems, the thought is domestic and humble, but often a genuine note of feeling is struck, an appreciation of friendship or nature. Thus Dach's *carpe diem*, his 'Mey-Liedchen', is entirely lacking in erotic suggestion, but sweetly invokes the harmony of nature:

> Still zu seyn von Feld und Püschen,
> Von dem leichten Heer der Lufft,
> Da sich jedes will vermischen,
> Jedes seines Gleichen rufft,
> Hört man in den Wäldern nicht
> Wie sich Baum und Baum bespricht?

Whether because of religious scruples about the justification of secular poetry altogether, or for other reasons, the secular poetry of the middle of the century is remarkably lacking in individuality and depth of experience. The poetry of Zesen, Rist, Harsdörffer, Klaj, Birken and the rest is, however, extraordinarily rich in formal and verbal experiment, in complex rhythms, rich rhymes, sonic expressiveness (assonance and onomatopoeia). Some of Zesen's early love-poems have a simple and sincere accent, but most of his work is little more than a display of images, sounds and rhythms, like his 'Maienlied' ('Glimmert ihr Sterne, Schimmert von ferne') with its welter of images and dancing movement. Formal exuberance of the same sort is found in Klaj's work, in the varied metre and inner rhymes of 'Vorzug des Frülings':

> Im Lentzen da gläntzen die blümigen Auen,
> die Auen, die bauen die perlenen Tauen. . . .

Punning, recommended by Harsdörffer, is often indulged in, as in Zesen's sonnet ('Klüng-getichte'):

> O trautes härts! was härts? vihl härter noch als hart . . .

This virtuose manipulation of words and rhythms was a real enrichment, but it runs riot and replaces or drowns thought and feeling. Even in so sincerely intended a poem as Klaj's 'Teutschland' (from his oratorio-like play *Herodes der Kindermörder*), his grief over the desolation of his country is blurred by the virtuosity of the form.

The early poems of Caspar Stieler are a rare respite in the storm of formal elaboration. His *Die Geharnschte Venus* (pseudonymous, 1660) moves within the pastoral-Petrarchian convention, but repeatedly Stieler discovers the exhilaration of a truly imaginative line—'Ich gieng einmahl im Traum zu Schiffe' or

> Die Nacht,
> die sonst den Buhlern fügt und süsse Hoffnung macht. . . .

Stieler can be vigorously impertinent and tenderly humorous, ironical and exuberant, and at times movingly simple. There is genuine experience in his regret for the countryside:

> Mir klingt der sanffte Drescher-schlag
> in Ohren noch, wenn in dem frühen
> die Morgen-treume reiner ziehen . . .
> Wie gerne wär' ich einmahl mein . . .

The mingled humour and tenderness of *Das angenehme Gespenst*, borne on light cadences, closes with rare delicacy:

> Sie liebten sich in der seltnen Reinligkeit.
> Gleich wie
> Geschwister ie
> sich keusch erfreut.

The musicality of Stieler's verse was promoted by the melodies which were printed with the poems, and he does not include complicated metres or profound themes such as might be unsuitable for sociable singing. The absence of sombre pomp, the preference for the tender, the humorous, the 'galant' lyric, is more marked in Saxony than elsewhere, though no other poet reaches Stieler's grace.

The later part of the century was indeed dominated by the poets of the so-called Second Silesian School, Hofmannswaldau, Lohenstein, Hallmann, Neukirch, and others. The movement and lightness of the earlier Baroque is replaced by a heavy pomp, rich in rhetorical figures of speech. There is a pedantic search for effects through far-fetched and elaborately detailed images, through pointed contrasts. With Hunold or Corvinus the playfulness of Zesen or Harsdörffer turns into a frigid erotic frivolity. Characteristic of the times were the 'Heldenbriefe' of Hofmannswaldau, imitations of Ovid's *Heroides*, rhetorical verse-epistles exchanged between the legendary heroes of love. The prestige of this late Baroque remained great for decades, and Neukirch's collections were published in many volumes. The influence of its grandiose rhetoric is still marked in Günther and Haller though here the impact of genuine personal experience and thought controls the extravagance of metaphor, the bombast, and the craving for piquancy and *pointe*. A more sober trend expressed in the criticism of satirists like Rachel, the moral didacticism of Christian Weise, the rationalism of Thomasius, slowly enters into the lyric itself, and the work of Barthold Brockes, moral and philosophical in its intention, precise in its description of nature as a demonstration of divine wisdom and law, founds the new lyricism of the Aufklärung.

Religious Poetry

The religious verse of the whole period follows the same stylistic and metrical principles as the secular except that in general classical mythology is replaced by Biblical imagery. Petrarchian images like Venus and Cupid and Psyche are employed, but the love-dialectic, here applied to the relationship of the soul to Christ, moves within the great antitheses of God and man, eternity and time, life and death, essence and semblance. Much of the religious poetry suffers from the same formalism as the secular. But it suffers far less from an estrangement of form from content, for in the religious poetry men were expressing a genuine heart-felt experience shared in the religious service and community. We find that poets who, in their secular poetry, never win through to a genuine statement, like Harsdörffer or Hofmannswaldau, can write religious poems that communicate emotion; while the secular poetry of Rist, though not without quality, never touches the grandeur of his 'O Ewigkeit, du Donner Wort', that springs from a quaking soul.

The Hymn

Since the hymn was so deeply rooted in the Protestant service, and the sixteenth-century hymn therefore so integral a part of worship, the form of the Protestant hymn changed rather slowly. Since too the hymn was written for communal worship, some of the more individualistic features of Baroque poetry could find little place in it. Thus Martin Rinckart's great hymn 'Nun dancket alle Gott' is a full-throated congregational hymn of praise in Luther's manner. Yet considerable change took place. The hymns of Paul Gerhardt, the greatest of the Lutheran hymn-writers of the century, are more personal and reflective than earlier. His version of 'Nun dancket alle Gott' is a gentle submissive appeal and prayer. 'Befiehl du deine Wege' is an inward-turned meditation. There is profound stillness in the subtle cadences and stanza-form at times that belongs to the new achievements of Baroque style:

> Nun ruhen alle Wälder,
> Vieh, Menschen, Städt und Felder,
> Es schläfft die gantze Welt . . .

Even more markedly Baroque is the mighty hymn 'O Haupt vol blut und Wunden' built as it is on a series of antitheses— God who is despised and rejected, bright eyes, coloured cheeks, red lips that are pale in death; the believer who finds his life in this death, his joy in this pain. Yet we rarely find in Gerhardt the rhetorical intensification and piling on of images that is customary in the secular verse.

Rist, also a Lutheran clergyman but one who stood in the main stream of the new culture, is more typically Baroque than Gerhardt. The grandeur of 'O Ewigkeit, du Donner Wort', its solemn march and elevated tone, the great antithesis of time and eternity, are Baroque in the best sense.

But in this long hymn Rist tries to intensify the effect by new images of terror—plagues and prisons, tyrants, the damned, the torments of devils, etc.—until what opens as the cry of a tormented soul turns into an overloaded display, Baroque in the bad sense. Like many of the surviving Baroque hymns, it is now used in a very abbreviated form. Rist's 'Char-freytagsgesang' is an even more elaborate set of variations on the five wounds of Christ.

Throughout the century there is a conflict between traditional and new forms, between simple confession of faith and display, between simplicity and learning, the outcome of which is sometimes successful sometimes not. Thus Johann Heermann's religious poems are weighted down by flat Alexandrines; but he wrote a Sapphic ode in German, 'Hertzliebster Jesu, was hast Du verbrochen' that is one of the greatest hymns. Through the sustained rhythm of the long pentameters, in a stanza of three long lines followed by a shorter fourth, he created a grave, flowing, religious meditation. On the other hand, in many hymn-writers the influence of the Petrarchian tradition promotes an over-sweet dalliance.

Versifications of Biblical texts for use in the Church service are common, particularly among Calvinist poets. Paul Schede's (Melissus) translation of Marot's Psalm-renderings (1572), in which rhymed pentameters and Alexandrines were used, was indeed an important step towards the new principles of metre. Opitz, in his renderings, used a great variety of stanza-forms and metres. The Song of Solomon was particularly popular, for the sensuousness of the imagery, the exaltedness of the emotion, and the allegorical interpretation all fitted the Baroque taste. It is surprising to find the Baroque influence so strong in the hymns of sectarians and pietists, yet Gottfried Arnold's versifications of the *Song of Solomon* are full of Petrarchian sweetness and rich in complex stanza forms. So too is the *Himmlische Libes-Küsse* (1671) of the eccentric sectarian Quirin Kuhlmann, whose prophetic zeal against orthodoxy and worldly authority brought him to martyrdom. But in that strangest of works, *Der Kühl-Psalter* (1684–6), he abandoned 'petrarcisiren' for 'Davidi-siren'. Drawing on the metaphorical resources of the Bible and the mystics, he makes strange composites and injects into his terms idiosyncratic meanings that are often obscure, yet at times convey the agony and rapture of a faith for which words seem inadequate.

Catholic hymns lack the resonance of the Protestant since they were never so central in the service. Versifications of the liturgy like those of B. Christelius display trends that are characteristic of the Catholic religious lyric.

The Religious Lyric

Nearly all meditative verse of the Baroque moves within a Christian framework, but by religious lyric I mean devotional verse, directly concerned with the experience of faith. It is distinct from the hymn in being a personal lyrical utterance not intended for congregational use, though there is evidently no sharp distinction.

It is here that the Catholic character of the Romance sources of the Baroque lyric comes most into play, and we must properly begin with the Catholic lyric. In the rhapsodic verse of the Spanish mystics, St John of the Cross and St Theresa, who themselves revive elements of medieval mystical poetry, we find decisive influences: Christ and the Church, or Christ and the believer, are bridegroom and bride, the raptures of faith are expressed in the opulent language and imagery of personal love. These features penetrated the early Catholic hymn, and through Catholic books of devotion, often translated by Protestants, became widely known.

The new type of Catholic religious verse was established by the Jesuit Friedrich von Spee in his volume *Trutz-Nachtigall* (written c. 1630), the extended title of which claimed it to be without precedent. He expresses the Christian situation in pastoral form, in the Petrarchian conventions; Christ 'der schöne Gott' is the bridegroom of the soul, the shepherd

Daphnis; his lips are coral, his tears are pearls. The tone is tender, idyllic, elegiac, rather than awed, the conceits tend to playfulness. Spee fails altogether with such exalted themes as the Holy Trinity, but his poem on Christ in the crib, 'Der Wind auf leeren Strassen,' is a most delicate evocation of the idyllic scene, achieved by a mastery of metrical modulation, metaphor and assonance.

Angelus Silesius (Johannes Scheffler), whose *Heilige Seelen-Lust* (1657) he gave the sub-title of *Geistliche Hirten-Lieder der in ihren Jesum verliebten Psyche*, raised this religious Petrarchism to its highest pitch. Typically Baroque is the extended image of the bee feeding on Christ's wounds, making honey from these 'roses', a traditional conceit; for here we see how the allegorical meaning overshadows the natural object. We are not meant to visualize the object described, but only to grasp what it emblematically means. But in several of these poems Silesius rises to an intense pathos of devotion, with a complex yet powerful lyrical movement. His

> Jesu, du mächtiger Liebes-Gott
> Nah' dich zu mir. . . .

is one of the greatest German lyrics. Here the ardour of physical love, the implications of the Venus-Cupid image, are utterly absorbed in the spiritual experience. Through a very complex stanza in which the short lines wonderfully hold the sweep of emotion in meditation, the poem moves majestically to a fulfilment in love and trust.

The Protestant lyric, more preoccupied with problems of life and death, time and eternity, never rises to such heights of rhapsodic devotion. Humble surrender to God's will takes its place, as in Fleming's delicate

> Lass dich nur nichts nicht tauren
> mit trauren,
> Sey stille . . .

In its vocabulary this poem has no obviously Baroque traits, but the intricacy of its form, the poised and hovering short lines, indicate that self-communing and self-exploration that lies beneath the Baroque endeavour.

Representative in a different way is Andreas Gryphius, whose whole work with minor exceptions is religious in inspiration. Not for him the bliss of rhapsodic devotion or serene submission. He was racked by the spectacle of human suffering, the thought of death and the transience of life; his faith is asserted in fear and trembling which only the hope of eternity allays. His verse is troubled, dramatic, never reaching the sweet confidence of song. Much of it is embedded in the events of the ecclesiastical year, Advent or Lent, a crystallization of the appropriate sermon. It is solemn and learned, clothed in the dignity of the Alexandrine, where the heaviness of the caesura interprets the severity of his thought, and the grandiose metaphors, the high rhetorical style fit the elevation of the themes of sin and redemption, despair and hope. There is much repetition, much rhetoric, in the Baroque manner, but also an intensity of feeling that redeems his verse from bombast, and that creates in some instances poems of high quality. In the four sonnets on the Times of Day unusually evocative descriptions are in each case followed by general religious reflections; 'Abend' has a remarkably musical elegiac movement, while the agitated dactyls of 'Mitternacht' convey the terror of night and sin; even the hope of salvation is shaken by the fear of 'des erschrecklichen Gottes Gerichte'.

The religious ode was much favoured, but generally in the hands of a Klaj or Rist, it is a shapeless collection of reflections giving opportunity for elaborate figures of speech and imagery. The intensity of Gryphius's religious feeling, monotonous though it is, enabled him to write the only great odes of his time. He uses (as in the choruses of his plays) the Pindaric form of two identical strophes followed by an episode (Satz, Gegensatz, Abgesang), and profited both by the metrical discipline this imposed and by the dramatic contrast and final resolution that the form invited. In the great ode 'Ich irrte gantz allein' the first strophe describes him lost and alone in desolation and night; the horror deepens in the antistrophe, death, destruction, and Hell threaten him, around him thunders

> Der auf den schwachen Geist zu hart erhitzte Gott.

The episode in calmer rhythms brings release: in God's omnipotent love there is hope. Unfortunately, as often, Gryphius goes on to expand, and further strophes recapitulate instead of developing the theme, and seek to intensify by piling on images of terror.

There are numerous Baroque lyrics which successfully express the feeling of transience, the hope and trust in God, but no other poet finds so large and profound a sublimity as Gryphius. Others, when they aim so high, often fall into triviality or bombast. Zesen's religious odes contradict their theme in their form; even when describing the sufferings of Christ he indulges in over-sweet images and metrical virtuosity. Klaj wrote a curious set of poems on the Passion, Resurrection, and Ascension of Christ. They are oratorios intended for declamation, and include a variety of forms that are all external glitter. There is a general tendency to stir feeling through a more and more detailed description of the physical horror of Christ's suffering, reaching its peak in Lohenstein's religious verse that combines elevated pomp of diction with a harrowing evocation of the putrescence of the crucified Christ.

This combination of an almost erotic sweetness with an almost sensational cult of physical suffering is a profound characteristic of Baroque religious poetry—indeed of Baroque religious art. First established in the Catholic poetry, it pervades for some time the Protestant equally. It was preserved in hymns for long after the Protestant lyric had taken on a more moral and sober tone, as we can see from the texts of Bach's oratorios, and it remained for long in the hymns and religious verse of pietism and the more fundamentalist sects. Its terminology still lingers on in the hymns of the Salvation Army.

Mystical Verse

All the verse discussed so far moves securely in the theological framework of the orthodox churches. But in Silesia, in circles influenced by the mystical thought of Valentin Weigel and Jakob Böhme, a different type of meditative verse arose. It is still Baroque in its pointedly antithetical style, but it is not ornate in imagery or language and its theme is the reconciliation of the great antitheses of God and man, eternity and time, within the soul. Daniel von Czepko, who also wrote secular pastoral poetry in the Petrarchian vein, was the first to distil this mystical thought into the form of the pointed distich:

> Was laufst du in den Stall: geh in dein Hertz und Ruh:
> Einmahl ist dorte Gott gebohrn, hier immer zu.

In his *Monodisticha* (1655) he finds numerous variations for the thought that the All is to be found by emptying oneself of all; that the source of movement lies in the stillness of the soul which discovers God everywhere:

> Schau alle Ding in Gott, und Gott in allen an,
> Du siehst, dass alles sich in ihm vergleichen kann.

Angelus Silesius was a friend of these Silesian mystics, but after conflict with the Lutheran authorities joined the Catholic Church which was more tolerant of mystical rhapsody. He adopted the distich in his *Geistreiche Sinn und Schlussreime* of 1657 which became widely known in the enlarged form of *Der Cherubinische Wandersmann* (1674 and 1675). Silesius revels in the boldest paradox, but the simplicity of image and statement gives the thought an unrivalled intensity:

> Der Abgrund meines Geists rufft immer mit Geschrey
> Den Abgrund Gottes an; sag, welcher tiefer sey.

Time and place have only a subjective reality:

> Nicht du bist in dem Orth, der Orth der ist in dir!
> Wirfstu ihn auss, so steht die Ewigkeit schon hier.

> Du selber machst die Zeit: das Uhrwerk sind die Sinnen:
> Hemstu die Unruh nur, so ist die Zeit von hinnen.

Theological truths are allegories of the inner life:

> Der Himmel ist in dir, und auch der Höllen Qual:
> Was du erkiest und wilst, das hastu überall.

God cannot be grasped in intellectual formulations, but only by turning inwards, by man becoming 'wesentlich': 'Je mehr du nach Ihm greiffst, je mehr entwird Er dir'. And all the rationalist and dogmatic structure of theology seems to crumble when Silesius writes:

> Ich weiss dass ohne mich Gott nicht ein Nu kan leben,
> Werd' ich zu nicht Er muss von Noth den Geist auffgeben.

> Ich bin so gross als Gott, Er ist als ich so klein:
> Er kan nicht über mich, ich unter Ihm nicht seyn.

In one aspect, this great work sums up the criticism of dogmatic theology, the search for a justification of inner experience that we can follow through from the humanists, from Sebastian Franck or Paracelsus. The thought comes directly from the theosophic mysticism of Böhme and the Protestant sects, and it lived on in the pietism of Gottfried Arnold. For Silesius it confirmed the Catholic belief, but it is more truly the most intense expression of that personal, anti-dogmatic search for a metaphysical meaning of existence that culminated in the German idealistic philosophy of the following century.

Altogether, the lyric of the seventeenth century, both secular and religious, documents a process of the greatest significance. In it men gave dignity to personal life, sometimes by merely rhetorical means, but more essentially by making of it the expression of their most personal and deepest feeling. Through it they freed the self from the established social and theological values even though this emancipation and enlargement of the self was achieved only in the imaginative world of poetry and did not find, until the maturity of the Aufklärung, a philosophical justification.

XI

SATIRE

SATIRE has in the seventeenth century nothing like the central position it occupied in the sixteenth. It is not deeply embedded in popular thought and feeling and did not create representative figures like the 'Narr', Till Eulenspiegel, or Reynard the Fox; nor is it bold and intellectually penetrating like the Humanist satire. Its best achievements come from the periphery of the new Baroque culture and are rather provincial and old-fashioned in outlook. Satirical elements in comedy and narrative are also less pungent and pervasive. We can distinguish two main forms of satire, one in some respects linking on to the sixteenth-century tradition, the other that is more peculiarly Baroque; one more discursive and descriptive, the other more witty and epigrammatical.

Discursive Satire

Aegidius Albertinus (1560–1620) was an official of the Munich court and deeply engaged in Counter-Reformation polemics; he translated a number of Spanish works of religious edification as well as the picaresque novel *Gusman de Alfarache* (1615), strengthening the moral through anecdotes and examples. His main satirical work is *Lucifers Königreich und Seelengejaidt* of 1616; in it he enumerates all possible human weaknesses not simply as follies but as evil. The work is a product of that gloomy period in which devilish forces were imagined as being very real and tangible, the period of the witch-trials, and lacks the urbanity of the Baroque. In several ways, however, it introduces Baroque methods and themes. There is a continual call to religious conversion, a stress on the joys of Heaven; and though he is often clumsily direct, he writes in a prose that is at times colourful, and that can rise to a declamatory pathos.

J. M. Moscherosch (1601–69) held responsible administrative posts in the Strassburg area and suffered much hardship in the turmoil of the Thirty Years War. The most important work of this Protestant, who won great prestige through his learning, was an adaptation of the Spanish Catholic Quevedo's *Visions* published in 1640 (enlarged 1642) under the title of *Gesichte Philanders von Sittewalt*—which earned him admission to the Fruchtbringende Gesellschaft as 'der Träumende'. The first part sticks fairly closely to Quevedo and satirizes rather general 'follies' (Moscherosch uses Brant's term) like the 'Venus-Narren', quacks, lawyers, courts and courtiers. The second part is more original and contemporary. Here Moscherosch attacks the 'Alamodewesen', the foreign manners, clothes, and language adopted by the fashionable. He holds up in contrast to this the rough and crude sincerity of the Ancient Germans, and indeed he proclaims in his 'Vorrede', addressed to his 'Teutsch gesinnter Lieber Leser', that he wished to restore 'die Alte Teutsche Redligkeit'. Here he unfolds a real satirical style. He uses a mobile prose, sometimes describing the appearance of the persons criticised, using dialogue, even dialect, to demonstrate their character, and enlivening his account by conversations. He is discursive, sometimes long-winded and over-learned, but the satire is rich and lively. It is characteristic of Moscherosch that, for anecdotes and themes, he goes back to sixteenth-century writers as well as to the Classics and to Spanish and Italian moderns; just as he decorates his account with poems and verses from German popular sources as well as from the new Petrarchian tradition. Eulenspiegel himself puts in an appearance.

In the last 'Vision', 'Soldaten-Leben', Moscherosch composed a little masterpiece. In place of the very loose thread that capriciously strings together the earlier themes, here we have a consistent narrative. Philander, fleeing from envious rivals, is kidnapped by a band of soldiers and takes part in

their exploits. Skirmishes, raids, retreats are vigorously described, the suffering of peasants and civilians, the frustrated
attempts of the higher officers to maintain law and order.
The terse, drastic narrative is a unique commentary (if we
except Grimmelshausen's *Simplicissimus*) on the chaos of the
time, when authority was flouted and soldiers were indis-
tinguishable from marauders. The story gets dispersed
towards the end as more discursive satire of a commissary and
a Jew breaks its unity, but the main part shows the best of
a new narrative technique, a remarkable grasp of action and
an expressive use of dialogue (a glossary of thieves' slang is
added); satire is embedded in situation and event, and is
more telling than any moralistic commentary. Here again we
see Moscherosch's ambiguous position within the Baroque.
There are obvious Baroque elements, learned and fantastic
interludes, even modish poems, and the story shows a verbal
and narrative skill that goes beyond any narrative prose of
earlier times; but in its drastic realism, its attentiveness to
common life and 'vulgar' characters, it links on to the sixteenth century.

   Johann Lauremberg's *Veer Schertz Gedichte* (1652) is the
work of another outsider. Lauremberg (1590–1658), a professor of medicine and mathematics in Rostock and Denmark,
wrote in High German courtly plays in the pastoral vein
with interludes of peasant comedy. In his old age he turned
against the Baroque mode and composed these four satires
in Low German, and though he uses in the main the Alexandrine, he often falls into 'Knittelvers'. The form of his satire
illustrates his intention to commend the simplicity of old
ways and old style. With great good humour he describes and
mocks at the new courtly modes, the 'Alamodische Kleder-
Dracht', the fashionable linguistic impurities ('dat Frantzoes-
ische Duedsch'), the craving for titles, and in the last satire,
the inflated conceits of the Baroque poets; he praises in
contrast the good sense and language of the common man,
the old traditions, and defends Low German (with a reference
to *Reinke de Vos*). His form, a mixture of anecdote, description,

G L—E

and pithy comment, goes back to Brant; but his satire is limited to manners and modes and is too relaxed and good-humoured to have much bearing; it is provincial in the best sense but also rather philistine.

J. B. Schupp (1610–61) is an outsider too. A very learned man, 'Hauptpastor' from 1649 in Hamburg, he was absorbed in his pastoral duties and expressed great scorn for the formal preoccupations of Opitz. Sturdily outspoken, he became involved in bitter controversies with his clerical colleagues. In his sermons, which were too popular for the liking of his colleagues, as in his writings, he used a vigorous style enlivened by anecdote that was called undignified and scurrilous by his critics. It is characteristic that he defended himself by the example of Luther; his language has indeed something of the drastic turns of speech and idiom, the outspokenness of the sixteenth century. On the other hand, he is often demonstratively learned and fond of classical figures; for instance he puts one of his works of self-defence in the form of a dialogue on Parnassus where Apollo is his mouthpiece.

His satire is ebullient, witty, anecdotal, and often a means to ventilate his own grievances, as when he satirized the pirating of books or the belief in prognostications. His most accomplished satire is *Corinna* (1660), an attack on sexual licence. This ancient theme, so often dealt with, is treated in a new and striking fashion. He tells the story of the seduction and fall of a whore, her evil life, her horrible end, diseased and abandoned. It is a colourful picture of manners and morals in his home town and typically Baroque in the contrast between the sordid realism of Corinna's end and the elevated pathos of her confession and repentance. The story is overloaded with learning and moralizing, but it indicates once again the trend to embody the moral in a story. The work was indeed sharply attacked by theologians on the grounds that it made vice seem too attractive, it pleased too much; and Schupp defended himself with the typically Baroque argument that art must please as well as edify, and that to get people to take their moral medicine one must 'überziehen mit Zucker die Wahrheit'.

Epigrammatical Satire

Discursive satire continued in many forms, in the homilies of Abraham a Santa Clara (1644–1709) with their riot of anecdote and verbal elaboration, in the polemical writings of Thomasius with their caustic wit. But a different type of satire also flourished in this century.

Opitz defined 'Satyra' as a genre in which vices were castigated with 'höffliche reden und schertzworte', meaning by the latter term 'stachlige und spitzfindige reden'. Thus he reckoned the epigram to be the characteristic form of satire, the latter being 'ein lang Epigramma'. He showed in his *Poemata* his delight in the witty brevity of the epigram, translating many from the Latin, though the material he uses for his own epigrams is usually only chosen for the sake of the form. He translated from the Latin several of the satirical epigrams of John Owen, a didactic writer who enjoyed much prestige in Germany and who used this classical form to deride the faults and vices of his time. Many of the Baroque poets wrote rhymed epigrams of this type, but they demonstrate literary skill and verbal wit rather than moral and satirical energy.

One great epigrammatical satirist emerged, however, Friedrich von Logau (1604–55), who published a first collection in 1638 and an enlarged edition in 1654 entitled *Salomons von Golaw Deutscher Sinn-Getichte Drey Tausend*. Logau, a Silesian nobleman in the service of petty Silesian dukes, was chafed by the wretchedness of his position and his domestic life. But though unhappy experiences made him bitter, they did not prevent him from finding a secure objective basis for his criticism. His choice of the epigrammatic form with its polished terseness helped too to eliminate subjective elements from his satire. His verbal dexterity, pointed brevity, subtle manipulation of verse and phrase and balancing of contrasts, all belong to the Baroque, as does also the patriotic fervour of his criticism of false cultural fashions; but his use of homely phrases, of provincialisms, his avoidance of bombast and conceits, his suggestive reticence, stand in great contrast to Baroque trends and reveal the hollowness and inner contradictions in the Baroque aspiration to create a German culture through imitation of the foreigner.

Thus Logau adds a dimension to the usual attacks on foreign fashions, for he gets to the moral attitude beneath the habit:

> Alamode-Kleider, Alamode Sinnen;
> Wie sichs wandelt aussen, wandelt sichs auch innen.

> Diener tragen in gemein ihrer Herren Lieverey;
> Solls dann seyn dass Frankreich Herr, Deutschland
>   aber Diener sey?
> Freyes Deutschland schäm dich doch dieser
>   schnöden Knechterey.

He satirizes the emptiness of wordy patriotism:

> Deutsche Sinnen sind gefallen, deutsche Reden
>   sind gestiegen;
> Scheint also, man lass an Worten mehr als Thaten
>   ihm genügen.

The hollowness of German patriotism is, he sees, due to the lack of unity in Germany, by which he means both political disunity and the estrangement of the different classes:

> Deutsch zu reden, deutsch zu schreiben sind die Deutschen
>   jetzt beflissen;
> Wie sie sich recht Deutsch bekleiden, künnen sie zur
>   Zeit nicht wissen,
> Biss zum kleiden, wie zum reden, eine Gnoszschaft sie
>   beschlissen.

Thus his criticism of courts and courtiers is sharp and applies to the courtly poets too:

> Anders seyn und anders scheinen;
> Anders reden, anders meinen. . . .

Von des Hofes Hofe-Leben hab ich manchmal
    viel gelesen.
O, das Lesen ist nur besser, als dass selbsten
    da gewesen.

And he writes bitterly of the suffering peasantry:

Was gab der Deutsche Krieg für Beute?
Viel Grafen, Herren, Edelleute;
Das Deutsche Blut ist edler worden
Weil so geschwächt der Bauer-Orden.

Ein Soldat kan durch verzehren
Sich ernähren?
Und ein Landman durch erwerben
Muss verterben?

Of the Peace of Westphalia, so extravagantly praised by other
poets:

Solcher Fried ist schwerlich gut
Der nicht Bauern sanffte tut.

He comments sardonically on the rivalry between the confessions; as often, his pointed satire is not merely negative,
but full of positive suggestion, opening into wide horizons:

Luthrisch, Päbstisch, und Calvinisch, diese Glauben
    alle drey
Sind vorhanden, doch ist Zweiffel, wo das Christentum
    dann sey.

Man kan zwar alle Kirchen schlüssen,
Doch nie die Kirchen im Gewissen.

Logau's satire is not aggressive or didactic, but caustic and
sardonic, opening up reflection, not giving lessons. From one
point of view it is the work of an outsider who knows his
powerlessness and isolation, who makes a solitary challenge:

Leser, wie gefall ich dir?
Leser, wie gefellst du mir?

His response to the evils of the world is despondent not active:

> Das beste, das ein Mensch in dieser Welt erlebet,
> Ist, dass er endlich stirbt, und dass man ihn begräbet.

But his satire also strikes aptly at the roots of the misfortunes of his times, at the evils within society and the evasions and false consolations of his contemporaries. His work went against the grain of the new culture and was largely ignored until, significantly, Lessing acclaimed both his purpose and his art.

In view of the great quantity of satire in these centuries, it is surprising to find the schoolmaster Joachim Rachel calling his *Teütsche Satyrische Gedichte* (1664) the first German satirical poems. What he means is that they are the first to be built on the model of the satires of Juvenal or Persius: each long poem is an extended treatment of a single theme, written in smooth Alexandrines and indeed adopting images and epigrammatical turns (that are often directly translated) from the Latin authors. The themes of most of the satires—the faults of women, parents, false friends, etc.—are very general; only in the last, 'Der Poet' added in 1667, did Rachel write an independent satire on a specific contemporary theme. Here, while defending the practice of poetry, Rachel attacks the triviality of much occasional poetry and takes a middle way on purism, satirizing not only the 'Mischmasch' of foreign borrowings but also the excessive purism of a Zesen. There is a prosaic rational tone in his satire, and this, combined with the 'correctness' of his diction and metre, made the work much admired, but there is no bite or penetration in it. Its academic complacency still recommended it to Gottsched, and it was not till the generation of Lessing that satire again began disquietingly to probe common assumptions and values.

XII

THE DRAMA

TILL late in the seventeenth century there were still no public theatres where actors, writers, and audience might have established a stable co-operation, and still of course no great metropolis where a cultural élite could have formed. The different social status of audiences, the different environments and purposes of performances, religious and geographical differences meant that the dramatic work of the period is heterogeneous.

At the top of the social scale, a few small theatres were built for court entertainment, and periodically occupied by Italian or French singers, dancers, and players; only occasionally were German plays produced here, for specific festive occasions. At the other end of the scale, itinerant players in the tradition of the Englische Komödianten travelled from town to town setting up their temporary stage in public rooms. As time passed they enriched their repertoire with adaptations of German and foreign, above all French plays, but still appealed to the populace by their sensationalism and crude farce. The cultured despised their plays, and society treated the players as outcasts; one of their most enterprising 'Prinzipale', Velten, was refused the last rites as he lay on his death-bed in Hamburg in 1692. Not till Gottsched made his alliance with the Neuber troupe did a cultural leader seek the co-operation of the itinerant players.

The educated middle class writers borrowed motifs here and there from the 'Wanderbühne'; they wrote plays for courts and texts to be performed in churches; their central endeavour was still, however, a drama for occasional performance at schools and universities, to be acted by students before the assembled notabilities and burghers. A serious religious and didactic purpose inspires these school-plays, and it is only in this framework that Baroque tragedy finds its form. But musical drama, oratorio and opera, was also considered to be a literary form, and many Baroque writers wrote oratorio and opera texts. Indeed the first public theatres built in Germany (by share-holding burghers) were the opera theatres at Braunschweig and Hamburg, where the rage for opera amongst the burghers, much opposed by the more puritanical clergy, gave occupation to literary adepts like Neumeister and Hunold, composers like Händel and Telemann. It was Gottsched again who put an end to this last exuberant expression of the Baroque spirit.

The 'Ordensdrama'

The school drama of the seventeenth century is formally linked with that of the sixteenth, but its character changed profoundly. Its main features were established by the Jesuits. The 'Schlusskomödie', the culminating event of the school year, became a great act of missionary 'propaganda' performed before a brilliant assemblage of nobles, notabilities and burghers. The authors are teachers and professors, and several show great dramatic and theatrical gifts. Other Orders, notably the Benedictines, adopted the custom too, and by the middle of the century great expense was lavished on productions; well-equipped stages were built in schools and universities. The plays are all in Latin, but their spectacular incident and staging and comic interludes had a popular appeal.

The Benedictine *Holofernes* (Salzburg, 1640) shows some of the cruder features of the new type. The action is reduced to its simplest and most sensational aspects. It is interrupted by allegorical figures and scenes, King David and Synagogue warn Israel, Venus and Cupid besiege Holofernes' camp, denizens of Hell rejoice over the expected downfall of the Jews, and strangely enough, Phoebus and Neptune in a 'Marine Chorus' lead Bethulia to the Cape of Good Hope. Comic relief is afforded by farcical interludes among the common soldiers. Judith herself appears only in the last act, and the play concludes with the death of Holofernes; the theme is more his spectacular punishment than Judith's spiritual victory.

The Jesuits used to the full such spectacle, allegorical and supernatural figures, comic interludes, but they combined them all in a more intense action in which behind the actual characters a metaphysical drama is fought out, culminating in the victory of the true faith. Jakob Bidermann's *Cenodoxus* (first produced 1602, published 1609, translated into fluent German Knittelvers in 1635) was a decisive step forward. Bidermann dramatizes here the ill fate of a proud, impious, hypocritical doctor of Paris who dies unrepentant and three times rises from his bier to announce in anguish his damnation; in the last scene his friends all drive home the moral and turn from this world. There is skilful delineation of Cenodoxus's hypocrisy and heartlessness, but no attempt to show any development in the characters. The struggle between evil and good is fought out between allegorical figures, his Guardian Angel and his Conscience on one side, Self-Love and Hypocrisy on the other, between Christ and the Devil. The central issue is not moral but religious, the outcome an ascetic repudiation of the world, the flesh, and the Devil. The play turns on sensationally used supernatural elements, and comic interludes of servants (taken from Plautus) do not seriously break the unity of action.

It is clear that the concentrated unity of action in this play, the dignity of diction, and the clarity of delineation, owe much to the Classical drama, though in every other way it is unclassical. It closely corresponds in this with Jesuit dramatic theory which set itself the task of reconciling traditional Poetics with the requirements of the Society. Jakob Masen's *Palaestra* of 1654 is the most authoritative statement. He insists on the unity of action, but allows time and place to vary according to the needs of the plot. He widens the concept of verisimilitude to include any illusion that imposes its power, thus justifying the use of the supernatural. His supreme concern for religious drama leads him to interpret Aristotle's 'pity and terror' as religiou3 emotions, and thus he legitimizes the happy consummations that both religious and moral teaching required.

By the middle of the century the stage had so far developed as to allow for the greatest virtuosity in production. Tragedies of saints and martyrs predominated, and the use of painted scenery, movable sets, flying machines, lighting effects, fireworks, allowed the most spectacular and impressive scenes of supernatural intervention, sudden transformations from peril to safety, scenes in Hell and Heaven, together with illusionistic realism in scenes of horror and torture. The sung choruses developed into intermezzos with ballet and music; comic interludes abounded. Curiously and characteristically, as in Baroque pictorial art, princely authority is glorified in elaborate scenes while at the same time the transience of earthly glory, its dependence on blind fate, is a dominant theme. This dazzling sensual-supersensual drama reached its height in the work of Nicolaus Avancini (1612–86), many of whose plays were written for festivities of the Imperial family. Simon Rettenbacher (1634–1706), the greatest of the Benedictine playwrights, preferred romantic subjects from antiquity like Perseus and Ulysses and was less allegorical in method; but the theme is still the transience of worldly glory combined with the same awe before the great in station, driven by their passions, subject not to any moral judgement but only to an inscrutable Deity whose instrument is Fortuna.

Baroque Tragedy

Urged on by their missionary zeal, the Jesuits showed great sureness of purpose in creating a new form of Baroque religious drama. The problem was much more difficult for the Protestant Opitz with his greater respect for classical and Renaissance models. He accepted from Scaliger and Heinsius the principle that tragedy presents the disasters of majesty. In the preface to his translation of Seneca's *The Trojan*

Women he formulates the decisive theme that tragedy, depicting those who are subject to 'das blosse Glück', helps the common man to withstand misfortune with greater fortitude; he has chosen to translate this play, he tells us, because here we see examples of great fortitude. With this, and his later translation of Sophocles's *Antigone*, Opitz came near to the martyr drama, though unlike the Jesuit drama his ideal is Christian-stoic, his form is pure, the action is simple, the Alexandrines he uses dignified and reserved. The insecurity of his taste is evident when Opitz came nearer the contemporary theatre in his translation of an Italian *Judith*. For this, mainly in lyrical metres, a 'Singspiel', is a courtly artifice in which the seriousness of the religious theme is lost in modish elegance.

Andreas Gryphius, the greatest dramatist of the Baroque, had by contrast the closest links with the contemporary school-drama. He translated a martyr play, *Felicitas*, by a French priest, and in Leyden came into close touch with the work of the Dutch playwright Joost van den Vondel whose biblical play *De Gebroeders* he translated and whose severe and concentrated form he adopted. His own plays were written for school production, for a Protestant stage that had taken over some of the splendour of the Jesuit, with scenic and lighting effects, changes of scene, supernatural figures. They were theatrically so effective that three of them, *Leo Armenius*, *Catharina von Georgien*, and *Papinianus* were taken into the repertoire of the Wanderbühne.

The inconstancy of fortune, the transience of happiness and glory, is the one theme of Gryphius's tragedies; the tragic hero is such by virtue of his constancy and fortitude in the face of disaster. Two of his heroes are Christian martyrs—Catharina, Charles I—and the stoic integrity of Papinianus, who remains faithful to his 'Gewissen', is near-Christian. But he gives this theme an unparalleled force, a felt pathos deriving from his country's sufferings in war and religious conflict, to which he refers in the preface to his first play *Leo Armenius* (c. 1646). His heroes are all (except in one case) exalted persons, and as is usual, courts are the settings; as is usual, the sacred dignity of their office makes them remote from normal beings. Yet with Gryphius they appear in their vicissitudes and their heroism as representatives of man, in whom the great metaphysical issues are heightened by being stripped of the petty paraphernalia of bourgeois life. This concentration is enhanced by the severity of the form. There are no secondary plots, no comic interludes to throw into relief the social dignity of the highly placed. There are slight changes of scene, but the action is compressed into twenty-four hours so that there is no relaxation of tension. Each of the five acts is a dramatic unity rounded off by choruses. Gryphius uses throughout an expressive Alexandrine, lofty and rhetorical, though for the choruses he uses more lyrical metres, often in the form of the Pindaric ode, sung by courtiers, imprisoned virgins, murdered kings and so forth. Occasionally he uses a little allegorical scene in the place of the chorus, and *Catharina von Georgien* opens with an impressive soliloquy by 'Ewikeit' pronounced in a setting described as follows: 'Der Schau-Platz liegt voll Leichen, Bilder, Cronen, Zepter, Schwerdter, etc. Über dem Schau-Platz öffnet sich der Himmel, unter dem Schau-Platz die Helle'. Allegorical figures do not, however, intervene in the action, and supernatural figures, ghosts, appear only as the visions of distressed minds.

The action and theme of *Catharina von Georgien* (1647) and *Ermordete Majestät oder Carolus Stuardus* (1649) are simple; the heroes, victims of the evil lusts and false beliefs of their adversaries, accept their fate with constancy and dignity, noble and passive martyrs. Papinianus is determined to remain the true servant of the co-emperors Geta and Bassianus, but the rivalry of the two makes his uprightness his doom. More complex and dramatic is the first play *Leo Armenius*. Leo has usurped the Byzantine throne. A new usurper, Michael Balbus, is discovered, but Leo postpones his execution because of his reverence for Christmas. Balbus escapes from prison, disguises himself as a priest and murders Leo at the altar. The problem of earthly power is treated here in a typically Baroque fashion. Usurpation is evil and, though Leo is a usurper, yet Balbus is no less evil in overthrowing the usurper; on the earthly plane there is no solution to this problem, and the only 'moral' is Leo's repentant recognition that he deserves his fall because of his former sin. In *Carolus Stuardus* the ghost of Stafford cries: 'put not your trust in Princes' and Charles proclaims that Majesty is 'Schatten, Rauch und Wind'; yet the play glorifies royalty and legitimacy. In *Papinianus* (1659) the rival emperors Bassianus and Geta (and after the latter's murder, his mother Julia) are both evil in their ruthless lust for power, and yet the highest ambition of the morally ideal Papinianus is to serve them; only in one respect may he resist, in that he will not publicly exonerate Bassianus from the guilt for the murder he has committed.

Thus the drama is metaphysical. Violence rules the world, right and religion are disregarded and overthrown; but the true issue is the religious one, and in making his peace with God and conscience, in turning from this world to the next, the tragic hero finds truth and bliss. As a consequence, there is little attention in the plays to purely human relationships either in the world of power or in personal life, little really human interplay, no variety and mobility of attitude, no penetration or inventiveness of thought. There are violent and bloody events, sudden changes of fortune and mood, but the characters are generalized and fixed and their passions sway between blind energy and passive submission, their reflexions move within the broad alternatives of earthly ambition and religious devotion. The grandiose Alexandrines with their heavy caesura admirably express this generalized pathos of their situation, but are not suited to more subtle probing and thought, and rhetorical devices, the excessive use of stichomythia, blur psychological truth, though they may powerfully express the sufferings of man caught in the great antithesis of eternity and time—there are moments of supreme pathos as for instance in *Papinianus* when on the murder of Geta the chorus of attendants cries out in horror and accompanies Julia's lamentations with an alternating dirge. Gryphius's plays fulfil the possibilities and illustrate the limitations of Baroque tragedy. They lack human variety and specificity, truly dramatic action, in spite of their theatrical event, moving scenes, and clarity of structure: the overriding concern for the metaphysical situation of man makes purely human relationships and consummations irrelevant.

These matters do assert themselves, however, in the one 'bürgerliches Trauerspiel' that Gryphius wrote. *Unglücklich Verlibete (Cardenio and Celinde)* 1650, originally planned as a story, is a tragedy of false love and lust with contrasting pairs of true lovers and false, and indeed there is here, expressed in Alexandrines that keep nearer to ordinary speech, some investigation of different types of feeling. But once again the plot leads to a religious crisis provoked through supernatural agencies, and the outcome is renunciation of the world:

Wol dem; der jeden Tag zu seiner Grufft bereit.

In the use of a witch, the apparition of ghosts, an eerie graveyard setting, and a visionary scene in which Death advances threateningly on Cardenio, in the sudden conversions and the repudiation of the world, this play is very near to the Jesuit tradition.

Gryphius established a type of drama that continued in Silesia, but his high earnestness was lost, and the tragedies of Lohenstein, Hallmann, and Haugwitz show features comparable to those in the later Jesuit drama—a love of grand spectacle, of stagey effects, startling changes of fortune, courtly splendour and crude horrors. By far the ablest of these writers was Daniel Casper von Lohenstein. He took his subjects from classical and oriental sources and thus deprived himself of a Christian hero, but his theme is the uncertainty of fate, most strikingly illustrated by the fall of the great: 'Gewalt und Fall sind Schwester'. The mighty figures he preferred to depict belong to times of decay and disintegration, a Sophonisbe or a Cleopatra, and he dwelt upon exotic opulence and customs, adding learned notes. Blood-curdling scenes abound, like that in *Sophonisbe* (1680) where the Carthaginian queen prepares to offer up her son to Astarte and Roman soldiers are ritually slaughtered. Typical of the Baroque are the uneasily combined themes of the transience of power with the adulation of power; in his *Cleopatra* (1661) the fall of Antony and Cleopatra is balanced by the victory of Augustus in whom power, supported by 'Vernunft', is glorified and who nobly celebrates at the end the immortal fame of Antony. In the final chorus 'Danube and Rhine' foretell that the Habsburgs will rival Augustus, and the thought of earthly glory obliterates any other moral.

Lacking the tragic philosophy of Gryphius, Lohenstein is obsessed by the doom that falls upon his heroes, who, mainly women, are borne along by violent and fatal passion. Feeling tosses them this way and that; in one scene Sophonisbe is determined to kill herself, to abandon herself to slavery, to take up the struggle against the Romans. The action sways violently with these violent changes of feeling. Thus *Cleopatra* gives him his best opportunity, and this play was republished several times up to 1733. Following the same sources as Shakespeare, he depicts a woman abruptly changing from love to deception, protesting in the most extreme rhetoric her love for Antony while she is plotting with Augustus, and making the same extravagant love-declarations to Augustus as she makes to Antony. There are the elements of a psychological tragedy here. But Lohenstein's psychology is stereotyped, and the generalized hyperbolic language he uses obscures the individuality of situation and character. His verse is, it is true, more flexible, less constantly rhetorical than that of Gryphius. But it is, especially at moments of pathos, bombastic, overladen with images and conceits, and as a result we cannot detect any difference between sentiments that are meant to be truly felt and those meant to be assumed. Lohenstein is moving towards a more secular conception of tragedy, but is still too enmeshed in Baroque ideas and language to produce anything more than a hybrid.

Baroque Comedy

Comedy in the seventeenth century shows an even greater uncertainty of intention and form than tragedy. Opitz gave the perfunctory definition that it treats of affairs among the 'gemeine Leute', weddings, deceitful servants, love-affairs, miserly old men, etc., but he wrote no exemplary model of what was in his mind. Later critics recognize that comedy is satirical in intention, but suggest like Masen that its gaiety demands that only minor foibles should be satirized. The frequent use of such terms as 'Freuden-Spiel' or 'Schertz-Spiel' indicates in fact strong disinclination for satirical comedy. The most prominent form of comedy is a courtly elegant play, usually allegorical and pastoral in form, composed for festivities at courts, the birthday of a prince, a wedding or an alliance. There is practically no plot, and all ends with the apotheosis of the prince. Music and ballet are introduced to heighten the decorous gaiety of the occasion. Such are the 'Festspiele' written by Klaj, Harsdörffer, and Birken to celebrate the Peace of Westphalia, or the group of plays written by Rist to mourn for or celebrate peace (*Irenaromachia*, 1630, *Das Friedewünschende Teutschland*, 1647, and *Das Friedejauchtzende Teutschland*, 1653). Gryphius's *Majuma* (1657), in the same allegorical style, includes many songs. There was no end to such courtly celebrations (Goethe was still to write several). They may have some poetic charm, there is the delight of disguise, but there is no characterization and no drama; any reference to the realities of war, to real politics, would have been considered improper, and a Rist or Gryphius can only smuggle in a critical comment.

Even the courtly audience must have felt this type of play to be insipid and Rist enlivened his by adding little peasant comedies as interludes between the acts of the allegory. In this he was linking up with farces of the Englische Komödianten (he was one of the few Baroque writers to describe with approval their performances) and with the peasant comedies of Heinrich Julius of Braunschweig. He used dialect, and the scenes are neat, drastic, and amusing; a charming sketch in his tragedy *Perseus* (1634) shows a corporal drilling three wretched recruits and setting them an example by running away as the battle approaches. The more ambitious interludes in the allegorical *Teutschland* plays enlarge the peasant satire by introducing a windbag and braggart, Sausewind, who reveals more and more the features of Philipp Zesen, a very rare and rather malicious example of satire of a bourgeois. Other writers followed suit, but no other writer reached the artistry of Gryphius's *Die gelibte Dornrose* (1660). This, a complete little play, is woven in with *Das verlibte Gespenst*, a translation of a comedy by Quinault, as a rustic counterpart to the elegant formalism of the latter. It likewise deals with the victory of true love over parental folly, and the characterization of the peasant men and an old wise-woman who all speak broad dialect is excellent. There are the beginnings of a satire of the upstart peasant in the magistrate, Aschenwedel, but this fades out as it is he who arranges the happy ending. Dornrose herself is unfortunately rather pallidly virtuous and it is characteristic of the Baroque attitude to the peasantry that she who is to claim our sympathy, speaks in literary German.

Apart from this interlude, Gryphius wrote two independent comedies *Absurda Comica oder Herr Peter Squentz* (1658) and *Horribilicribrifax* (1663). The former, based on Shakespeare's Pyramus and Thisbe scenes, was derived from an intermediary German source; the appearance of Pickelhäring betrays the influence of the Englische Komödianten. Gryphius's artisans do not speak in dialect, but he catches with delightful irony their mode of expression and thinking. Since the theme of Oberon and Titania is omitted, Bottom's part is changed, and Gryphius enriches the play with Lollinger, a weaver who is a self-important Meistersinger learned in literary art. There are references to Hans Sachs, and the play and production of *Pyramus*, of which Lollinger is part-author, are a delicious good-humoured satire on the

Meistersinger plays and players: as the king observes 'Wenn sie besser wären, würden wir so sehr nicht drüber lachen'.

Horribilicribrifax takes up again the theme of the braggart, pretending to courage and wealth and shown up at the end as a penniless coward. Here, however, despite the skill with which Gryphius satirizes the language and behaviour of such persons, he makes his purpose over-complicated. There are three girls whose false or true love we are to follow, two honourable and scarcely distinguishable lovers and two braggarts who seek a good match, one who affects French and the other Italian (a companion spouts Spanish), while there is another rival, a pedantic village schoolmaster who overflows with Latin and Greek. With this riot of jargon and crowd of persons, the plot is very summary and scenes succeed one another in a rather haphazard way. There is an interesting conflict of character suggested in two of the 'good' lovers, Palladius and Caelestina, but it is resolved all too abruptly. This fixedness of character, which does not change but only asserts itself more emphatically in different situations, we can recognize as belonging to the Baroque; those nobly born are consistently courteous (even stilted) and good, the upstarts are grotesquely foolish. There is no true social satire, only laughter over the role people play—and consequently, at the end, even the braggarts are rewarded, not punished. It is typical of the Baroque that, until the end of the century with Reuter and Weise, the only satirical comedy is aimed at the peasantry, the artisans and the braggart outsider. The nobility was, by definition and custom, above criticism, and the writers refrain from satirizing themselves or the middle class—perhaps because they lacked the self-confidence and social independence that self-criticism requires.

Opera and Oratorio

We have seen that for Opitz 'lyrica' were texts to be sung, yet also poems with their own style and form. The Baroque writers sought to create texts of poetic value for several types of musical composition, choruses in tragedies and Biblical plays, songs in comedies, and whole texts for operas and oratorios. Both these latter forms were created in the seventeenth century, and by the end of the century enjoyed in their different ways probably a greater popularity than any other dramatic form.

Like the 'Freuden-Spiel' the opera is Italian and courtly in origin, and during most of the century it remained what W. Flemming calls 'ein Luxusgeschöpf des barocken Absolutismus'. Opitz with Heinrich Schütz as his composer gave the Germans their first opera *Dafne* (1627), adapted from the Italian, an elegant pastoral artifice; his *Judith* (1635), also adapted from the Italian, was the first example of the heroic (biblical) opera. Gryphius planned an opera text (*Piastus*), Birken, Schirmer, Neumark all wrote opera-texts for production at courts. Harsdörffer composed a curious spiritual opera, *Seelewig*, infusing the pastoral artifice with a religious content—nymphs and shepherdesses have such names as Seelewig, Sinnigunda, Herzigilda, etc. Anton Ulrich of Braunschweig included two opera texts in his novels. In the last third of the century the rage for opera seized the middle class, and while Italian works and companies dominated Catholic Bavaria and Austria, and French opera prevailed in Dresden, in the north, particularly in Hamburg, a large number of German operas were composed. Here, where Händel composed his first four operas, text writing became a professional activity of literary men, and Christian Hunold, a poet and novelist of some quality, wrote a great number. Here too Barthold Feind and Hunold wrote theoretical works claiming the superiority of opera as a 'Gesamtkunstwerk' in which poetry, music, dance and decorative art were combined. Here too the first public theatre was built for operatic performances.

The chief substantial contribution of the poets to opera was the provision of lyrical texts of singable and expressive character, for which they could use all their new technical resources, all the varieties of metre, stanza, poetic dialogue, echo-songs, etc. But they did not create a form that as a text had any dramatic power. There was no prescription in the Aristotelian Poetics for opera, and writers could blithely follow the taste of the audience and the composers. In the pastoral-allegorical tradition, questions of verisimilitude did not arise; all moved in a wondrous world and the music leaped from one situation to the other. In the later part of the century, when, as in tragedy, legendary and pseudo-historical heroic themes became popular, the words simply had to provide the basis for stock situations: heroic determination, unhappy love, tyrannical passion, sensual and chaste love, etc. etc. The plot is a nonsensical absurdity, the words a conventional artifice; only the music of a Telemann or a Händel could turn such nonsense into works of delight. Gottsched made short work of the literary pretensions of the opera-writers.

Oratorio likewise came from Italy as a grandiose representation in honour of a saint, performed in church. It was taken over by Protestant composers, notably by Heinrich Schütz, and his Passions, in which instrumental introductions provide the framework for unaccompanied singing, established the form—the biblical text is sung in recitative by the Evangelist, the high points being elaborated by choral singing. Later composers added numerous arias, and choral hymns well-known to the congregation, and developed the instrumental introductions and intermezzos—this was the form that Bach adopted. Well-known seventeenth century hymns were used, and poets were called on too for arias and cantatas. Later we find Brockes versifying even the text of the Evangelist and the cantata form became popular in its own right as a free verse-meditation upon a biblical text, that long remained Baroque in form and language.

The most remarkable literary manifestation of the oratorio was, however, composed for speaking, not for music. Johann Klaj, probably at Harsdörffer's instigation, wrote three pieces on the Resurrection, Ascension and Passion of Christ (1644–5). The fourth of the series, *Die Geburt Christi* (1650), shows the full development of this Baroque form; it was produced in church. The biblical account, built out with reflections and exhortations, is rendered in elaborate Alexandrines. More lyrical verse, in a variety of metres, is used for characters like Gabriel, Mary, and Joseph. All this was declaimed by Klaj himself. Choruses were sung from time to time by the choir and accompanied by instruments. The work is divided into four acts each one of which closes with a sung chorus, a duet between 'Engel' and 'Dichter' bringing the piece to an end. Though the work created a powerful effect on the congregation and found imitators, it did not establish a new form. It is remarkable evidence of the versatility of expression that the Baroque poets had developed, but for the sublime effects at which Klaj aimed through the use of rhetoric and piled metaphors a better instrument was there, music, and the musical oratorio survived his challenge.

New Trends

Towards the end of the century there are signs of dissatisfaction with the unreality, fantastic illusionism and bombast of late Baroque drama and opera. As in other genres, there is no sudden break; Baroque taste was only slowly replaced by new values in the early decades of the eighteenth century. In the work of Christian Reuter (1665–1712?) and Christian Weise (1642–1708) Baroque traits run along with the beginnings of the new; they are harbingers of the coming cultural dominance of Protestant Saxony.

Reuter's comedies, like Weise's owing something to the popularity of Molière on the Wanderbühne, are new in that actual bourgeois society is satirized. They were written in 1695–6 while Reuter was a student at Leipzig and are a gay persiflage of his landlady 'Frau Schlampampe' and her children. The stock phrases and violent temper of the landlady are exuberantly ridiculed, the flirtatious daughters' absurd aping of fine phrases and fine manners and the son's crude braggadoccio (a reflection of Molière's Les Précieuses Ridicules). Amusing and apt as the satire is, it lacks resonance,

for the family is tested only against the pranks and judge-
ments of frivolous and heartless students who themselves are
not criticized. As in his other comedy *Graf Ehrenfried*, a satire
on an impoverished class-proud nobleman, there is a new
and impertinent note in Reuter's plays, though it is rather
capricious, personal and unsubstantial. His sallies led to his
dismissal from the university and lost him the patronage of
the nobility, and his later works, poems and a Passion-text,
show a return to the normal Baroque manner. Even in *Graf
Ehrenfried* there is a proliferation of operatic elements, in
strong distinction to his earlier novel *Schelmuffsky*, in which
he not only satirizes the vulgar braggart but with it the
whole genre of the heroic adventure-story.

Christian Weise's work is altogether more stolid, less pro-
vocative than Reuter's, but in many ways he heralds a new
era. He too was a Saxon, a schoolmaster, first at the
'Ritterakademie' at Weissenfels, then, from 1678 to his retirement, headmaster at the 'Gymnasium' of Zwickau, his birth-
place. He is the last of the great schoolmaster-playwrights,
and with astonishing industry for many years he wrote three
plays to be produced on successive nights, a biblical piece,
a 'political' (historical) play, and a comedy; he wrote too
much conventional verse, novels, and many works of edification. His object with his plays was the time-honoured one of
providing useful moral instruction and practice in deportment and speech, and in many ways his plays show a
characteristic Baroque intention. The social supremacy of
the nobility is a fixed principle, their behaviour and their
concerns are held up as a model. The prince is beyond
criticism, and favouritism, deception, capricious manipulation of his subjects are his unquestioned right. The unctuous
flattery the courtiers use, their preoccupation with status and
promotion, their stilted language, are all intended to be
exemplary; this was the sort of behaviour and language his
pupils, particularly the aristocratic pupils, were to acquire.
Submission, the hope of aristocratic favour are commended
as the highest virtues of the middle class, while the peasantry

are treated throughout as beasts who, if God had not wisely ordained them to live in 'Hunger und Kummer', would overthrow all order. Weise chose rebellion as his theme in many of his plays, and always the rebels appear vicious in their personal as well as political behaviour.

In the form of his plays Weise goes back, however, to an older and popular tradition. He wanted to give parts to as many pupils as possible and thus his plays are crowded (in *Masaniello* 78 speaking parts, not counting attendants) and hence full of dispensable scenes and undifferentiated characters. From the Wanderbühne he took the clown, Pickelhäring or Allegro or Passetems, introducing through them light relief and using them too for moralizing comments. His plots therefore lack the high tension and pathos of the Baroque, and indeed are often undramatic and flat.

But in other ways Weise reveals a more direct revulsion from Baroque drama. He writes in prose because, as he says in *Von Verfertigung der Komödien und ihrem Nutzen* (1708), people do not speak in verse in ordinary life. His prose is often long-winded, stilted, sententious, but it is often lively and fresh, not far from ordinary speech, and above all with more varied tones than Baroque dramatic verse, for his speakers can qualify, make humorous comments, even satirize themselves. This prose is well suited to the discussion of practical questions of behaviour, of practical rules of life, and indeed here we find the greatest contrast to the Baroque. For even in many of his biblical plays, Weise is not concerned with the great earth-Heaven antithesis, with metaphysical problems, but with earthly existence. It is a change of preoccupation that is not polemical, that arose naturally from his moral concern as a practical educator; but here and there we find significant reversals of Baroque tenets. In *Der Niederländische Bauer* (1700), a comedy in which a peasant is persuaded he is a prince (taken probably from *The Taming of the Shrew* as performed on the Wanderbühne), a nobleman reflects on the honoured theme that life is a shadow, a dream, a heavy travail in pursuit of uncertain favours. But when his friend suggests that the life of 'Staats-Leute' must therefore be sheer folly, he answers that after all one should be grateful if the night brings a pleasant dream; even if the moment is transient, yet one is glad if it is happy—a sober correction of Baroque exaltation. And in the same play, when the drunken frolics of the peasant lead the noblemen to reflect that there is an absolute distinction between nobleman and peasant—'eine Gattung von leibhafftigen Vieh'—one of them objects: 'Ich möchte fast also raisoniren: Wir sind alle Bauern; Doch welcher den Bauer im Hertzen verbergen kan, dass er nicht an das Tage-Licht kommen kan, der wird ein qualificierter Hoffmann genennet'; upbringing is more significant than birth!

Such thoughts might be intended simply as views Weise proposed for discussion. There is a more emphatic message in the best of his political plays, *Masaniello* (1683). It treats of a rebellion in Naples, led by Masaniello, a violent and brutal butcher who rages in madness and meets a well-deserved end. Legitimacy triumphs and its alternative is shown to be violence and disorder. What is curious about the play is that while the King of Spain remains beyond criticism—indeed, ignorant of the causes and course of the revolt, he does not appear in the play—there is sharp criticism of his Vice-Roy and the nobility. We learn that the burghers have been burdened by taxes and dues until their life is unbearable, all for the sake of the personal enrichment of the nobles; and the practical policies of the Vice-Roy, his deceptive promises, are shown to be heartless and immoral. Thus, though the rebellious artisans and tradesfolk act in a brutal and senseless manner and their leader grows drunk with power and eventually goes mad, there is sympathetic understanding of their plight.

One further play of Weise's deserves attention as demonstrating this (as yet hesitant) movement of sympathy for the commoner. *Die Unvergnügte Seele* (1688) is, like Molière's *Le Misanthrope* to which it is clearly indebted, a work that is neither comedy nor tragedy, but near to the 'drame sérieux' of the eighteenth century. There are many traditional comic elements in it, notably the clown Passetems and small scenes with peasants and a Jewish jeweller. But it is a study of a pathological hypochondriac, a man to whom marriage, friendship, high office and wealth only bring vexation and despondency; in all situations he comes to the conclusion 'Ich bin unvergnügt'. He becomes a hermit, he seeks the solace of philosophy, all to no purpose. Ultimately he finds in private domestic bliss the contentment he seeks:

> Gott im Herzen, die Liebste im Arm,
> Eins macht selig, das andre macht warm.

There is a certain amount of social satire in the play—the undue fuss of weddings, the petty intrigues of court-life, the burdens of the rich—but it is only the hypochondria that turns these into serious issues. What is important about the play is that, in spite of the ridicule of this unfounded melancholy, we have here an extended study of a 'humour', while the fact that Vertumnus is a nobleman is only of secondary importance; the action is directly translatable into bourgeois terms. And the outcome is not only bourgeois in form—the pious domestic family—but here most strikingly a moral ideal is held up in which religion serves the moral purpose. The Baroque antithesis of God and man, eternity and time, no longer prevails; here is asserted the ideal of the moral values and the social world of the Aufklärung.

XIII

THE NOVEL

THE numerous narrative forms of the sixteenth century—
fable, anecdote, romance, legend, exemplary tale—are reduced in the Baroque period to one main endeavour, the
novel: i.e. a long coherent story of one or several characters,
that follows their fates through vicissitudes to some sort of
stable outcome. Incidents may abound, but are to be inte-
grated into the progressive story. How great a change in
the narrative tradition this meant is indicated by the pre-
dominance of foreign models and the slowness with which an
equivalent German novel emerged. The poverty of theory is
equally striking. The novel was continually attacked on the
grounds of its immorality, and as a consequence most
discussions of it were concerned with its message rather than
its form. Most writers resolved the conflict between the
stipulations of theologians and moralists and the unquench-
able delight in love and adventure stories by creating heroes
of ideal virtue, and many salved their conscience by using
Biblical figures, a Joseph or a Samson, as their heroes. The
modest claim of Fischart (who himself translated a part of
the *Amadis de Gaulla*) that the novel is a moral fable, becomes
more complex as the Baroque taste became more marked.
Morhof is uncertain whether novels are not useless and
immoral, but approves them if they can be made 'nutzlich
und lehrreich'—it became indeed a practice to stuff them
with all sorts of historical information and practical admonishment. The Preface of Duke Anton Ulrich of Braunschweig's *Aramena* (1669) sums up the most usual defence:
novels should lead to 'Gotteserkenntnis' and to virtue, but
also inculcate aristocratic manners and courtly speech; they
make truth sweet by the 'Honig der angedichteten Um-

stände'. The form of the novel is rarely discussed. Traditional prescriptions for the epic lead critics to say the story should start in the middle, and Birken recommends 'die Mänge und Mängung der Geschichten', i.e. the weaving of many incidents in the plot.

Such theoretical comments apply to a type of courtly idealistic novel that closely corresponds to the general principles of the Baroque Poetics. There is, however, another type, more realistic and plebeian, that runs along with it in uneasy companionship and more and more in rivalry. We will examine the two streams separately.

The Courtly Novel

When the Spanish romance, Montalvo's *Amadis de Gaulla* (1508), was translated (from a French version) in 1569, it won an immense popularity. By 1594 the translation ran into many volumes. It surpassed the German romances in the sensationalism of the heroic adventures, the richness of incident, the piquancy of the rather crude love affairs, the skilfully renewed tension to which the interventions of supernatural creatures, fairies and sorcerers, contribute. It was to the German translation of this work that Opitz referred in *Aristarchus* as a proof of the potential dignity of German letters. Equally aristocratic, but much more courtly, was the new pastoral of Sannazaro (*Arcadia*) and Montemayor (*Diana*)—the latter, translated in 1619, became an admired example for the Germans. Courtly society appears in the guise of shepherds and shepherdesses in an idyllic countryside, spinning love affairs and composing lyrics. Here for the first time there is a subtle differentiation of character and feeling. The frank artifice of the pastoral disarmed the reproach of immorality, and Opitz himself could publish an improved translation of Sidney's *Arcadia*, a work in the same vein. Honoré D'Urfé's *L'Astrée* (1607–23), a work of huge dimensions, gave the pastoral full novel form, weaving many love-stories together and providing a psychological study of various types of character and courtly love (translated 1615–

1617). A further step was taken by John Barclay in his *Argenis* which Opitz translated from the original Latin (1626–31). In this highly stylized political novel, adventures and love-affairs are subordinate to an overriding glorification of the absolute monarch, and an elaborate account of the means by which the absolute prince maintains his divine power and authority. The two themes, courtly love and manners and the politics of the absolute prince, are the centre of the novels of Mlle de Scudéry and other French novelists which were translated, several by Zesen. These novels are often set in remote times and places; it is characteristic that the taste now awakened for the fantastic and erotic adventures of the late Greek novel, above all of Heliodorus's *Aethiopian Histories.*

Overwhelmed by this great flood, the German writers took many years before they could match the foreigners—the pastorals of Opitz, Harsdörffer, Rist, etc., are meagre and not in novel form. The first notable novelist in this vein, Philipp von Zesen, is also one of the most original. His *Adriatische Rosemund* (1645) is a psychological novel of love with pastoral scenes and elegant conceits in the style of D'Urfé and Scudéry. He recognizes the originality of his enterprise and justifies it in the 'Vorrede' on the grounds that the Germans now, after so many translations, read 'gaern von der Libe' and that this is 'eine keusche libesbeschreibung'. But the novel is also in a sense a realistic work, even with autobiographical references. Its milieu is the aristocratic society of Amsterdam of which city Zesen was an honorary Freeman. Markhold, a Silesian Junker, a Protestant, falls in love with the daughter of a refugee Venetian nobleman, Rosemund, a Catholic. But the father refuses to allow them to marry unless Markhold engages to bring up any daughters in the Catholic faith and this Markhold cannot do. Rosemund falls into a decline and dies.

This serious theme is, however, wrapped up in artifice. Numerous incidental tales and extensive discussions spread out the simple tale. All is told in a most elaborate, precious style, and there are many descriptions of fashionable dress

and elegant rooms. Rosemund in distress withdraws to a hermitage, and this is the idealized pastoral of Mlle de Scudéry,
a cottage whose walls are hung with tapestries in 'bleu
mourant' and a life spent in expressing her grief in verses.
Zesen's elegance is the extreme of preciosity, his learning is
demonstrative and tedious. But the book is unusually sensitive to states of feeling and their physical expression. Above
all, it is a rare presentation of a real and serious issue: the
conflict between natural feeling and confessional pressures,
an elegiac plea for the rights of love.

Zesen later repented of his early dalliance with love, and
his two last novels are taken from Biblical story. *Assenat*
(1670), the story of Joseph, is as he calls it 'eine heilige und
weltliche Staatsgeschichte', the story of Joseph's shrewd
grasp of the principles of statecraft, in which the amorous
wiles of Potiphar's wife and Joseph's own love-marriage are
hallowed by their Scriptural source. The whole moves in an
aristocratic courtly world. Zesen's language here is less
precious than in his youth, but it is highly pointed, anti-
thetically balanced. In *Rosemund* from time to time a vigorous colloquial phrase pleasantly breaks the artifice; here,
however, all is stylized and elevated. Zesen's *Simson* (1679) is
written in the same elevated pointed style, and here again
Zesen could combine a piquant love-story with a political
action.

Most of the succeeding novelists find a religious or moral
theme to justify their interest in love and adventure. The
moral of *Amadis*, whose hero is only mighty, is condemned as
'schandsüchtig'; it is the virtuous hero who now overcomes
all dangers and wins his true love. In adversity he trusts in
God who inscrutably works through the mysteries of fate; he
wields power like a God, his policies are beyond his subjects'
criticism and he must be worshipped as divine. The novels
are monstrous in form and size. A. H. Buchholtz's *Des
Christlichen Teutschen Gross-Fürsten Herkules . . . Wunder-Geschichte* of 1659–60, with its continuation of 1665, illustrates
the double theme of religion and extravagant patriotism.

Herkules, a German prince, pursues his beloved through a fantastic world, frustrated by fateful accident and sustained by Christian faith. Clumsy and pedantic in style, the work is full of religious and moral edification. Duke Anton Ulrich of Braunschweig's *Die durchleuchtige Syrerin Aramena* (1669–73) is more courtly and political in tone. While here again the union of the princess with her princely lover (a Celt, i.e. a German), achieved after a series of fantastic adventures, is ascribed to divine Providence, the novel gives many practical lessons in princely policy. *Octavia, Römische Geschichte* (1685–1707) is a story of princely martyrdom and gives an opportunity for much historical information. There is considerable clear-sighted exposition of princely statecraft in these works, and in spite of their unwieldy size, the various characters have a consistent individuality; but the innumerable and far-fetched incidents are beyond all belief.

Fantastic as the world of these novels is, there are many veiled references to contemporary figures and events. The same is true of Daniel Casper von Lohenstein's *Grossmüthiger Feldherr Arminius* (1689–90). Here the ideal German, the Herman who overthrew Varus, appears as the modern absolute monarch, courteous in love and address, pious, a master of political strategy, heroically stoical under the blows of an inscrutable fate. Lohenstein dedicated his work as a model to the German nobility; in his bourgeois readers he assumes his own worship of rank, but adds for their delectation, in an elaborate bombastic style, innumerable disquisitions on historical, political, and moral matters.

These novels were widely read well into the eighteenth century; but still more popular was *Die Asiatische Banise* (1689) by H.A. von Zigler und Kliphausen, a novel that provoked many imitations, still delighted Goethe's contemporaries, and had a successful career in dramatic form. It is based on travellers' tales of recent events in Pegu (in the East Indies), and contains much curious information concerning customs, religion, etc. Its theme is the conflict between an evil tyrant, Chaumigrem, and the upright prince

Balacin who loves Chaumigrem's prisoner, the beautiful and chaste Banise, and in the end slaughters Chaumigrem, marries Banise, and brings peace, plenty, and piety to the suffering people. This is the usual scheme of the aristocratic novel, and as is usual, the heroes are immaculate, the villain a bloodthirsty monster. The style is overloaded with bombastic figures of speech, and the chief characters always express themselves in an exaggerated, absurdly stilted rhetoric. But the novel is much more skilful than most. It is relatively short, and Zigler, employing delaying tactics in his narrative, creates moments of climax that hold the reader in suspense. The most violent and sensational actions occur, massslaughter is described in blood-curdling detail, and the heroes are continually in urgent danger; in the end, Banise is rescued from being sacrificed when Balacin, disguised as a priest, plunges the sacrificial knife into Chaumigrem's heart. Though the main characters are unrelievedly exalted in all they do and say, there is a more natural tone in some minor characters, and pleasant relief is provided by Scandor, Balacin's servant, a subdued version of Sancho Panza.

In certain novels of the late seventeenth and early eighteenth centuries, a more frivolous tone replaces the pathos and pedantic earnestness of *Arminius* or *Banise*. Christian Hunold's *Die verliebte und galante Welt* (1700) or August Bohse's *Der Liebes-Irrgarten* (1696), piquant stories of aristocratic love written in a less bombastic style, are, however, as remote from any contemporary reality as the far-fetched tales of ancient Greeks, Germans, Syrians, or the imaginary travels that fascinated readers with their sensational incidents and exotic information. In Christian Reuter's *Schelmuffskys Reisebeschreibung* (1696) this whole type of courtly novel is gaily parodied: the hero is complacently stupid, his love-affairs are imaginary, the description of the places he visits trivial and false. Reuter's hero is the son of a landlady, a charlatan who apes the manner of a nobleman and takes in the rich bourgeois he meets on his travels, in spite of the crudity of his speech and behaviour. It is the first satire on the taste for the high-flown, though it is directed at the aping of the nobility, not the nobility itself, and is, like Reuter's comedies, grotesque and farcical rather than penetrating.

The courtly novel in Germany is almost completely devoid of artistic quality, above all because the world in which it is set is so remote from any reality. It is assumed that princes are, as Lohenstein called them, 'irdische Planeten' moving beyond the experience and judgement of ordinary mortals; their manners and speech, their mode of feeling, their principles had therefore to be idealized; their prestige gained in accordance with their unnaturalness. The novels were based on a gaping wonder and worship, not on a search for understanding; and all the trappings, all the informative disquisitions on remote and outlandish matters, ministered to wonder not knowledge. This remoteness from the reality of the world of power is artistically much more disastrous in the novel than in tragedy, disturbing as it is there too, for instance in Lohenstein's plays. The generalizing character of high tragedy can tolerate stylization and rhetoric, while the novel, using the medium of prose and pretending to an elaborate exactitude in its descriptions of manners and feelings, suffers all too strikingly from the contrast between its pretensions and its psychological and social untruth. These courtly novels bear painful witness to the thwarted longing for splendour and grandeur in the subordinate and submissive German bourgeoisie.

The Plebeian Novel

Just as the Germans found in the Spanish *Amadis* a model for the idealistic aristocratic novel, so they adopted likewise its plebeian opposite from Spain, the picaresque novel. Both Spanish types correspond to German sixteenth-century forms—the chivalrous romance and the anecdotal rogue-story of Eulenspiegel or Hans Clawert—but so far outshone them as almost to obliterate their memory. The Spanish 'Schelmenroman'—*Lazarillo de Tormes* (1554) and Aleman's *Gusman de Alfarache* (1599) are the first and outstanding examples—describes the underworld of servants and rogues, forced to use all their inventiveness in their uncertain running fight with their masters and society. The tricks the 'picaro' gets up to win our amused sympathy for the underdog, and since he tells the story himself, the reader sees the masters (clergy, noblemen, lawyers, etc.) through eyes that keenly discern the mean reality of a man beneath the appearance of office or pretension. The satirical and plebeian character of these tales is hardly modified by the somewhat perfunctory edifying comments that give them a veneer of respectability.

When Aegidius Albertinus, a severe Catholic moralist, translated *Gusman* (1615), it is not surprising that he damped down the impertinence and gaiety of the original by extensive moralizings which culminate, in a continuation (by 'Freudenhold'), in the religious conversion of the 'Landstörzer.' Nicolaus Ulenhart's translation of a picaresque tale of Cervantes, *Isaak Winterfelder und Jobst von der Schneid*, is much fresher and realistically adapted to German circumstances, but in his translation of *Lazarillo* (also 1617) Ulenhart cuts out all satire of the Catholic clergy. The genre became popular in Germany, but as with the courtly novel, it was some time before true German equivalents were written, and the best, Grimmelshausen's *Ertzlandstörtzerin Courasche* and *Der seltzsame Springinsfeld* (1670), are only offshoots from his major novel. The influence of the Schelmenroman was absorbed in a somewhat different form, its gay impertinence was given moral depth.

The first step was taken by Moscherosch in the last section of his *Gesichte Philanders* (1642), the 'Soldatenleben'. The story-teller here is a learned official, temporarily a refugee, who throws in his lot with a group of marauders. In the end he repudiates them, and he always remains at a moral distance from the rough soldiers, but for some time he also participates in their exploits and communicates some of the keen excitement of events, admiring the skill and ruthlessness with which they despoil peasants and civilians. The realistic description of this underworld of the Thirty Years War, of its organization, manners, and speech, is startlingly new; almost without parallel too is the vigour of the narrative in which for a long stretch the imagination is absorbed without the vexations of moralizing interruptions (which interfere with the story in its later stages).

The one great novel of the seventeenth century is in this vein, *Der Abentheurliche Simplicissimus Teutsch* (1669), by a writer, Grimmelshausen, who stands on the plebeian fringe of the Baroque culture. He was the son of a baker and innkeeper, captured as a boy by the Imperial forces and thrown about by the war, and leaving the army only in 1649. He held posts as a bailiff of large estates and kept an inn, spending the last years of his life as 'Schultheiss' of a small town; without much schooling, he came into contact with the new culture only late in life. He had no direct links with the men of learning of his times, but living in the North of the Black Forest came into touch with the work of Alsatians like Moscherosch. As with Moscherosch, elements of the older Alsatian satirists like Brant, Murner and Fischart live on in his work, and much local folk-lore. His is the only work of the seventeenth century which is embedded in a living native tradition, the only imagination that freely uses the motifs that the tangled world around him offered.

Grimmelshausen's work is not anti-Baroque. Amongst his voluminous writings are a Biblical novel and two novels in the courtly mode. His *Keuscher Joseph* is, however, much more plainly written than Zesen's, and in the two romances *Dietwald und Amelinde* and *Proximus und Lympida* the tone of a naïve popular legend modifies the courtly elegance which was his purpose. Even in *Simplicissimus*, so uncourtly and un-Baroque in many respects, there are unmistakable Baroque elements.

The hero of *Simplicissimus* is brought up by foster-parents on a farm in Spessart. As a child he sees his presumed parents tortured and the farm despoiled by marauding soldiers; running into the forest, he lives for some years with a hermit who christens him Simplicius (Simplex) and gives him pious instruction. On the death of the hermit, he wanders into the world. He becomes a page and fool to the Swedish governor of Hanau, the sport of the heartless noble officers, but quickly learning the ways of the world, turns his presumed simplicity to his own advantage. Captured by Croatian skirmishers, he passes from troop to troop and meets a true and a false friend, Hertzbruder and Olivier. In the Imperial army he becomes a skilled and enterprising soldier, famed as the 'Jäger von Soest', and wins booty that he deposits with a Cologne merchant. He is captured but allowed out on parole and has various love-affairs. Forced to marry a girl he has seduced, he goes to get his property, finds the merchant is bankrupt, and travels to Paris as the companion of two noblemen. Here he again cuts a fine figure, but on the way back he is struck down by smallpox and loses all his money and his good looks. He falls among plundering marauders, and joins Olivier, now a footpad, whose ill-gotten gains he inherits. Hertzbruder rescues him from his evil life, and they make a pilgrimage to Einsiedeln where he joins the Catholic Church. Their fortunes are now promising, and they take up arms again in the Imperial army; but Hertzbruder is wounded and dies. Simplex meets his foster-parents again and learns from them that the hermit was his father. He sets up as a farmer and marries again, unwisely. There follow various fantastic adventures. He explores the Mummelsee and learns from the king of the water-sprites about the structure of the earth. He travels to Russia, Korea, Japan, and ultimately back to the Schwarzwald; in pious repudiation of the 'world' he retires to a hermitage. A last (sixth) book was added for the second edition in which Simplex's 'Wanderlust' entices him out again into the world. He is captured by pirates in the Mediterranean, freed, shipwrecked, and cast on to a desert island in which he finds a new pious hermitage, the first Robinson Crusoe, who however, unlike Defoe's, refuses to return to the temptations of the world.

It is a story rich in incident, rooted in the common life of the times, recalling indeed in many incidents Grimmelshausen's own experiences. Despite the moral of renunciation, it expresses a great avidity for experience, a delight in the multifarious confusions of life, that links Grimmelshausen with the sixteenth rather than the seventeenth century. When he departs from the field of direct experience, for instance in the adventures in Paris or the travels to the East, his account is conventional and perfunctory, but in the main part it is not only lively in narrative but brilliantly evocative of situations and attitudes. At the same time, the narrative technique is remarkably sophisticated. While on the one hand Grimmelshausen skilfully establishes the historical authenticity of characters and happenings, on the other he freely allows himself imaginative combination and invention. His sometimes ironical authorial comments on the truth of incidents (e.g. on the witches' sabbath that Simplex observes) show a more subtle understanding of the nature of fiction and illusionism, of the sovereignty of the fictional writer, than is to be found in any German contemporary.

As in the picaresque novel, the hero narrates his own story, but Grimmelshausen is far more successful than his predecessors in fusing the double standpoint of the person who experiences the adventures and the chronicler who, having acquired experience, learning, and a moral philosophy, can distance himself from his earlier experiences and even add learned and moralizing comments. These comments, inclining to a complacent and diffuse bombast, do indeed at times disfigure the style. At times, too, an inappropriate awareness is attributed to the youthful hero; it is for instance psychologically false that this simple lad sees the world of war as a tree bearing with all its weight on the peasants and labourers that nourish its roots, its trunk and branches swarming with rapacious soldiers and crowned at the top by a 'cavalier'—a typical Baroque emblem. But it is Grimmelshausen's great achievement that he can dispense with such direct or indirect commentary. He is able to identify himself with his hero at the different levels of his experience, describing the world as he himself experienced it, and embodying his criticism and his moral in the realistic situation and the mode in which the hero responds to his changing situations. When the child observes the despoiling of his peasant home, his incapacity to understand the wanton cruelty and destruction makes it all the more vivid and horrifying; the balanced contrast of the soldiers' actions and his naïve misinterpretation gives a realistic psychological depth to the Baroque antithetical form; similarly the uncomprehending naïvety of the boy at the Hanau headquarters brings out with remarkable force the heartlessness of the aristocratic officers. So also the evident enjoyment with which the exploits of the 'Jäger von Soest' are described interprets the thoughtless self-confidence of the young soldier. There is a striking episode in which Simplex, lying in ambush, meets a half-crazed man who imagines himself to be Jupiter coming to punish the world. Simplex in his practical realism mocks him, telling him that all his punishments—war, famine, plague—will only hurt the innocent and profit the evildoers. When Jupiter cries that he will send a 'Teutscher Held' to force the princes to cease from war, Simplex tells him the hero will only add to the strife. Yet this humorous interlude suggests more insistently than any moralizings would have done that there is more in the idealism of this flea-ridden madman than in the cynical commonsense of Simplex.

The explicit moral of the novel, the deceitfulness of fortune, the vanity of worldly ambitions, is typically Baroque; but its plebeian character, its drastic and impertinent delight in the common world, its gay and sly humour and earthy wisdom are anti-Baroque. It was perhaps the more robust features that made the novel immensely popular, for its imitations all lack the moral and psychological depth of *Simplicissimus*; even Grimmelshausen's own continuations, the 'Simplicianische Schriften' are much coarser, and his *Courasche* shows no inkling of the human and social tragedy of Brecht's *Mutter Courage*. *Simplicissimus* had no true successors, but contributed greatly to the liberation of the novel from the pretentious solemnities of the courtly mode.

The Satirical Novel

Towards the end of the century, the turn from the stilted unrealistic novel takes various forms without creating any work of outstanding quality. In Johann Beer's numerous novels, fantasy and satire, idyll and realism, are curiously combined. Beer, an innkeeper's son who became a court-musician, shows an unusual gift for the poetry of landscape, often heightened by musical festivities. But idealized love-affairs, pranks, popular superstitions, and romantic episodes, are mingled haphazardly, following the whimsy of his imagination. Beer laughs at the pretensions of aristocracy, the stuffy philistinism of the bourgeois, and shows his predilection for the social underdogs, those who live by their wits. His novels are important as a protest against the cultural and moral conventions of the time, but are not concentrated and shaped.

Eberhard Werner Happel was another writer who did not fit into the establishment; the impoverished son of a defrocked clergyman, he led an irregular life as a tutor, editor and writer. Most of his novels are in the 'galant' tradition, feeding the taste for exotic love-stories in far-off lands; his only memorable work is his last, *Der Academische Roman* of 1690. It too is stuffed with information and irrelevant anecdotes, and he gives no account of academic life in the exact sense. His main purpose is the description of the various types of students—the drunkards, the squabblers, rioters, the women-chasers, the elegants, and the few serious students. Though there are here elements of social satire in the humorous predicaments he narrates, the style is grotesque and the form undisciplined. Like Reuter's *Schelmuffsky* it is in theme and manner a protest against the unrealistic courtly romance, yet it is only its reverse and does not anticipate a new form for the novel.

There is much more of the future in Christian Weise's *Die*

drey aergsten Ertz-Narren of 1672, just as his plays anticipate Aufklärung comedy and tragedy. It describes a journey through contemporary Germany. A nobleman has to put portraits of the three greatest fools in his gallery, and he travels with his tutor and a painter to find them. It is scarcely a novel. The three travellers only observe and learn, they do not experience, and their relations to one another remain unchanging: the nobleman is noble and educable; the tutor wise, learned, and respected; the painter, treated as a servant, liable to comic errors. But they observe the manners around them, the follies of the bourgeois world, presented in a series of character-sketches and little incidents. There are occasional references to larger matters such as warfare, but the satire is confined in general to the personal follies of fops, braggarts, misers and wastrels, peasants, and bourgeois who ape their betters, etc. The moral is very practical; the 'klare und helle Vernunfft' that the tutor complacently recommends is based on the practical virtues of common life; there is indeed a puritanical streak in the criticism of jollifications like Carnival and Christmas mumming. Similarly, the language is sober, clear, rational, without fuss and, in spite of tedious discussions, in general lively and alert.

The limitations as well as the strength of the Aufklärung novel are here anticipated. Gone are the sensationalism, the far-fetched ambitions of the Baroque novel; the exalted notion of fate, the tension between religious and worldly values, have faded; though a nobleman is travelling, all attention is on the bourgeois world, and the one question is, how can a man best manage in this world. Religion is now a guide to practical moral life and directs the bourgeois to his own limited affairs. The social structure is accepted without question, the bourgeois is to remain submissive; but he is not to bother himself, neither in emulation nor in criticism, neither in imagination nor in practice, with the higher world; his own limited world is his proper concern. This security of aim is paralleled by the sobriety, unpretentiousness, and serenity of the form of Weise's novel; there is no high emotion, no fantasy, no grotesque exaggeration, but cool observation, sober judgement, and self-discipline. In Weise's whole work, in his moral writings, his religious and political dramas and his comedies, and in his novels, the middle class begins to find the formulation of its own values, soberly and rather humbly turning to its own concerns, not challenging the courts and nobility and their culture, but finding the imaginative forms corresponding to its own way of life. This change did not occur suddenly, and the ambiguous social attitude of the middle class meant for some time a wavering of taste between the extravagant courtly novel and the sober domestic tale, between a high and a plain style, an ambiguity characteristic of the early Aufklärung. Not till the times of Lessing and the Sturm und Drang did the middle class free itself from subservience and timidity.

XIV

TRANSITION AND ASSIMILATION

No great political event or dramatic social change signals the
end of the Baroque culture, and Aufklärung trends only gradually infiltrated a society still broken into numerous political
units, still rigidly stratified, and divided by different religious
creeds and churches. German Baroque architecture, sculpture,
painting and music, indeed reached their greatest heights in
the eighteenth century. While, as we have noted, there was a
significant interpenetration of Catholic and Protestant trends
throughout the seventeenth century, at the end they begin to
diverge. The great centre of late Baroque literature was Silesia,
a territory including many Catholic principalities, deeply
affected by the Counter-Reformation and owing allegiance to
the Catholic emperor; Nürnberg, though a free and Protestant
city, also cherished a special relationship with the emperor
and here too the tradition of the 'Pegnitzschäfer' lingered for
long. The Baroque tastes, though taking more secular and
Rococo forms, continued to prevail in Catholic lands, in
Austria and Bavaria, and at such Catholic courts as Dresden.
Aufklärung trends asserted themselves however in Protestant cities at a distance from courts, at centres like Hamburg,
Halle, and above all Leipzig; an important contribution
came once more from Protestant Switzerland.

The early Aufklärer did not challenge the authority of religion and the church but sought to find a rational, philosophical basis for belief; God became for them not a miraculous, transcendental experience, but the source of order in
nature and the universe, and religion became the spring of
social morality, a sober rule of life, not the proclamation of
the vanity of the world. They did not challenge the authority
of the prince or the social superiority of the aristocracy, but

they turned their attention to the common life of the bourgeoisie with its humble joys and sorrows, its practical wisdom. The exuberance, the pathos, the self-exaltation of the Baroque, the disorders of fancy and the brooding imagination, were viewed with suspicion, commonsense began to reign in literature as in life; only in the religious ecstasies, anxieties, and introspection of the Pietists did imagination continue to challenge commonsense. Nothing contrasts more sharply with the extravagant and tortured imagination of the Baroque than the flat, complacent rationalism of Christian Wolff and Gottsched, the philosophical and literary authorities of the early Aufklärung. But it was their achievement, enriched by a liberating stream of thought from England and France, that laid the foundation for the independence of mind and spirit of Lessing, Kant, Herder, and Goethe who, boldly seeking to assert middle-class values as general human principles, probe disquietingly into themselves and the philosophical and moral foundations of their world.

But there was not only rupture and change. Gottsched admired and commended the work of such men as Opitz and Rachel, and even composed a Reinecke Fuchs; the fable-writers fell back again on their predecessors of the sixteenth century. Above all, the full maturity of German literature in the Goethe period, through a confluence of many different sources, was sealed by the discovery of the living traditions of the preceding centuries. The splendour of Luther's Bible was now assimilated, the drastic vigour of his style; the simplicity and urgency of folksong, the disrespectfulness and alertness of Eulenspiegel and Reinecke Fuchs and the picaresque novel, the wood-cut plasticity and self-reliant confidence of Hans Sachs. Götz von Berlichingen provided an image of stalwart independence for Goethe, as Michael Kohlhaas did for Kleist. The naïve charm of the chivalrous romances captivated Goethe, Tieck and the Romantics. The metaphysical drama of Dr Faustus now captured the German imagination, never to release its hold. Nor were the subtler virtues of the Baroque ignored. Lessing rediscovered the pointed epigrams of Logau, J. E. Schlegel commended the tragedies of Gryphius. The tender hymns of Gerhardt found successors in the religious poems of Hölty or Claudius. The inward dedication of sectarians, pietists, and mystics, their courageous devotion to their inner light, now found a full moral affirmation, while the mystical doctrine of a Böhme enriched, with the Romantics, modern metaphysical thought. The courtly and pastoral tradition also found a place, while the Baroque theatre survived in Austrian writers, from Grillparzer to Hofmannsthal. And the German lyric from Goethe onwards, though in some respects so different from that of the Baroque, yet owes something of its great range and variety to the tradition of Opitz and Fleming, for it was they who, discovering a great range of metrical and stanza forms and a new world of epithet and image, immensely widened the resources of the poet, and in so doing proclaimed the worth of the experience their poems celebrate. They re-established the idea of the poet, and with it enlarged and justified the sphere of personal experience, even if much of their poetry is only formal play.

Thus the literature of the sixteenth and seventeenth centuries has become assimilated into modern culture, which still continues to draw on some or other of its achievements. The scholarly study of this literature, which began in the early nineteenth century with such men as Jakob Grimm, Görries, or Uhland, has not been merely the discovery of the literary forms and tastes of a past epoch, nor is its purpose fulfilled with the re-discovery of works of high artistic quality: it belongs and contributes to modern German culture which, nurtured on this older literature, has made of it a living tradition.

Select Bibliography

CONTENTS

1. GENERAL WORKS OF REFERENCE

Allgemeine Deutsche Biographie, 1875 ff., contains valuable biographical and bibliographical material.

W. Kosch, *Deutsches Literatur-Lexikon*, 4 vols, 1949–58, gives further bibliographical information with lists of secondary studies.

P. Merker and W. Stammler, *Reallexikon der deutschen Literaturgeschichte*, 4 vols, 1925–6, now appearing in a revised edition, by W. Kohlschmidt and W. Mohr, contains authoritative articles on themes and subjects.

Since these works should always be consulted, it has not been thought necessary to refer to them in the following bibliography.

Valuable information on current scholarly work is contained in *The Year's Work in Modern Language Studies*, published annually by The Modern Humanities Research Association.

2. COLLECTIONS OF TEXTS AND ABBREVIATIONS

Excellent reprints of texts are available in the following series, with valuable introductions and notes. They are referred to in the later parts of the bibliography under the symbols indicated.

LV   *Bibliothek des Litterarischen Vereins in Stuttgart*, 1843 ff. (many of these volumes are now being reprinted).

DD   *Deutsche Dichter des 16. Jahrhunderts*, 1868 ff.

DD(17) *Deutsche Dichter des 17. Jahrhunderts*, 1869 ff.

Nd   *Neudrucke deutscher Litteraturwerke des 16 und 17 Jahrhunderts*, 1876 ff. (continued in a new series, Neue Folge, 1961 ff.).

DN   *Deutsche Neudrucke, Reihe Barock*, 1965 ff.

DNL   *Deutsche National-Litteratur*, 1882 ff.

LLD   *Lateinische Litteraturdenkmäler des 15. und 16. Jahrhunderts*, 1888 ff.

DL   *Deutsche Literatur in Entwicklungsreihen*, 1928 ff. (Not all the 'Reihen' in this collection are complete. The following series are relevant: *Humanismus und Renaissance; Reformation; Volkslied; Volks- und Schwankbücher; Barocklyrik; Barockdrama; Deutsche Selbstzeugnisse.*)

The following abbreviations have been used:

Pal	*Palaestra;* a long series of valuable literary studies, like the following:
Germ. Stud.	*Germanistische Studien.*
DVLG	*Deutsche Vierteljahresschrift für Literaturwissenschaft und Geistesgeschichte.*
Ztschr.f.dt.Phil.	*Zeitschrift für deutsche Philologie.*
MLR	*Modern Language Review.*
Ztschr.f.dt.B.	*Zeitschrift für deutsche Bildung*
GRM	*Germanisch-Romanische Monatsschrift.*
Mod. Phil.	*Modern Philology.*

In titles, the following abbreviations have been used:

Gesch.	Geschichte
dt.	deutsch (in various inflexions)
J.	Jahrhundert
Ztalter	Zeitalter
diss.	Dissertation
Gesam.Schr.	Gesammelte Schriften

Titles of works are often given in abbreviated form; it was usual in the sixteenth and seventeenth centuries to give works very long titles.

3. SUBJECT BIBLIOGRAPHIES

This part of the bibliography corresponds to the fields of the different sections. References to texts, and collections of texts, are included when these are not listed under Personal Bibliographies.

Political and Economic Histories

P. Rassow (ed.), *Dt. Gesch. im Überblick*, 1953.

G. Mann (ed.), *Von der Reformation zur Revolution*, 1964 (Propyläen Weltgesch.7).

G. Barraclough, *The Origins of Modern Germany*, 1946.

E. L. Woodward, *The Age of Reformation*, 1938.

K. Brandi, *Dt. Gesch. im Ztalter der Reformation und Gegenreformation*, 2 vols, 1927–30.

P. Rassow, *Die politische Welt Karls V*, 1934.

M. Ritter, *Dt. Gesch. im Ztalter der Gegenreformation*, 2 vols. 1889–95.

E. Gothein, *Staat und Gesellschaft des Ztalters der Gegenreformation*, 1908.

C. V. Wedgwood, *The Thirty Years War*, 1938.

R. Kötschke, *Grundzüge der dt. Wirtschaftsgesch. bis zum 17 J.*, 1923.

A. Dopsch, *Wirtschaftliche und soziale Grundlagen der europäischen Kulturentwicklung*, 2 vols, 1923–4.

G. Schmoller, *Dt. Städtewesen in älterer Zeit*, 1922.

C. Brinkmann, *Agrarkrisis and Agrarkonjunktur in Mitteleuropa vom 13. bis zum 19. J.*, 1935.

R. Ehrenberg, *Capital and Finance in the Age of the Renaissance*, 1928 (*Das Ztalter der Fugger*, 1896).

T. E. Rabb, 'The Thirty Years War and the German Economy', 1962 (*Journal of Modern History*, 34)—a useful summary and bibliography.

G. Caro, *Sozial- und Wirtschaftsgesch. der Juden im Mittelalter und in der Neuzeit*, 2 vols, 1908–20.

Humanism

A few texts are given in DL *Humanismus und Renaissance*, 1 and 2, and *Selbstzeugnisse*, 1, 4, and 5, with informative introductions.

J. Huizinga, *The Waning of the Middle Ages* (1924), 1956 (Pelican).

R. Stadelmann, *Vom Geist des ausgehenden Mittelalters*, 1929.

W. Andreas, *Deutschland vor der Reformation*, 1932.

W. Andreas, 'Die Kulturbedeutung der dt. Reichsstädte zu Ausgang des Mittelalters,' 1928 (*DVLG* 6).

L. Geiger, *Renaissance und Humanismus in Italien und Deutschland*, 1882.

W. Dilthey, *Weltanschauung und Analyse des Menschen seit Renaissance und Reformation*, 1918 (*Gesam. Schr.* 2).

R. Newald, *Probleme und Gestalten des dt. Humanismus*, 1963.

K. Burdach, *Reformation, Renaissance, Humanismus*, 1926[2].

W. E. Peuckert, *Pansophie*, 1956[2].

W. E. Peuckert, *Die grosse Wende*, 1948.

P. Joachimsen, *Geschichtsauffassung und Geschichtsschreibung unter dem Einfluss des Humanismus*, 1910.

R. Wackernagel, *Humanismus und Reformation in Basel*, 1924.

E. Trunz, 'Der dt. Späthumanismus als Standeskultur', 1931 (*Dt. Barockforschung*, ed. Alewyn, 1965).

Religion and the Churches

A. Hauck, *Kirchengesch. Deutschlands,* 5 vols, 1896–1920.
A. Ritschl, *Gesch. des Pietismus,* 3 vols, 1880–6 (reprinted 1965).
W. Wiswedel, *Bilder und Führergestalten aus dem Täufertum,* 2 vols, 1928–30.
J. Lortz, *Die Reformation in Deutschland,* 2 vols, 1939–40.
L. von Muralt, *Stadtgemeinde und Reformation in der Schweiz,* 1930.
M. Preger, *Gesch. der dt. Mystik,* 3 vols, 1874–93.
A. K. E. Holmio, *The Lutheran Reformation and the Jews,* 1949.
B. Duhr, *Gesch. der Jesuiten in den Ländern dt. Zunge in der ersten Hälfte des 17 J.,* 2 vols, 1907–13.
A. Tholuck, *Das kirchliche Leben des 17 J.,* 1861.
W. von Schröder, *Studien zu den dt. Mystikern des 17 J.,* 1917.
E. Troeltsch, *Die Soziallehren der christlichen Kirchen,* 1911 (*Gesam. Schr.* i).
Reprints of pamphlets are given in the valuable collections:
O. Schade, *Satiren und Pasquillen aus der Reformationszeit,* 3 vols, 1863.
O. Clemen, *Flugschriften aus den ersten Jahren der Reformation,* 4 vols, 1907–11.

Culture and Education

G. Steinhausen, *Gesch. der dt. Kultur,* 2 vols, 1913.
H. Gumbel, *Dt. Kultur von der Mystik bis zur Gegenreformation,* 2 vols, 1936–9.
B. Haendcke, *Dt. Kultur im Ztalter des 30j. Krieges,* 1906.
A. Dock, *Der Souveranitätsbegriff von Bodin bis zu Friedrich dem Grossen,* 1897.
W. Flemming, *Dt. Kultur im Ztalter des Barock,* 1940.
M. von Boehn, *Die Mode: Menschen und Moden im 16 J.,* ed. Kardorff, 1964.
M. von Boehn, *Die Mode: Menschen und Moden im 17 J.,* 1913.
E. Buchner, *Das Neueste von Gestern,* vol. 1, 1911 (an interesting selection of broadsheets, newspaper items etc.).
F. Paulsen, *Gesch. des gelehrten Unterrichts,* 2 vols, 1919–21[3].
A. Matthias, *Gesch. des dt. Unterrichts,* 1907.
A. Heubaum, *Gesch. des dt. Bildungswesens seit der Mitte des 17 J.,* 1905.

Literary Histories and Studies

W. Stammler, *Von der Mystik zum Barock, 1400–1600*, 1927 (1950[2]).
—— *Dt. Philologie im Aufriss*, 3 vols, 1957 (1962[2]).
G. Müller, *Dt. Dichtung von der Renaissance bis zum Ausgang des Barock*, 1927 (1957[2]).
K. Gysi (and others), *Gesch. der dt. Literatur:* vol. 4, *Von 1480 bis 1600*, 1961; vol. 5, *Von 1600 bis 1700*, 1963 (this Marxist work contains very useful bibliographical and biographical material).
R. Newald, 'Dt. Literatur im Ztalter des Humanismus', 1953 (*DVLG* 23).
R. Newald, *Die dt. Literatur vom Späthumanismus zur Empfindsamkeit, 1570–1750*, 1951.
J. Bächthold, *Gesch. der dt. Literatur in der Schweiz*, 1892.
H. Heckel, *Gesch. der dt. Literatur in Schlesien*, 2 vols, 1929.
G. Ellinger, *Gesch. der neulateinischen Literatur Deutschlands im 16 J.*, 2 vols, 1929.
P. Böckmann, *Formgesch. der dt. Dichtung*, vol. i, 1949.
A. H. Kober, *Gesch. der religiösen Dichtung in Deutschland*, 1919.
K. Viëtor, *Gesch. der dt. Ode*, 1923.
G. Müller, *Gesch. des dt. Liedes*, 1925.
W. Kayser, *Gesch. der dt. Ballade*, 1936.
F. Beissner, *Gesch. der dt. Elegie*, 1941.
K. Holl, *Gesch. des dt. Lustspiels*, 1923.
H. H. Borcherdt, *Gesch. des Romans und der Novelle in Deutschland*, vol. i, 1926.
O. Mann, *Gesch. des dt. Dramas*, 1960.
J. Klein, *Gesch. der dt. Lyrik*, 1957.
A. Closs, *The Genius of the German Lyric*, 1962[2], Paperback, 1965.
W. Weisbach, *Barock als Kunst der Gegenreformation*, 1921.
P. Hankamer, *Dt. Gegenreformation und dt. Barock*, 1935, 1964[2].
C. von Faber du Faur, *German Baroque Literature*, 1958.
R. Stamm (ed.), *Die Kunstformen des Barockztalters*, 1956.
K. Borinski, *Balth. Gracian und die Hofliteratur in Deutschland*, 1894.
E. Vogt, *Die gegenhöfische Strömung in der dt. Barock-literatur*, 1931 (*Dt. Barockforschung*, ed. Alewyn, 1965).
I. Weithase, *Die Darstellung von Krieg und Frieden in der dt. Barock-dichtung*, 1953.
E. K. Horwood, *The Impact of the Thirty Years War on the Writers of the Time*, diss. Melbourne, 1956.

O. Frankl, *Der Jude in den dt. Dichtungen der 15, 16, und 17 J.*, 1905.

C. I. Gebauer, *Gesch. des französischen Kultureinflusses auf Deutschland von der Reformation bis zum 30j. Krieg*, 1911.

K. H. Wels, *Die patriotischen Strömungen in der dt. Literatur des 30j. Krieges*, 1913.

C. H. Herford, *Studies in the literary relations of England and Germany in the 16th century*, 1886 (reprint 1966).

G. Waterhouse, *The literary relations of England and Germany in the 17th century*, 1914.

A penetrating and comprehensive review of the history and present position of Baroque scholarship is given in:

R. Alewyn (ed.), *Dt. Barockforschung*, 1965.

Language

Contemporary grammars:

V. Ickelsamer, *Ein Teütsche Grammatica*, 1534.

J. Claius, *Grammatica Germanicae linguae*, 1578.

A. Buchner, *Einleitung zur dt. Poeterey* (circulating from 1638, published by Prätorius, 1665).

C. Queintz, *Dt. Sprachlehre Entwurf*, 1641.

—— *Dt. Rechtschreibung*, 1645.

J. G. Schottel, *Ausführliche Arbeit von der Teutschen Haubt Sprache*, 1663.

J. M. Rist, *Rettung der edlen teutschen Hauptsprache*, 1642.

P. Zesen, *Hoochdt. Spraach-übung*, 1643.

D. G. Morhof, *Unterricht von der Teutschen Sprache und Poesie*, 1682.

C. Stieler, *Der Teutschen Sprache Stammbaum und Fortwuchs*, 1691.

(Nearly all the Poetics of the seventeenth century include expositions of grammar and orthography.)

Histories and studies:

A. Bach, *Gesch. der dt. Sprache*, 1961[7].

Hugo Moser, *Dt. Sprachgesch.*, 1955[2].

R. Priebsch and W. Collinson, *The German Language*, 1958[4].

T. Frings, *Die Grundlagen des meissnischen Deutsch*, 1936.

K. Brooke, *An Introduction to Early NHG*, 1955.

P. Hankamer, *Die Sprache, ihr Begriff und ihre Deutung im 16 und 17 J.*, 1927.

A. Daube, 'Anfänge einer dt. Sprachlehre im Zusammenhang der dt. Geistesgesch.', 1942 (*ZfdB* 18).

J. Erben, *Grundzüge einer Syntax der Sprache Luthers*, 1954.

H. Bach, *Laut- und Formenlehre der Sprache Luthers*, 1934.

H. Gumbel, *Dt. Sonderrenaissance in dt. Prosa*, 1930.

The Printing Press—Books, Broadsheets, Newspapers

K. Schottenloher, *Bücher bewegten die Welt*, 2 vols, 1951.

K. Schottenloher, *Flugblatt und Zeitung*, 1922.

F. Kapp and J. Goldfriedrich, *Gesch. des dt. Buchhandels*, 5 vols, 1886–1903.

A. Götze, *Hochdeutsche Drucker der Reformationszeit*, 1964.

J. Scheible, *Die Fliegenden Blätter des 16 and 17 J.*, 1850.

R. Muther, *Die dt. Bücherillustration der Gotik und Frührenaissance*, 2 vols, 1884.

M. Geisberg, *Die dt. Buchillustration in der ersten Hälfte des 16 J.*, 1930.

G. Eckhard, *Das dt. Buch im Ztalter des Barock*, 1930.

H. von Zwiedenek-Südenhorst, *Zeitungen und Flugschriften in der ersten Hälfte des 17 J.*, 1873 (Programm Graz).

L. Salomon, *Gesch. des dt. Zeitungswesens*, vol. i, 1900.

J. Kirchner, *Das dt. Zeitschriftenwesen*, part I, 1942.

W. Schöne, *Die dt. Zeitung des 17 J. in Abbildungen*, 1940.

Selections of newspaper items are given in the following:

E. Buchner, *Das Neueste von Gestern*, vol. i, 1911.

E. Weller, *Die ersten dt. Zeitungen* (LV 3, reprinted 1962).

Satire in the sixteenth century

See under Brant, Murner, Hutten, Erasmus, Sachs, Wickram, Fischart.

A number of satirical writings are reprinted in O. Schade, *Satiren und Pasquillen aus der Reformationszeit*, 3 vols, 1863; and in DL *Reformation* 2.

In addition the following texts:

(anon.), *Reinke de Vos*, 1498 (DNL 19).

(anon.), *Epistolae obscurorum virorum*, 1515 (probably by Crotus Rubianus and Hutten); ed. with an English translation by

F. G. Stokes, 1909 (1964²). *Briefe der Dunkelmänner*, ed. Amelung, 1965.

(anon.), *Ein kurtzweilig lesen von Dyl Ulenspiegel*, 1515 (Nd 55–6, DNL 18).

K. Scheidt, *Fr. Dedekinds Grobianus*, 1551 (Nd 34–5).

(anon.), *Das Lalebuch*, 1597 (Nd 236), and its close relations *Die Schiltbürger*, 1598, and *Grillenvertreiber*, 1603.

Studies:

W. Gaedick, *Der weise Narr in der Literatur von Erasmus bis Shakespeare*, 1928.

M. Held, *Das Narrenthema in der Satire am Vorabend und in der Frühzeit der Reformation*, diss. Marburg, 1945.

B. Könneker, *Die Narrenidee im Ztalter des Humanismus*, 1966.

Volkslied and Gesellschaftslied of the sixteenth century

Texts:

L. Erk and R. Böhme (ed.), *Dt. Liederhort*, 3 vols, 1893–4.

R. von Liliencron (ed.), *Die historischen Lieder der Deutschen vom 13 zum 16 J.*, 4 vols, 1865–9.

R. von Liliencron (ed.), *Dt. Leben im Volkslied um 1530* (DNL 13).

J. Meier (ed.), *Dt. Volkslieder mit ihren Melodien*, 1935 (Dt. Volksliederarchiv).

DL *Volkslied*, vols 1 and 2.

Georg Forster, *Ein ausszug guter alter und newer Teutscher liedlein*, 4 parts, 1539, 1540, 1549, 1556 (Nd 203–6).

(anon.), *Etliche hübsche Berkreien*, 1531 (Nd 99–100).

Studies:

A. Heusler, *Dt. Versgesch.*, 3 vols, 1925–8, vol. 3.

H. Mersmann, *Das dt. Volkslied*, 1922.

G. Pohl, *Der Strophenbau im dt. Volkslied*, 1921 (Pal 136).

M. Platel, *Vom Volkslied zum Gesellschaftslied*, 1939.

J. Schopp, *Das dt. Arbeitslied*, 1935.

G. P. Jackson, 'The rhythmic form of the German folksongs', 1915–16 (*Mod. Phil.* 13–14).

H. Mersmann, *Grundlagen einer musikalischen Volksliedforschung*, 1922 (Archiv für Musikwissenschaft).

Meistersang

See under Sachs, Wickram, Probst.

Texts:

Die Meisterlieder des Hans Folz, ed. Mayer, 1908.
Nürnberger Meistersinger-Protokolle 1575–1689 (LV 213–14).
Nürnberger Meistersinger-Protokolle 1595–1605, with *Das Gemerkbüchlein* of Hans Sachs (Nd 149–52).
Meisterlieder der Kolmarer Handschrift (LV 68).
Adam Puschmann, *Gründtlicher Bericht des Deudschen Meistergesangs*, 1571 (Nd 73).
G. Münzer (ed.), *Das Singe-buch Adam Puschmans*, 1906 (with the original melodies).
J. C. Wagenseil, 'Von der Meister-Singer Holdseligen Kunst', 1697 (Anhang to *De civitate Noribergensi commentatio*).
C. Spangenberg, *Von der Musica und den Meistersängern* (LV 62).

Studies:

A. Heusler, *Dt. Versgesch.*, vol. 3, 1928.
W. Hofmann, *Stilgeschichtliche Untersuchungen zu den Meisterliedern des Hans Folz*, 1933.
H. P. Heinen, *Die rhythmisch-metrische Gestaltung des Knittelverses bei Hans Volz*, 1966 (Marburger Beiträge zur Germanistik 12).
R. Weber, *Zur Entwicklung und Bedeutung des dt. Meistergesangs im 15 und 16 J.*, diss. Berlin 1921.
A. Taylor, *The literary history of Meistergesang*, 1937.
W. Stammler, 'Die Wurzeln des Meistergesangs', 1923 (DVLG 1).
H. O. Burger, *Die Kunstauffassung der frühen Meistersinger*, 1936.
B. Nagel, 'Der Bildausdruck der Meistersinger', 1940 (*Ztschr. f. dt. Phil.* 65).
H. Lütcke, *Studien zur Philosophie der Meistersinger*, 1911.
B. Nagel, *Der dt. Meistersang*, 1952 (is a comprehensive study, and lists a full bibliography of texts and studies).

The Hymn in the sixteenth century

See under Luther.

Texts:

P. Wackernagel, *Das dt. Kirchenlied von den ältesten Zeiten bis zu Anfang des 17 J.*, 5 vols, 1864–77.

Das evangelische Gemeindelied (DL *Reformation* 4).
R. Wolkan, *Das dt. Kirchenlied der böhmischen Brüder im 16 J.*, 1891.
R. Wolkan, *Die Lieder der Wiedertäufer*, 1903.
J. Westphal, *Das evangelische Kirchenlied nach seiner gesch. Entwicklung*, 1925[6].

Studies:

K. Böhm, *Das dt. evangelische Kirchenlied*, 1927.
R. Sellgrad, *Welt und Mensch im dt. Kirchenlied vom 16 bis zum 18 J.*, diss. Köln, 1955.
There are many valuable articles in *Realencyclopädie für protestantische Theologie und Kirche* and *Lexikon für Theologie und Kirche.*

The Fable

See under Waldis, Sachs.

Texts:

H. Steinhöwel, *Esopus*, c. 1476 (LV 117).
(anon.), *Reinke de Vos*, 1498 (DNL 19).
Erasmus Alberus, *Das buch von der Tugent und Weissheit*, 1550 (Nd 104, DNL 19)—49 fables, many of them from Aesop.
G. Rollenhagen, *Der Froschmeuseler*, 1595 (DD 8-9, DNL 19).

Studies:

H. Badstüber, *Die dt. Fabel von ihren ersten Anfängen*, 1924.
W. Kayser, *Die Grundlagen der dt. Fabeldichtung des 16 und 18 J.*, 1932 (Herrigs Archiv 86).
E. Voss, *Die Lebensbezüge von Fabel und Schwank im 16 J.*, diss. Rostock, 1945.

The Anecdote (Schwank)

See under Sachs, Wickram, Krüger.

Texts:

Schwänke des 16 J. (DNL 24) includes selections from Wickram and Pauli.
J. Pauli, *Schimpff und Ernst*, 1522 (DNL 24).

(anon.), *Ein kurtzweilig lesen von Dyl Ulenspiegel*, 1515 (Nd 55–56, DNL 18).

H. W. Kirchhoff, *Wendunmut*, 1563 (DNL 24).

(anon.), *Das Lalebuch*, 1597 (Nd 236).

Studies:

A. Jolles, *Einfache Formen*, 1930.

G. Kuttner, *Wesen und Formen der dt. Schwankliteratur des 16 J.*, 1934 (Germ. Stud. 152).

Legend and Romance

See under Wickram.

Texts:

DL *Volks- und Schwankbücher*, vol. 1, includes *Hug Schapler, Pontus und Sidonia, Die Haimonskinder*, and *Trojas Zerstörung*.

(anon.), *Fortunatus*, 1509 (Nd 240–1, DL *Volks- und Schwankbücher* 7).

(anon.), *Historia von Dr. Johann Fausten*, 1587 (Nd 7–8); of the many editions, that by R. Petsch, 1911[2], is the best.

(anon.), *Der gehörnte Siegfried*, 1726, together with *Das Lied vom Hürnen Seyfried*, c. 1560 (Nd 81–82).

There are many editions of the Volksbücher with modernized spelling, e.g. those by K. Simrock, 1865–67, R. Benz, 1911–24, H. Mohr, 1918.

Studies:

L. Mackensen, *Die dt. Volksbücher*, 1927.

W. Liepe, *Elisabeth von Nassau-Saarbrücken. Entstehung und Anfänge des Prosaromans in Deutschland*, 1920.

S. Sachse, *Motive und Gestaltung des Volksbuchs von Fortunatus*, diss. Würzburg, 1955.

E. M. Butler, *The Fortunes of Faust*, 1952.

W. E. Peuckert, 'Faust' (*Pansophie*, 1956[2]).

F. Stroh, 'Volksbuchprobleme (Lalebuch)', 1935 (*Euphorion*, 36).

A. Paucker, 'Das dt. Volksbuch bei den Juden', 1961 (*Ztschr. f.dt. Phil.* 80).

A. Paucker, *The Yiddish versions of the German Volksbuch*, diss. Nottingham, 1959.

Fastnachtspiel and Schuldrama

See under Reuchlin, Gegenbach, Manuel, Waldis, Gnaphaeus, Salat, Birck, Macropedius, Sachs, Naogeorgus, Wickram, Probst, Frischlin, Ayrer.

Texts:

R. Froning (ed.), *Das Drama des Mittelalters* (DNL 14, 3 vols).

E. von Keller (ed.), *Fastnachtspiele aus dem 15 J.* (LV 28, 29, 30, 46), reprinted 1964.

R. Froning (ed.), *Das Drama der Reformationszeit* (DNL 22), reprinted 1965.

T. Tittmann (ed.), *Schauspiele aus dem 16 J.* (DD 2 vols).

J. Bosshart (ed.), *Schweizerische Schauspiele des 16 J.*, 3 vols, 1890–3 (*Schweiz. Schauspiele*).

A. E. Berger (ed.), *Die Schaubühne im Dienste der Reformation* (DL *Reformation* 5, 6).

M. Sommerfeld (ed.), *Judith-Dramen des 16/17 J.*, 1933 (*Judith-Dramen*).

(anon.), *Eccius dedolatus*, 1521 (DL *Reformation* 2).

(anon.), *Karsthans*, 1521 (DL *Reformation* 2).

J. Agricola, *Tragedia Johannis Huss*, 1538.

J. Cochlaeus (Vogelsang), *Ein heimlich Gespräch von der Tragedia Joh. Hussen*, 1538 (Nd 174).

T. Stimmer, *Spiel von zwei Eheleuten*, 1580, ed. Witkowski, 1915.

M. Hayneccius, *Hans Pfriem*, 1582 (Nd 36).

J. Stricker, *De Düdesche Schlömer*, 1584 (DL *Reformation*, 6).

(anon.), *Das Endinger Judenspiel*, 1616 (Nd 41).

Studies:

M. J. Rudwin, *The Origin of the German Carnival Comedy*, 1906.

R. Stumpfl, 'Der Ursprung des Fastnachtspiels', 1934 (*Ztschr. für den Deutschunterricht*, 48).

H. Holstein, *Die Reformation im Spiegelbilde der dramatischen Literatur*, 1886.

D. van Abbé, *Drama in Renaissance Germany and Switzerland*, 1961.

H. Wyss, *Der Narr im Schweizerischen Drama des 16 J.*, 1959.

H. Beck, *Das genrehafte Element im dt. Drama des 16 J.*, 1929 (Germ. Stud. 6).

H. Holstein, *Das Drama vom verlorenen Sohne*, 1880.

J. Maasen, *Drama und Theater der Humanistenschulen in Deutschland*, 1928.

P. Stachel, *Seneca und das dt. Renaissancedrama*, 1907 (Pal 46).

K. Goedeke, *Everyman, Homulus, und Hecastus*, 1865.

R. Tarot, 'Literatur zum dt. Drama und Theater des 16 and 17 J.', 1963 (*Euphorion*, 57) gives an extensive review of literature on the subject.

A. Köster, *Die Meistersingerbühne des 16 J.*, 1920.

C. H. Kaulfuss-Diesch, *Die Inszenierung der dt. Dramen an der Wende des 16 and 17 J.*, 1905.

R. Stumpfl, 'Die Bühnenmöglichkeiten im 16 J.', 1929–30 (*Ztschr.f.dt. Phil.* 54–5).

H. Kindermann, *Theatergeschichte Europas*, vol. 2, *Renaissance*, 1959.

Englische Komödianten and the Wanderbühne

See under Ayrer, Braunschweig (Heinrich Julius).

Texts:

A. Cohn, *Shakespeare in Germany in the 16th and 17th Centuries*, 1865 (texts, English translations, and introduction).

Die Schauspiele der E.K. in Deutschland (DD 13).

Die Schauspiele der E.K. (DNL 23), ed., with a valuable introduction, by W. Creizenach.

Das Schauspiel der Wanderbühne (DL *Barockdrama* 3).

Studies:

W. Richter, *Liebeskampff 1630 und Schaubühne 1670*, 1910 (Pal 78).

J. Bolte, *Die Singspiele der E.K. und ihrer Nachfolger in Deutschland*, 1893 (Theatergesch. Forschungen 8).

R. Genée, *Lehr- und Wanderjahre der dt. Schauspielkunst*, 2 vols, 1882.

E. Devrient, *Gesch. der dt. Schauspielkunst*, vols. 1 and 2, 1848.

M. Fehr, *Die wandernden Theatertruppen in der Schweiz*, 1949.

J. Bolte, *Das Danziger Theater im 16 und 17 J.*, 1895.

A. Baesecke, *Das Schauspiel der E.K. in Deutschland*, 1935.

S. Mauermann, *Die Bühnenanweisungen im dt. Drama bis 1700*, 1911 (Pal 102).

R. Pascal, 'The Stage of the E.K.', 1940 (*MLR* 35).

Much valuable information is contained in the series Theatergeschichtliche Forschungen.

The Sprachgesellschaften

Contemporary histories:

G. Neumark, *Der Neu-Sprossende Teutsche Palmbaum oder Ausführlicher Bericht von der Hochlöblichen Fruchtbringende Gesellschaft Aufstieg*, 1668.

P. von Zesen, *Das hochdt. Helikonische Rosenthal: das ist der Deutsch gesinnten Genossenschaft Ertzschrein*, 1669.

J. Herdegen (Amarantes), *Historische Nachricht von dess löblichen Hirten- und Blumen- Ordens an der Pegnitz Anfang und Fortgang*, 1744 (published posthumously, to celebrate the centenary of the foundation of the Nürnberg Blumenorden).

C. von Höveln, *Teutscher Cimber-Schwan*, 1667 (account of Rist's Elbschwanenorden).

Valuable collections of documents and letters are published in the following:

G. Krause (ed.), *Der Fruchtbringenden Gesellschaft ältester Ertzschrein*, 1855.

T. Bischoff (ed.), *Festschrift zur 250 jährigen Jubelfeier des Pegnesischen Blumenordens*, 1894.

Altes und Neues aus dem Pegnesischen Blumenorden, 3 vols, 1897.

Studies:

F. W. Barthold, *Gesch. der Fruchtbringenden Gesellschaft*, 1848.

O. Denk, *Fürst Ludwig von Anhalt-Cöthen und der erste dt. Sprachverein*, 1917.

K. Dissel, *Ph. von Zesen und die Deutschgesinnte Genossenschaft*, 1890.

H. Schultz, *Die Bestrebungen der Sprachgesellschaften des 17 J. für Reinigung der dt. Sprache*, 1888.

C. Pranger, *Ein Jahrzehnt dt. Sprachreinigung 1640–50*, diss. Freiburg 1922.

The Poetics

Texts (the place of publication is given, as this usually indicates a local grouping):

M. Opitz, *Buch von der dt. Poeterey*, Breslau 1624 (Nd I—facsimile 1963).

A. Buchner, *Kurzer Wegweiser zur dt. Tichtkunst*, compiled Göze, Jena 1663; otherwise

A. Buchner, *Anleitung zur dt.* Poeterey, compiled Prätorius, Wittenberg 1665, ed. Szyrocki, 1965. The latter is the more genuine, and goes back to earlier work circulating in MS in the late 1630s.

P. Zesen, *Dt. Helikon*, Wittenberg, 1640, enlarged 1649 and still further in *Hochdt. Helikon*, 1656.

J. B. Schupp, *Ineptus orator*, Marburg, 1640, translated by J. B. Kindermann as *Der ungeschickte Redner*.

J. P. Titz, *Zwey Bücher von der Kunst, Hochdt. Verse und Lieder zu machen*, Danzig 1642.

J. G. Schottel, *Teutsche Vers- oder Reim Kunst*, Wolfenbüttel 1645.

—— *Ausführliche Arbeit von der Teutschen Haubt Sprache*, Braunschweig 1663.

J. Rist, *Rettung der Edlen Teutschen Hauptsprache*, Hamburg 1642.

M. Rinkart, *Summarischer Diskurs oder Teutsche Prosodia*, Leipzig 1645.

G. Harsdörffer, *Poetischer Trichter, die Teutsche Dicht- und Reimkunst in sechs Stunden einzugiessen*, 3 parts, Nürnberg 1647, 1648, 1653.

—— *Frauenzimmer-gesprechspiele*, 8 vols, Nürnberg 1641–9.

J. Klaj, *Lobrede der Teutschen Poeterey*, Nürnberg 1645 (a short extract DL *Barocklyrik* 2).

S. von Birken, *Teutsche Rede-bind und Dicht-Kunst, mit geistlichen Exempeln*, Nürnberg 1679.

J. H. Hadewig, *Kurtze und richtige Anleitung, wie ein teutsches Getichte könne verfertiget werden*, Lübeck 1650.

J. Masen, *Palaestra eloquentiae ligatae*, 3 parts, Köln 1654 (brief selections in DL *Barockdrama* 2).

A. Moller, *Tyrocinium Poeseos Teutonicae, das ist Eine Einleitung zur Dt. Verss- und Reimkunst*, Helmstedt 1656.

A. Tscherning, *Unvorgreiffliches Bedencken über etliche missbräuche in der dt. Schreib- und Sprach-Kunst, insonderheit der edlen Poeterey*, Lübeck 1658.

G. W. Sacer, *Nützliche Erinnerung wegen der Dt. Poeterey*, Stettin 1661.

—— *Reime dich, oder ich fresse dich*, Nordhausen 1673 (pseudonym, H. Reinhold).

J. B. Kindermann, *Der dt. Poet*, Wittenberg 1664.

G. Neumark, *Poetische Tafeln oder Gründtliche Anweisung zur Teutschen Verskunst*, Jena 1667.

G. Treuer, *Der dt. Dädalus oder Poetisches Lexikon*, Berlin 1675.

D. G. Morhof, *Unterricht von der Teutschen Sprache und Poesie*, Kiel 1682.

A. A. von Haugwitz, *Prodromos poeticus oder poetischer Vortrab*, Dresden 1684.

A. C. Rotth, *Vollständige Dt. Poesie in Drey Teilen*, Leipzig 1688.

C. Stieler, *Dichtkunst—eine ungedruckte Poetik*, ed. Bolte (Sitzungsber. der Preuss. Akad. der Wiss., 1926).

C. Weise, *Curiöse Gedancken von dt. Versen* (1691), Leipzig 1702.

M. D. Omeis, *Gründliche Anleitung zur Teutschen accuraten Reim- und Dicht-Kunst*, Nürnberg 1704.

J. C. Männling, *Der Europaeische Helikon*, Stettin 1705.

B. Neukirch, 'Vorrede von der dt. Poesie', 1725 (preface to his anthology of poems).

E. Neumeister, *Die Allerneueste Art, zur Reinen und Galanten Poesie zu gelangen*, Hamburg 1707 (the long preface is by C. Hunold-Menantes).

B. Feind, 'Gedancken von der Opera,' Hamburg 1708 (in his volume *Dt. Gedichte*).

C. Thomasius, *Höchstnötige Cautelen*, Halle 1713 (chapters 8 and 9).

G. W. Leibniz, *Unvorgreiffliche Gedanken betreffend die Ausübung und Verbesserung der Teutschen Sprache*, written 1698, first published 1717 (*Dt. Schriften*, vol. 1, 1916).

J. von Sandrart, *Academie der Bau-, Bild- und Mahlerey-Künste*, Nürnberg, 1675–79 (ed. and abridged by A. R. Peltzer, München 1925).

Studies:

See under Personal Bibliographies.

K. Borinski, *Die Poetik der Renaissance und die Anfänge der literarischen Kritik in Deutschland*, 1886.

B. Markwardt, *Gesch. der dt. Poetik*, vol. 1, 1937.

B. Hathaway, *The Age of Criticism. The late Renaissance in Italy*, 1962.

G. Brates, 'Die Barockpoetik als Dichtkunst, Reimkunst, Sprachkunst', 1928 (*Ztschr.f.dt.Phil.* 53).

J. Dyck, *Dichtkunst, Barockpoetik und rhetorische Tradition*, 1966.

W. Juker, *Die Theorie der Tragödie in den dt. Poetiken des 17 J.*, diss. Heidelberg 1924.

K. Holl, *Gesch. der Lustspieltheorie von Aristoteles bis Gottsched*, vol. 1, 1910.

M. L. Wolff, *Gesch. der Romantheorie*, 1915.

E. Neustädter, *Versuch einer Entwicklungsgesch. der epischen Theorie in Deutschland*, 1928.

M. Staege, *Gesch. der dt. Fabeltheorie*, 1929.

U. Wendland, *Die Theoretiker und Theorien der sogen. galanten Stilepoche und die dt. Sprache*, diss. Greifswald 1930.

The Baroque Lyric

In addition to items in the Personal Bibliographies, the following contemporary works and anthologies:

P. Schede (Melissus), *Die Psalmen Davids*, 1572 (Nd 144–8).

J. Regnart, *Kurtzweilige Teutsche Lieder*, 1576 (ed. Eitner, 1895).

C. von Schallenberg, *Gedichte*, c. 1600 (LV 253).

T. Hock, *Schoenes Blumenfeld*, 1601 (Nd 157–9).

J. W. Zincgref, *J.W.Z's und anderer dt. Poeten auserlesene Gedichte*, 1624 (Nd 15).

(anon), *Venus-Gärtlein*, 1656 (Nd 86–9).

B. Neukirch, *Herrn von Hofmannswaldau und anderer Deutschen auserlesene Gedichte*, 7 vols, 1695–1727 (the two first volumes Nd Neue Folge 1 and 16).

Modern anthologies:

Barocklyrik, 3 vols, ed. Cysarz (DL *Barocklyrik*), reprinted 1964.

Das dt. evangelische Kirchenlied des 17 J., ed. Fischer and Tümpel, 3 vols, 1904–15.

Dt. Gedichte des 16 und 17 J., ed. Milch, 1954.

German lyrics of the 17th century, ed. Closs and Mainland, 1940.

Tränen des Vaterlands. Dt. Dichter aus den 16 und 17 J., ed. Becher, 1954.

Barock, Liebeslyrik der Deutschen, ed. Grützmacher, 1965.

Die dt. Literatur, vol. 3 (*Barock*), ed. Schöne, 1963—contains selections of prose and drama as well as lyrics.

Die hist.-politischen Volkslieder des 30j. Kriegs, ed. Bartsch, 1882.

Die Lieder des 30j. Krieges, ed. Weller, 1855, reprint 1967.

Studies:

M. von Waldberg, *Die galante Lyrik*, 1885.

—— *Die dt. Renaissance-Lyrik*, 1888.

R. Velten, *Das ältere dt. Gesellschaftslied unter dem Einfluss der italienischen Musik*, 1914.

G. Ellinger, *Gesch. der neulateinischen Lyrik Deutschlands*, *1929*.

H. Cysarz, *Dt. Barockdichtung*, 1924.

R. H. Thomas, *Poetry and Song in the German Baroque*, 1963.

K. Vossler, *Das dt. Madrigal*, 1898.

E. R. Keppeler, *Die pindarische Ode in der Poesie des 17 und 18 J.*, *diss.* Tübingen 1911.

R. Hossfeldt, *Die dt. horazische Ode von Opitz bis Klopstock*, *diss.* Köln 1961.

F. W. Wentzlaff-Eggebert, *Das Problem des Todes in der dt. Lyrik des 17 J.*, 1931 (Pal 171).

M. L. Wolfskehl, *Die Jesusminne in der Lyrik des dt. Barock*, 1934.

A. Joseph, *Sprachformen der dt. Barocklyrik*, 1930.

I. Ziemendorff, *Die Metapher bei den weltlichen Lyrikern des dt. Barock*, 1933.

E. Schubert, *Augustus Bohse und die Galante Zeit*, 1911.

K. Berger, *Barock und Aufklärung im geistlichen Lied*, 1951.

M. Windfuhr, *Die barocke Bildlichkeit und ihre Kritiker*, 1966 (Germ. Abhandlungen 15).

Satire in the Seventeenth century

See under Moscherosch, Lauremberg, Logau, Schupp, Rachel.

Studies:

H. Klamroth, *Beiträge zur Entwicklungsgesch. der Traumsatire im 17 und 18 J.*, *diss.* Bonn 1912.

E. Urban, *Owenus und die dt. Epigrammatiker des 17 J.*, 1900.

R. Levy, *Martial und die dt. Epigrammatik des 17 J.*, 1903.

H. E. Wichert, *J. B. Schupp and the Baroque Satire in Germany*, 1952.

Baroque Drama

See under Bidermann, Opitz, Rist, Gryphius, Lohenstein, Avancini, Rettenbacher, Reuter, Weise.

A valuable selection of texts is provided DL *Barockdrama*, 6 vols, edited with excellent introductions by W. Flemming (1, *Das*

Schlesische Kunstdrama; 2, *Das Ordensdrama;* 3, *Das Schauspiel der Wanderbühne;* 4, *Die Komödie;* 5, *Die Oper;* 6, *Oratorium und Festspiel*).

Studies:

W. Benjamin: *Ursprung des dt. Trauerspiels,* 1928 (*Schriften,* 1955, vol. I).

G. Brates, *Hauptprobleme der dt. Barockdramaturgie,* 1935.

R. Alewyn, *Vorbarocker Klassizismus und Griechische Tragödie,* 1926.

——, 'Der Geist des Barocktheaters', 1952 (*Festschrift für Strich*).

E. Lunding, *Das schlesische Kunstdrama,* 1940.

J. Müller, *Das Jesuitendrama in den Ländern dt. Zunge vom Anfang bis zum Hochbarock,* 2 vols, 1930.

W. Flemming, *Gesch. des Jesuitentheaters,* 1923.

K. Fischer-Neumann, *Die Dramentheorie der Jesuiten im Ztalter des Barock, diss.* Wien 1937.

F. Adel, *Das Wiener Jesuitentheater und die europäische Barockdramatik,* 1960.

K Moser, *Die Anfänge des Hof- und Gesellschaftstheaters in Deutschland,* 1940.

M. Enzinger, *Die Entwicklung des Wiener Theaters vom 16 zum 19 J.,* 2 vols, 1918–19.

A. Kutscher, *Das Salzburger Barocktheater,* 1924.

K. Holl, *Gesch. des dt. Lustspiels,* 1923.

H. Hartmann, *Die Entwicklung des dt. Lustspiels von Gryphius bis Weise, diss.* Potsdam Päd. Hochsch. 1960.

I. Schenk, *Komik im dt. Barocktheater, diss.* Wien 1946.

F. Hammer, *Das Zwischenspiel im dt. Drama bis auf Gottsched,* 1911.

A. Schöne, *Emblematik und Drama im Ztalter des Barock,* 1964.

R. Brockpähler, *Handbuch zur Gesch. der Barockoper in Deutschland,* 1964.

E. Wellesz, *Der Beginn des musikalischen Barock und die Anfänge der Oper in Wien,* 1922.

A. W. Bartmuss, *Die Hamburger Barockoper und die Bedeutung für Dichtung und Bühne, diss.* Jena 1925.

H. M. Schletter, *Das dt. Singspiel,* 1863.

A review of the literature on the subject is given in:

R. Tarot, 'Literatur zum dt. Drama und Theater des 16 und 17 J.', 1963 (*Euphorion,* 57).

The Baroque Novel

See under Opitz, Moscherosch, Zesen, Grimmelshausen, Buchholtz, Braunschweig (Anton Ulrich), Beer, Lohenstein, Zigler, Happel, Reuter, Weise.

Studies:

F. Bobertag, *Gesch. des Romans in Deutschland*, 1876.

A. Schultheiss, *Der Schelmenroman der Spanier und seine Nachbildungen*, 1893.

E. Jenisch, 'Vom Abenteuer- zum Bildungsroman', 1926 (GRM 14).

E. Turnher, *Das Formgesetz des barocken Romans*, 1959.

E. Cohn, *Gesellschaftsideale und Gesellschaftsroman des 17 J.*, 1921 (Germ. Stud. 111).

J. Prys, *Der Staatsroman des 16 und 17 J. und sein Erziehungsideal*, diss. Würzburg 1913.

O. Woodtli, *Die Staatsräson im Roman des dt. Barocks*, 1943.

A. Hirsch, *Bürgertum und Barock im dt. Roman*, 1934 (1957²).

J. Deuschle, *Die Verarbeitung biblischer Stoffe im dt. Roman des Barocks*, 1927.

G. W. Stern, *Die Liebe im dt. Roman des 17 J.*, 1932 (Germ. Stud. 120).

M. Oeftering, *Heliodor und seine Bedeutung für die Literatur*, 1901.

P. Hultsch, *Der Orient in der dt. Barockliteratur*, diss. Breslau 1936.

H. Meyer, *Der dt. Schäferroman des 17 J.*, diss. Freiburg 1928.

H. Singer, *Der galante Roman*, 1961.

A. C. Jungkunz, *Menschendarstellung im dt. höfischen Roman des 17 J.*, 1937 (Germ. Stud. 190).

4. PERSONAL BIOGRAPHIES AND BIBLIOGRAPHIES

Indicated below are the barest particulars concerning the life of the prominent writers, the region in which they worked, their religion and profession. Only their most important works are listed, usually with the date of their first publication (it must be remembered that many works were altered and enlarged in later editions). Modern editions are mentioned where they exist, and a list of the most important biographical and critical studies is included. For further information readers are referred to other works of reference already listed, and full bibliographies are to be found in many of the studies included here.

Abraham a Santa Clara (Joh. Ulrich Megerle), 1644–1709

The son of a peasant, born in Baden (S. Germany), Megerle attended the Jesuit College at Ingolstadt and the Benedictine University at Salzburg, entering the Augustinian Order in Vienna in 1662. He studied further in Prague and Italy, and from 1665 worked mainly in Vienna as a preacher, filling important posts in his Order. His many writings, like his sermons, combine a popular style, full of local idioms, fables, descriptive anecdotes, with Baroque pathos and religious exhortation.

Works:

Werke, ed. Bertsche, 2 vols, 1943–4.
Merks Wien, 1679 (Reclam).
Judas der Ertz-Schelm, 1685–95 (DNL 40—selections).
Wunderlicher Traum von einem grossen Narrennest, 1703 (Reclam).
Neun neue Predigten (Nd 278–81).
Neue Predigten (LV 278).

Studies:

C. Blanckenburg, *Studien über die Sprache A's a S.C.*, 1897.
W. Brandt, *Der Schwank und die Fabel bei A.a S.C.*, diss. Münster 1923.
M. Michel, *Die Volkssage bei A. a S.C.*, 1933.
G. Stiasny, *Das Wortspiel bei A. a S.C.*, diss. Wien 1939.

Agricola, Johannes (Schnitter), 1492–1566

Born at Eisleben, Schnitter studied theology in Wittenberg, and was one of Luther's staunchest supporters, though his radical leanings in theology later brought conflict with Luther, who censured his play on Huss. From 1538 he lived in Berlin as Court Preacher and Head of the Church of the Mark. His collection of German proverbs is a great storehouse of German idioms as well as proverbs, and includes many sayings that illustrate the common man's criticism of the mighty.

Works:

Tragedia Johannis Hus, 1538.
Sibenhundert und Fünfftzig Teutscher Sprichwörter, 1534. (DNL 25.
Reprint 1967).

Studies:

G. Kawerau *J.A.*, 1881.

Agricola, Rudolphus (*Hysman, Roelof*), *1443–85*

Born at Gröningen, Agricola studied at Louvain, Paris, and
several Italian universities, and became one of the leading
Humanist classical scholars. He lectured at Heidelberg on Greek,
Roman, and Hebrew in the last years of his life, and re-intro-
duced the study of classical philosophy. He composed a plan for
a classical education, recommending that German should be used
in the explanation of texts, and he was celebrated as a teacher by
many German Humanists.

Works:

De formando studio, first printed 1539.
De inventione dialectica libri III, first printed 1523, reprinted 1965
(brief selections DL *Humanismus und Renaissance* 2).

Studies:

H. van der Velden, *R.A.*, 1911.

Arnold, Gottfried, *1666–1714*

Born in Annaberg of a Lutheran family, Arnold studied theology
and philosophy in Wittenberg. As a tutor to a noble family in
Dresden, he came into contact with the Court Preacher P. J.
Spener, the founder of pietism, and came to believe that the truth
of religion lay in personal piety and was distorted by the orthodox
churches. He renounced his post as professor of history at Giessen
in order to write his *Ketzer-Historien*, a work of great learning in
which he defends heretics and sectarians as the true confessors
of Christianity. Forced to give up his parish at Allstedt, he was
later appointed to various parishes in Brandenburg. The *Ketzer-
Historien* remained a handbook of pietism throughout the

eighteenth century, and contributed greatly to the emancipation of thought from Protestant orthodoxy.

Works:

Unparteyische Kirchen- und Ketzer-Historien, 4 vols, 1699–70 (brief extracts DL *Selbstzeugnisse* 6).
Auswahl, ed. Seeberg, 1934.

Studies:

E. Seeberg, *G.A.*, 1923.

Avancini, Nicolaus, 1612–86

A member of a noble family of the Tyrol, Avancini joined the Society of Jesus, and became professor of rhetoric and philosophy in Graz and Vienna. He wrote numerous Latin plays for production at the university and for festive occasions before the Imperial court, ranging from themes of martyrdom to historical plays glorifying earthly majesty. Plays and productions represent the height of Jesuit Baroque, including spectacular scenes of battle and courtly pomp, and the intervention of supernatural beings, sorcerers, demons, angels. They are enlivened by comic interludes, ballet, and song. Avancini was also widely known for works of religious edification.

Works:

Tragediae, 5 vols, 1675.
Pietas Victrix, 1659 (DL *Barockdrama* 2).

Studies:

See works on the Jesuit Drama.

Aventinus (Turmaier, Johannes), 1477–1534

Born at Abensberg (Bavaria), Aventinus studied at Ingolstadt, Vienna, Cracow, and Paris, and became tutor to princes of Bavaria. He was a leader of the Bavarian Humanists, the founder (1516) of a literary society in Ingolstadt (under the inspiration of Celtis), and wrote a Latin grammar. From 1517 he was Court Historiographer, and composed *Annales Boiorum* in 1521, publishing a popular version in German in 1526, the *Bayrische Chronik*. It shows a careful scrutiny of documentary sources, and is particularly remarkable for the attention paid to the language and character of the Ancient Germans. Though Aventinus did not formally break with the Catholic Church, he sympathized with the Reformers in many things and his outspoken criticism of the papacy and Church practices led to his being imprisoned in 1528.

Works:

Sämtl. Werke, ed. Riezler, 5 vols, 1881–6.

Studies:

J. von Döllinger, *Aventin und seine Zeit*, 1877.

Ayrer, Jakob, 1543–1605

Born in Franken of a Protestant family, Ayrer had little education, practised law in Bamberg from 1570 to 1593, and from then was a legal official of the City Courts at Nürnberg. In this last period he wrote his plays, many in the Fastnachtspiel tradition of Hans Sachs and Peter Probst; others are based on school-plays by Frischlin and Macropedius, and some are dramatizations of romances and histories. Through the visits of the Englische Komödianten he was stirred to imitate them, and his *Sidea* has some affinity with Shakespeare's *The Tempest*, possibly being based on a common original. He also wrote, in the style of the Englische Komödianten, a group of Singspiele.

Works:

Dramen (LV 76–80).
Opus thaeatricum, 1618.
Comedia von der schönen Sidea, with other plays and Singspiele (DD *Schauspiele* 2).

Studies:

M. Wodick, *J.A.'s Dramen*, 1912.
K. Fouquet, *A.'s Sidea und Shakespeare's Tempest*, 1929.

Beer, Johann, 1655–1700

The son of a Protestant innkeeper at St Georgen (Austria), his family was driven by religious persecution to Regensburg. A gifted musical performer and composer, from 1676 Beer was employed as a musician at various Saxon courts, becoming 'Konzertmeister' at Weissenfels in 1685. He composed Singspiele and other musical entertainments for court festivals, and wrote technical and polemical works on many topics, often attacking the puritanism of the burghers. His novels, gay and exuberant, romantic and fanciful, show the Bohemian streak in his character and profession, and, written in great haste, are rather formless; among them is an imitation of Grimmelshausen's *Simplicissimus*.

Works:

Des abenteuerlichen Jan Rebhu artlicher Pokazi, 1680.
Narrenspital and *Jucundus Jucundissimus*, 1680, ed. Alewyn, 1957
   (Klassiker der Literatur und der Wissenschaft 9).
Die kurtzweiligen Sommer-Täge, 1683 (Nd 324).
Die teutschen Winter-Nächte, ed. (with preceding item) Winkler,
   1963.

Studies:

R. Alewyn, *J.B.*, 1932.
I. Hartle, *Die Rittergeschichten J.B.'s*, diss. Wien 1947.

Bidermann, Jakob, 1578–1639

Born at Ehingen, Bidermann joined the Society of Jesus in 1594 and studied philosophy and theology at Dillingen and Augsburg. From 1606 he taught rhetoric, then philosophy, at the Gymnasium at München, was professor of theology at Dillingen from 1615, and from 1624 was a high official of the Jesuit Order in Rome. He wrote Latin epigrams and other verse, a novel *Utopia* (plagiarized in German translation 1677), and many Latin plays for production at schools which established the themes and form of the Jesuit drama.

Works:

Ludi theatrales sacri, 1666, ed. Tarot, 2 vols, 1963 (DN 6, 7).

Cenodoxus, 1609. (Nd neue Folge 6; the contemporary German translation DL *Barockdrama* 2 and in *Dt. Dichter des Barock*, ed. Hederer, 1958).
Philemon Martyr, ed. and translated Wehrli, 1960.

Studies:

D. G. Dyer, *J.B.*, *diss.* Cambridge 1951.
M. Wehrli, 'J.B.'s Cenodoxus' (in *Das dt. Drama*, ed. B. von Wiese, i, 1958).
R. G. Tarot, *J.B.'s Cenodoxus*, *diss.* Köln 1960.

Birck, Sixt, 1501–54

Born at Augsburg, Birck studied at Erfurt and Tübingen, and joined the evangelical movement. From 1532–6 he taught at the Basel Gymnasium, and from 1536 to his death was headmaster of the Augsburg Gymnasium. In Basel he came into contact with the lively Swiss school drama of Kolross and Bullinger, and wrote many plays, in German and Latin, for school production. The subjects are taken from the Bible, and his intention is moral rather than polemical; he was one of the first to adopt classical forms.

Works:

Susanna, 1532 (*Schweiz. Schauspiele* 2; the Latin version LLD 3).
Judith, 1534 (*Judith-Dramen*; the Latin version LLD 8).
Josef, 1539 (in Latin).
Eva, 1539 (in Latin).

Studies:

E. Messerschmid, *S.B.*, 1955.

Birken, Siegmund, 1626–81

Birken's father was a Lutheran clergyman in Wildstein, Bohemia, forced by the war to migrate to Nürnberg in 1629, where he became Diakonus. Birken studied law and theology in Jena, travelled to Holland and England, and settled in Nürnberg in 1648, where he directed the plays for the Peace celebrations. A protégé of Harsdörffer's, he took an active part in Nürnberg literary life, writing several pastorals, joined the 'Pegnesischer Blumenorden' under the name of Floridan, and was elected to the Fruchtbringende Gesellschaft (as 'Der Erwachsene'). For his early works he used his father's name Betulius, but after his ennoblement in 1655 reverted to its original German form. He was a tutor to aristocratic and patrician families, and assiduous in his poetic tributes to the great who repaid him with their high esteem. From 1662 till his death he was president of the Blumenorden, and allowed members to bring their wives to the meetings. His later poetry is religious, and he illustrated his Poetics with examples taken from religious verse.

Works:

Floridans Kriges-und Friedens-Gedächtnis, 1650.
Passions-Andachten, 1653.
Norisches Hirtengespräche . . . *durch Floridan und Myrtillus*, 1667 (with Samuel Hund).
Todesgedanken und Todten-Andenken, 1670.
Pegnesis oder . . . *Feldgedichte*, 1673–9 (also contains pastorals by Harsdörffer and Klaj).
Der Norische Föbus, ein Winter Schäferspiel, 1677.
Teutsche Rede-bind und Dicht-Kunst . . . *mit geistlichen Exempeln*, 1679.

Studies:

G. Quedenfeld, *S. von. B.*, Programm Freienwalde 1878.
A. Schmidt, 'S. von B., genannt Betulius' (*Festschr. zur 250j. Jubelfeier des Pegnes. Blumenordens*, 1894).

Böhme, Jakob, 1575–1624

Born near Görlitz, the son of a poor peasant, Böhme settled in Görlitz as a cobbler. He came into touch with mystical and theosophical ideas circulating in sectarian groups, studied Paracelsus, and composed his own theosophical system in his *Aurora oder Morgenröte im Aufgang* (1612), which he was forbidden to publish and which brought on him violent attacks from the Görlitz 'Oberpfarrer'. He gave up his workshop in 1613 in order to devote himself to his religious enquiries, and travelled a good deal to like-minded believers, largely dependent on their support. From 1618 he was not prevented from publishing, and his ideas became the inspiration of the Silesian mystics; Abraham von Franckenberg published a selection from his writings in 1624. Hamann and the Romantics drew upon his ideas and his obscure, mysterious and expressive language. His works have been widely translated and are still authoritative among sectarian groups in various parts of the world.

Works:

Sämtl. Werke, ed. Kayser, 6 vols, 1920.
Aurora oder Morgenröte im Aufgang, written 1612, publ. in part 1634.
Beschreibung der drei Principien göttlichen Wesens, 1618–19.
Vom dreifachen Leben des Menschen, 1619–20.
De Signatura Rerum, 1621 (Everyman edition).

Studies:

W. E. Peuckert, *Das Leben J.B.'s,* 1924.
P. Hankamer, 'J.B.' (*Gestalt und Gestaltung,* 1924).
A. Koyre, *La Philosophie de J.B.,* 1929.
W. Struck, *Der Einfluss J.B.'s auf die englische Literatur des 17 J.,* 1936.
J. J. Stoudt, *Sunrise to Eternity,* 1957.
Werner Buddecke, *Die Jakob Böhme-Ausgaben.* Die Ausgaben in deutscher Sprache. Hainbergschriften, 5. Heft. Göttingen, 1937.
Werner Buddecke, *Die Jakob Böhme-Ausgaben.* Die Übersetzungen. Hainbergschriften, Neue Folge. Göttingen, 1957.

Brant, Sebastian, 1457?–1521

Brant's father was an innkeeper and town councillor of Strassburg, where he was born. He studied law at Basel, and later taught canon and Roman law there, and edited classical and German texts; he also composed verse in Latin and German. He returned to Strassburg in 1500, first as Syndicus, then from 1503 as town clerk; a warm adherent of imperial power, he was made an Imperial Councillor by Maximilian. Despite his criticism of the clergy, he remained faithful to Catholic beliefs. His *Narrenschiff* is a brilliant exposition of the manners and morals of the times as seen from the point of view of the enlightened but conservative burghers. The Knittelvers is lively with exemplary incident and popular turns of phrase, and numerous satirical woodcuts added to the vividness of the presentation. The book was one of the most popular and influential publications of the time, and called forth a host of translations and imitations.

Works:

Das Narrenschiff, 1494 (DNL 16; Nd neue Folge 5, Facsimile 1913).
Flugblätter des S.B., ed. Heitz and Schultz, 1915.

Studies:

R. Newald, *Elsässische Charakterköpfe aus dem Ztalter des Humanismus*, 1944.
T. Maus, *B., Geiler, und Murner, diss.* Marburg 1914.
H. H. Ebert, *Die Sprichwörter in B.'s Narrenschiff, diss.* Greifswald 1933.

Braunschweig, Herzog Anton Ulrich von, 1633–1714

Anton Ulrich reigned over the dukedom of Braunschweig-Wolfenbüttel as co-regent from 1685, and alone from 1704. Among his tutors were J. G. Schottel and S. von Birken. He was an energetic and capable ruler, and corresponded with Leibniz over the union of the Protestant Churches. He entered the Catholic Church in 1709, but guaranteed freedom of religious observance to his subjects. He wrote religious poetry, a pious-courtly Singspiel, *Daniel*, in honour of a Braunschweig prince, and two voluminous novels notable as expositions of the policy of the absolutist ruler. He was admitted to the Fruchtbringende Gesellschaft in 1659 as 'Der Siegprangende'.

Works:

Christ-Fürstliches Davids Harpffen-Spiel, 1667 (ed. Wendenbourg, 1856).
Daniel, 1663 (DL *Barockdrama* 5).
Die durchleuchtige Syrerin Aramena, 5 vols, 1669–73.
Octavia, Römische Geschichte, 6 vols, 1685–1711.

Studies:

C. Heselhaus, *A.U.'s Aramena*, diss. Münster 1939.
M. Schnelle, *Die Staatsauffassung in A.U.'s Aramena*, 1939.
E. Erbeling, *Die Frauengestalten in der 'Octavia' des A.U.*, 1939 (Germ. Stud. 218).
R. Fink, 'Die Staatsromane des Herzogs A.U,' 1941 (*Ztschr. für dt. Geisteswissensch.* 4).

Braunschweig, Herzog Heinrich Julius von, 1564–1613

Succeeding to the throne of Braunschweig-Wolfenbüttel in 1589, Heinrich Julius was a champion of absolutism and energetically centralised power in his own hands. A close collaborator of the emperor Rudolph II, he strove to maintain the unity of Germany. He was a patron of the arts and sciences, and himself a scholar and playwright. He invited the Englische Komödianten to Braunschweig in 1593, and wrote a number of plays and comedies in their style, breaking with the German tradition by writing in prose; the plays were performed by a company he formed from his own court-servants. The clown that Sackville created, Johan (Jan) Bouset, appears in several of his plays. His best play, *Vincentius Ladislaus*, a satire of a boastful soldier, was taken into the repertoire of the Englische Komödianten.

Works:

The plays, all written 1593–4, have been published LV 36 and DD 14. *Von einem Buler und einer Bulerin* is to be found also DL *Barockdrama* 3; *Vincentius Ladislaus* in DL *Barockdrama* 4 and DNL 22.

Studies:

R. Friedenthal, *H.J. als Dramatiker*, diss. München 1924.
A. H. J. Knight, *H.J. Duke of Brunswick*, 1948.

Buchholtz, Andreas Heinrich, 1607–71

The son of a Braunschweig clergyman, Buchholtz studied theology, and after some time as a professor of theology and pastor became in 1662 chief Lutheran clergyman in Wolfenbüttel. He wrote hymns, translated Horace's odes and *Ars poetica* (1639) and Lucian's satires, and in two heavily moral novels, recounting the wonderful adventures of ideal German princes, tried to stem the taste for Amadis-type romances.

Works:

Geistliche teutsche Poemata, 1651.
Des Christlichen Teutschen Gross-Fürsten Herkules ... *Wunder-Geschichte*, 2 parts, 1659–60.
Des Christlichen Königlichen Fürsten Herkuliskus ... *Wunder-Geschichte*, 1665.

Studies:

F. Stöffler, *Die Romane des A.H.B.*, *diss.* Marburg 1918.

Buchner, August, *1591–1661*

Born in Dresden, where his father held high office as a military engineer and architect, Buchner studied philosophy and law at Wittenberg. From 1616 he held professorships of poetry and eloquence and posts of authority in the university of Wittenberg, where he remained till his death. An able Latinist, he edited many of the classics, including Horace's *Ars Poetica*, and wrote much Latin poetry. He also lectured on ancient German poetry, and played a very active part in establishing the principles of German metrics, working in friendly collaboration with Opitz. He wrote a German Poetics that circulated in manuscript from 1638 and was published posthumously. Many of the German poets were his pupils, among them Queintz, Schottel, Gerhardt, Klaj, and Zesen. He was much respected by Ludwig von Anhalt, who sought his opinion in metrical and linguistic matters, and admitted him to the Fruchtbringende Gesellschaft in 1641 ('Der Genossene'), though he had often supported Opitz in opposition to Ludwig, basing metrical stress on the natural accentuation of speech. He was the first to establish the dactyl, anapaest, and spondee as German metrical feet, and the dactyl was known as 'die Buchner-art'. His letters were published as examples of style.

Works:

Wegweiser zur deutschen Tichtkunst, ed. Göze, 1663.
Anleitung zur deutschen Poeterey, ed. Prätorius, 1665. (This is the more genuine of the two posthumous versions of Buchner's Poetics. It has been edited by Szyrocki, 1965.) (DN 5.)

Studies:

H. H. Borcherdt, *A.B.*, 1919.

Canitz, Friedrich Rudolf Ludwig von, 1645–99

Born at Berlin of a noble Prussian family, Canitz studied at Leyden and Leipzig, and travelled in Italy, France, and England. After some administrative experience, he held high office at the Brandenburg court, undertaking a number of important diplomatic missions. French literature of the classical period appealed to him, and he translated scenes from Racine and some of the 'galant' writing of the time. He wrote poetry and satires, and the latter, elegant and sophisticated satires of court life, became much admired. They were published in 1700 after his death under the title *Nebenstunden unterschiedener Gedichte* (DNL 39). Reminiscent in style and method of Boileau, they mark the beginning of the sobriety of expression of the early Aufklärung.

Celtis, Conrad (Bickel), 1459–1508

Born in Franken, the son of a vintner, Celtis (Celtes) studied at many German and Italian universities, and became the leading classical scholar and Humanist of Germany. He lectured at many German universities, and founded societies in several places (Cracow, Wien, Heidelberg, Ingolstadt) for the study of classical literature. He edited many classical works, including Tacitus's *Germania*, and wrote an Art of Poetry (like all his works, in Latin). He contributed greatly to the patriotic interest in the German past, publishing the plays of the medieval nun Hrotsvitha which he discovered, and a scholarly history of Nürnberg; his plan for a history of Germany inspired others to collect materials and compose histories. He wrote much Latin verse, panegyrics, patriotic odes, and love-poems, the ease and vigour of utterance of which place him among the finest neo-Latin poets; his *Ludus Dianae* is the first court-masque written by a German. His influence on his Humanist contemporaries is incalculable.

Works:

Selections (with English translations), ed. L. W. Forster, 1948.
Briefwechsel, ed. Rupprich, 1934.

Ars versificandi, 1486.
Quatuor libri amorum, 1502.
Libri odarum quatuor, 1503.
Oratio in gymnasio in Ingolstadio, ed. Rupprich, 1932.
Ludus Dianae, 1501, ed. Pindter, 1955.
Urbs Norimbergensis, 1493–5.

Studies:

L. W. Spitz, *C.C.*, 1957.
F. Pindter, *Die Lyrik des C.C.*, diss. Wien 1930.

Czepko, Daniel von, 1605–1660

Born near Liegnitz, the son of a Lutheran pastor, Czepko studied at Leipzig and Strassburg and travelled widely. He was tutor to several noble families in Silesia, later an administrator in the small principalities of Brieg and Ohlau. He came into close contact with the Silesian sectarian mystics, and formed a circle in Breslau for discussion and religious exercises. He wrote some poetry in the Opitzian vein, but his main literary achievement is the *Monodisticha* in which he found a terse, balanced form in which to reflect upon the great antitheses of time and eternity, existence and the 'Nichts', man and God. Through his doctrine and his literary style he exercised an important influence on Angelus Silesius.

Works:

Geistliche Schriften, ed. Milch, 1930.
Weltliche Dichtungen, ed. Milch, 1932, both reprinted 1964.
Sexcenta Monodisticha Sapientum, 1647.

Studies:

H. Palm, *Beiträge zur Litgesch. des 16–17 J.*, 1877.
W. Milch, *D. von C.*, 1924.

Dach, Simon, 1605–1659

Born at Memel, Dach studied theology and philosophy at Königsberg, became a schoolmaster at the Cathedral School there in 1633 and professor of poetry at the university in 1639. His circumstances were narrow and humble, and his poetry reflects the simple joys and sorrows of a man closely attached to his family and near friends. He formed with Roberthin, the secretary to the courts of law, Robert Blum, a burgher who had a good voice, Heinrich Albert, the organist and composer, a circle ('Die Kürbis-Hütte') for poetry-reading and singing, the least pretentious of all the Sprachgesellschaften. His poems became known through the settings of Heinrich Albert (*Aryen*, 1638 ff.), and though Opitzian in form, they are distinguished by a simple sincerity that links them with folksong. His later poems are darkened by grief for the loss of many of his friends who died in the plagues from 1649 to 1654.

Works:

Gedichte, 4 vols, ed. Ziesemer, 1936–8.
Sämtl. Gedichte (LV 130).
Poetische Werke, 1966. Reprint 1967.
Gedichte des Königsberger Dichterkreises (Nd 44–7, and DNL 30).

Studies:

H. Böhm, *Stil und Persönlichkeit S.D.'s*, diss. Bonn 1910.
W. Ziesemer, *S.D.*, 1924.

Erasmus, Desiderius (Gerhards, Gerhard), 1469–1536

Born at Rotterdam, Erasmus studied in Holland, Paris and Italy. He became a priest, but was relieved of duties by a dispensation. He travelled widely and became the paragon and leader of the North European Humanists. A man of great scholarship, he edited many Greek and Latin classics, among them Euripides, Demosthenes, Aristotle, Plautus, Seneca and Livy. Deeply concerned over the religious and moral failings of the Church, he sought to restore the instruments of true faith and moral life through editions of the authentic texts of the Fathers of the Church (among them Augustine), and above all by his edition of the Greek New Testament (1516) upon which Luther based his translation. He defined his ideal of a Christian in *Enchiridion militis christiani* (1502), and boldly and wittily attacked follies, evils, and superstitions in Church and society in *Stultitiae Laus* (1509), translated 1534 by Sebastian Franck as *Lob der Narrheit*.

He continued the attack in his *Colloquia familiaria* (1519), a model of Latin style and of ironic satire. In his *Querela pacis* (1517) he sharply criticized the self-seeking warfare of secular and ecclesiastical princes. From 1514 till his death he lived chiefly in Germany, mainly at Basel where he died. He was looked on as the leader of the Humanist reform-movement, but feared and repudiated the violence of Luther's beliefs and actions, and sharply quarrelled with Luther on central theological questions. He maintained against Luther the freedom of the will, and put his trust in rational enlightenment; his works, written in a lucid and eloquent Latin, are addressed to the learned and those in authority, not to the common people.

Works:

Ausgewählte Werke, ed. Holborn, 1933.
Briefe, ed. Köhler, 2 vols, 1938, 1955.

Studies:

P. Smith, *Erasmus*, 1923.
J. Huizinga, *D.E.*, 1951 (in German translation).

Fischart, Johann, 1546?–90

The son of a wealthy Strassburg tradesman, Fischart travelled through Germany, the Netherlands, England, France and Italy, and acquired a vast store of indiscriminate knowledge; he took his doctorate at Basel in 1574. He worked as a lawyer in Strassburg and Speyer, finally as an administrator in Forbach. Tumultuous and undisciplined works poured from his pen, often aggressively polemical; many are adaptations and free translations. An exuberant imagination and humour are strangely married with a streak of conservative and Calvinistic puritanism, and while he satirized many superstitions, he himself contributed greatly to the belief in witchcraft through his translation (1581) of Bodin's *De la démonomanie* and his re-issue of the *Malleus Maleficarum* of 1489. His translation of Rabelais's *Gargantua*, the *Geschicht Klitterung* (1575), shows brilliant verbal inventiveness, and he paid tribute to new courtly trends by translating a book of *Amadis de Gaulla*. His *Jesuiterhütlein* is a violent attack on the Jesuits, who had established their first college in Alsace in 1580.

His skill in verse fable and anecdote is best exemplified in his *Flöhhaz* and *Eulenspiegel Reimensweisz*. Fischart is the most important satirist of the late sixteenth century.

Works:

Selections are given DNL 18₁ 18₂, 18₃, and DD 15.
Eulenspiegel Reimensweisz, 1572 (DNL 18₂).
Aller Praktik Grossmutter, 1572 (Nd 2).
Flöhhaz, 1573, enlarged 1577 (Nd 5, DNL 18₁, DD 15).
Geschicht Klitterung, 1575 (Nd 65–71; ed. Nyssen, 1963).
Das glückhafft Schiff von Zürich, 1577 (Nd 182, DNL 18₁, DD 15).
Jesuiterhütlein, 1580 (DNL 18₁).

Studies:

A. Hauffen, *J.F.*, 2 vols, 1921–2.
H. Sommerhalder, *J.F.'s Werk*, 1960 (Quellen und Forschungen, 128).

Fleming, Paul, *1609–1640*

Born in Saxony, the son of a Lutheran pastor, Fleming was educated at the Thomasschule in Leipzig where the composer Hermann Schein was one of his teachers. He studied medicine at Leipzig, and became renowned among his fellows as a poet in the new Opitzian style. He joined embassies sent by the Duke of Holstein to Moscow (1633–4) and to Persia (1635–7), the official account of which is contained in Adam Olearius, *Beschreibung der Neuen Orientalischen Reise* (DNL 28). He took his medical degree at Leyden in 1640, but died shortly after settling in Hamburg. He wrote lyrical poetry in both Latin and German, and was the first German to infuse the Petrarchian-Opitzian forms with a distinct personality and immediacy of experience; his religious and patriotic poetry shows the same distinctiveness of experience as his personal and love poems. He is perhaps the greatest lyric poet of the seventeenth century.

Works:

Lateinische Gedichte (LV 73).
Deutsche Gedichte (LV 82–3, DNL 28), both reprinted 1965.

Teutsche Poemata, 1642 (often republished in the seventeenth century, reprint 1967).
Lateinische Poemata, 1648.

Studies:

H. Pyritz, *P.F.'s deutsche Liebeslyrik*, 1932 (Pal 180).
H. Pyritz, *P.F.'s Suavia* (Museum für Philologie des Mittelalters und der Renaissance, 5).
E. Hartmuth-Müller, *Die Sprache P.F.'s*, 1938.
G. Ruggenberg, *P.F., Motive und Sprache*, diss. Köln 1939.
E.F.E. Schrembs, *Die Selbstaussage in der Lyrik bei Fleming, Gryphius, und Günther*, diss. München 1953.

Franck, Sebastian, 1499–1542

Born at Donauwörth, Franck became a Catholic priest in 1524, but joined the evangelical movement and became a preacher near Nürnberg. His sympathy with the sectarians led to a rupture with Luther, and from 1528 he moved about from place to place, Strassburg, Esslingen, Ulm, making a hard living as an artisan, printer and writer, and driven away by the hostility of Luther and Lutheran authorities. From 1539 till his death he found refuge in Basel where he composed a famous collection of German proverbial sayings. His moral and religious writings express his conviction that the essence of Christianity is the spirit of love and selflessness; he courageously opposed all rigid dogmatism, Catholic, Lutheran, Zwinglian, and even that of the sects, and vigorously reproved the arrogance of the learned and self-seeking, of the rich and powerful. His *Kriegbüchlein des Friedens* is a noble plea for peace in the realm, and shows a mastery of style unusual in this period. Sympathy for the poor and the oppressed, criticism of the intolerant and mighty, run also through Franck's chronicles; he was, however, always opposed to violence, putting his truth in an inward mystical piety and selfless love.

Works:

Chronika Zeytbuch und geschycht bibel (with an appendix 'Ketzerchronik'), 1531.
Paradoxa ducenta octoginta, 1534 (ed. Ziegler, 1909).
Kriegbüchlein des Friedens, 1539 (ed. Klink, 1929). Reprint 1967.

Erste namenlose Sprichwörtersammlung, 1532 (ed. Latendorf, 1876, reprint 1967).
Sprichwörter, 1541.

Studies:

A. Reimann, *S.F. als Geschichtsphilosoph*, 1921.
W. E. Peuckert, *S.F.*, 1943.
G. Müller, *S.F.'s Kriegbüchlein und der Friedensgedanke im Reformationsztalter*, diss. Münster 1954.

Franckenberg, Abraham von, 1593–1652

Born at Schloss Ludwigsdorf near Oels, of a noble Lutheran family, Franckenberg gave up his studies under the influence of a quietistic, mystical impulse gained from his reading of mystics, particularly Tauler. He gave up his estate, and henceforth lived privately, becoming the leader of the Silesian pietists and mystics. His attitude brought him into repeated conflict with the Lutheran authorities, and from 1641–9 he lived in the tolerant city of Danzig. After the Peace of Westphalia he returned to Ludwigsdorf where he died. He composed religious poetry and a number of pious tracts, all of a simple and heartfelt character, and also engaged in theosophical speculations and alchemistic studies. He was perhaps most important as the transmitter of Jakob Böhme's ideas. He published Böhme's work in Holland, and in 1651 wrote the story of Böhme's life. The influence of Franckenberg's doctrine is evident in the work of Czepko and Silesius.

Works:

Raphael oder Ertzengel, ed. Schneider, 1924.
Gründlicher und wahrer Bericht von dem Leben und Abschied des in Gott seelig ruhenden Jakob Böhme, 1651.

Studies:

G. Koffmanne, *Die religiösen Bewegungen in der evangelischen Kirche Schlesiens während des 17 J.*, 1900.
H. Schrade, *Beiträge zu den dt. Mystikern des 17 J.: A.v.F.*, diss. Heidelberg 1922 (contains a list of F.'s works).

Frischlin, Philipp Nikodemus, 1547–1590

Born in Württemberg, the son of a Lutheran pastor, Frischlin studied in Tübingen, and held a professorship there from 1568 to 1586, interrupted by some years as a schoolmaster. A skilled Latinist, he wrote in Latin many plays and epics, on classical, biblical, and legendary subjects. Several of the plays embody direct satire of his own times, particularly *Priscianus vapulans*, directed against academic pedantry, and *Julius redivivus*, an amusing confrontation of Caesar and Cicero with contemporary Germany. He translated five plays by Aristophanes into Latin. His somewhat scurrilous satire involved him in continual strife with the university and the state, and in 1586 he was forced to flee from Tübingen and moved restlessly from city to city. He was arrested in Mainz in 1590, and died attempting to escape from prison. His satirical plays are his best work, though their form is uncontrolled; the biblical and classical plays are little more than exercises in the conventional school-drama. *Frau Wendelgart* is the only extant play of several that he wrote in German.

Works:

Deutsche Dichtungen (LV 41).
Operum poeticorum pars scenica, 1585.
Priscianus vapulans, 1578.
Hildegardis magna, 1579.
Frau Wendelgart, 1579, ed. Kuhn and Wiedmann, 1908.
Phasma, 1580.
Julius Redivivus, 1572–85 (LLD 19).

Studies:

D. F. Strauss, *Leben und Schriften von N.F.*, 1856.
G. Roethe, *F. als Dramatiker*, 1912.
K. F. R. Fink, *Studien zu den Dramen des N.F.*, diss. Leipzig 1920.

Gengenbach, Pamphilus, 1480?–1524?

Born probably at Nürnberg, where he possibly learned Meistersang, Gengenbach settled in Basel as a printer. He does not seem to have printed for the Humanists, like Froben, and his literary works are in spirit and expression close to the common people, patriotic, moralistic with a rough humour, and combining an earthy commonsense with a naïve credulity. In a poem *Der Bundtschu* he condemns the violence of rebellious peasants, and his 'Meisterlied' *Fünf Juden* celebrates a recent anti-semitic pogrom. He wrote a series of Fastnachtspiele which embody his satirical gifts at their best. Several of his works show his sympathy with the evangelical movement, most drastically the dramatic dialogue *Die Todtenfresser*.

Works:

Schriften, ed. Goedeke, 1856.
Die Todtenfresser, 1521 (DNL 22).

Studies:

R. Raillard, *P.G. und die Reformation*, diss. Zürich 1936.
K. Lendi, *Der Dichter P.G.*, 1926.
W. Schein, *Stilistische Untersuchungen zu den Werken P.G.'s*, diss. Jena 1927.

Gerhardt, Paul, 1607–1676

Born at Gräfenhainichen, Saxony, where his father became Bürgermeister, Gerhardt studied theology at Wittenberg, tutored for some years, and from 1651 held livings near and in Berlin. A strictly orthodox Lutheran, he resigned his living when the Great Elector decreed the unification of the Lutheran and Reformed Churches, and was appointed at Lübben where he spent his last years. He learned the new principles of poetic expression at Wittenberg from August Buchner, and became the greatest hymn-writer of the seventeenth century. His first hymns, *Praxis pietatis melica*, appeared when he was still a young tutor, and were continually reprinted in enlarged editions. The first complete collection was published by J. G. Ebeling, the precentor at the Berlin Nicolaikirche, in 1667.

Works:

Gedichte, ed. Goedeke, 1877 (DD (17) 12).
Dichtungen und Schriften, ed. von Cranach-Sichart, 1957.

Studies:

E. Aellen, *Quellen und Stil der Lieder P.G.'s*, diss. Basel 1912.
T. B. Hewitt, *P.G. as a hymn writer*, 1918.

Gnaphaeus, Gulielmus (van de Voldersgraft, Willem), *1493–1568*

Born and brought up at The Hague, Gnaphaeus studied at Köln and returned home to become a schoolmaster. He was twice imprisoned for his evangelical sympathies, and for religious reasons left the Low Countries in 1528 to live in Germany. His attempts to settle in Elbing and Königsberg were frustrated by ecclesiastical hostility, and he found a refuge for the last twenty years of his life as secretary to the Countess of East Friesland. His Latin play on the theme of the Prodigal Son, *Acolastus*, was published in Antwerp in 1529 and with it he founded the School Drama. The form and characterization of Terentian comedy are skilfully adapted to the religious and moral purpose, and the language is supple and pointed. The play was immensely influential, and it had thirty-nine editions by 1581; it was translated into German in 1535. The play has been admirably edited, with an English translation, by W. E. D. Atkinson, 1964 (also LLD I): the 1535 Swiss–German translation is reprinted in *Schweizerische Schauspiele des 16 J.*, vol. 1.

Grimmelshausen, Hans Jakob Christoffel von, *1621?–76*

Born at Gelnhausen where his father was a baker and innkeeper, Grimmelshausen was carried off by soldiers in 1635 and seems to have been tossed between the opposing armies, later becoming a regimental clerk in the Imperial forces, leaving only in 1649. He became a bailiff on estates in the North Schwarzwald, an innkeeper, and from 1667 Schultheiss in Renchen where he died highly esteemed. A Protestant by upbringing, at some time he joined the Catholic Church. Without a regular education, he found a library on the estate of a Strassburg doctor for whom he worked, and through him came into touch with the literary life in Elsass, notably with the work of Moscherosch. He is one of the very few writers of the seventeenth century outside the learned professions and with no academic education, and some of his work belongs to popular almanach literature. He wrote biblical and legendary novels in the courtly vein, but plebeian elements of incident and expression contrast with the stiltedness and preciosity of his contemporaries. His great work is *Der abenteuerliche Simplicissimus*, the only lasting German novel of the seventeenth century, that immediately gained tremendous popularity and has never ceased to be reprinted. While this work has some Baroque traits, it links up with the realistic Picaresque tradition in that it is embedded in the life of the common people during the Thirty Years War, and indeed is in some respects autobiographical; it is distinguished by great narrative skill, keen delight in the actual world, and an exuberant fancy. Its success led Grimmelshausen to write sequels and related tales, usually referred to as the 'Simplicianische Schriften', which are coarser in texture; many other writers plagiarized him, helped by the fact that most of his works were published under pseudonyms.

Works:

Grimmelshausen's collected works were first published 1683–4, again in 1685–99, and 1713. Selections are given DNL 33–34–35.

Der Satyrische Pilgram, 1666–70.

Des Vortrefflich Keuschen Josephs in Egypten . . . Lebens-Beschreibung, 1669.

Dietwalds und Amelinden anmutige Lieb- und Leids-Beschreibung, 1669.

Der abenteuerliche Simplicissimus Teutsch, 1668 (Nd 302–9).

Der abenteuerliche Simplicissimus, 1669, ed. Kelletat, 1964 (Nd 19–25).

Trutz-Simplex oder . . . Lebensbeschreibung der Ertzlandstörtzerin Courasche, 1670 (Nd 246–8).

Der seltzsame Springinsfeld, 1670 (Nd 249–52).

Das wunderbarliche Vogel-Nest, 1672 (Nd 288–91).

Simplicianische Schriften (including 'Continuatio') (Nd 310–4).

Proximus und Lympida, 1673.

Studies:

K. C. Hayens, *Grimmelshausen*, 1933.

J. H. Scholte, *Der Simplic. und sein Dichter*, 1950.

R. Alewyn, 'Grimmelshausen-Probleme', 1930 (*Ztschr. für Deutschkunde*).

K. Fuchs, *Die Religiosität des J.J.C.G.*, 1935 (Pal 202).

R. Brie, *Die sozialen Ideen G.'s*, 1938 (*Germ. Stud.* 205).

C. A. Bloedau, *G.'s Simplic. und seine Vorgänger*, 1908 (Pal 51).

C. Lugowski, 'Literarische Formen und lebendiger Gehalt im Simplic.', 1934 (*Ztschr. für Dtkunde*).

L. Schmidt, 'Das Ich im Simplic'., 1960 (*Wirkendes Wort* 10).

G. Rohrbach, *Figur und Charakter* (*Simplic.*), diss. Bonn 1959.

C. Stucki, *G.'s und Zesens Josephsromane*, 1933.

E. Stilgebauer, *G.'s Dietwald und Amelinde*, 1893.

Gryphius, Andreas (Greif), 1616–64

Gryphius was born at Glogau of a Lutheran family, in a province riven by political and religious conflict, and his family suffered all the vicissitudes of war—devastation, plague, persecution, forced contributions, and expulsion. He lost his father, his step-father and mother had to flee from religious persecution, and his schooling was often interrupted. He found a more secure home in Danzig, where the different religions were tolerated. Like many Silesians, he studied in Leyden, whither he travelled as tutor-companion, staying from 1638 to 1644; in the later years he lectured on many topics. He accompanied another pupil to France and Italy, returning home in 1647. He then became legal adviser in Glogau to the Protestant provincial diet, and was often engaged in strenuous resistance to the encroachments of the Imperial power and the Counter-Reformation. Gryphius's poems and tragedies bear the stamp of the bitter sufferings of Germany in this period; a master of the formal rhetoric of the Baroque, he infuses it with a true and felt pathos. Much of his poetry is religious, and he invests his consciousness of the transience of life with a sombre majesty. He is the greatest dramatist of the Baroque age, and though his tragedies lack mobility and action, they movingly express the transience of earthly glory and the nobility of stoic renunciation and Christian faith. They were written for production at schools, but *Leo Armenius*, *Catharina von Georgien*, and *Papinianus* were taken into the repertoire of the Wanderbühne. The Prefaces to *Leo Armenius*, *Catharina*, and *Cardenio und Celinde* indicate his conception of tragedy. His comedies, particularly *Herr Peter Squenz*, show a gaiety and lightness of touch that contrasts with the tone of the rest of his work. He wrote too a number of Latin poems. He was a friend of Czepko and Hofmannswaldau, and was admitted to the Fruchtbringende Gesellschaft in 1662 as 'Der Unsterbliche'.

Gryphius was a scrupulous craftsman, and revised the texts of earlier editions of his poems for the collected works of 1657 and 1663. The plays *Leo Armenius, Catharina von Georgien, Carolus Stuardus*, and *Cardenio und Celinde* were first published in the *Deutsche Gedichte* of 1657.

Works:

Gesamtausgabe der deutschsprachigen Werke, ed. Szyrocki and Powell, 1963 ff. (in course of publication).
Lustspiele (LV 138); *Trauerspiele* (LV 162); *Lyrische Gedichte* (LV 171); *Lateinische und deutsche Jugenddichtungen* (LV 287)—these volumes were reprinted in 1961.
Sonn- und Feyertags-Sonette, 1639 and 1663 (ND 37-8).
Leo Armenius, 1646 (DNL 29).
Catharina von Georgien, 1647 (Nd 261-2).
Ermordete Majestät oder Carolus Stuardus, 1649, later revised, ed. Powell, 1955 (DD (17)4).
Unglücklich Verlibete (Cardenio und Celinde), 1650, ed. Powell, 1967² (DL *Barockdrama* 1).
Grossmüttiger Rechts-Gelehrter oder Sterbender Aemilius P. Papinianus, 1659 (DL *Barockdrama* 1 and Reclam).
Majuma, Freudenspiel, 1653 (DL *Barockdrama* 5).
Absurda Comica oder Herr Peter Squentz, Schimpfspiel, 1658, ed. Powell, 1957 (DNL 29, ND 6, Reclam).
Verlibtes Gespenst, Gesang-Spil, and *Die gelibte Dornrose*, Schertz-Spil, both of 1660 (DL *Barockdrama* 4).
Horribilicribrifax, Schertz-Spil, 1663 (Nd 3, DL *Barockdrama* 4, Reclam).

Studies:

M. Szyrocki, *Der junge Gryphius*, 1959.
M. Szyrocki, *A.G. Leben und Werk*, 1964 (these two volumes contain very full bibliographies).
F. Gundolf, *A.G.*, 1927.
W. Flemming, *A.G.*, 1965.
W. Jockisch, *A.G. und das literarische Barock*, 1930 (Germ. Stud. 89).
V. Manheimer, *Die Lyrik des A.G.*, 1904.

G. Fricke, *Die Bildlichkeit in der Dichtung des A.G.*, 1933.
F. W. Wentzlaff-Eggebert, *Dichtung und Sprache des jungen Gryphius*, 1936, 1966².
J. Pfeiffer, *A.G. als Lyriker*, 1956.
E. F. E. Schrembs, *Die Selbstaussage in der Lyrik des 17 J. bei Fleming, Gryphius, und Günther, diss.* München 1953.
I. Rüttenauer, *Die Angst des Menschen in der Lyrik des A.G.*, 1957.
W. Harring, *A.G. und das Drama der Jesuiten*, 1907.
W. Flemming, *A.G. und die Bühne*, 1921.
D. W. Jöns, *Das 'Sinnen-Bild' bei G.*, 1966 (German. Abhandlungen).
E. Geisenhof, *Die Darstellung der Leidenschaften in den Trauerspielen des A.G., diss.* Heidelberg 1958.
O. Nuglisch, *Barocke Stilelemente in der dramatischen Kunst von A.G. und D.C. von Lohenstein*, 1938.
E. Mannack, 'A.G.'s Lustspiele', 1964 (*Euphorion*, 58).
E. Lunding, 'Assimilierung und Eigenschöpfung in den Lustspielen des A.G.' (*Stoffe, Formen, Strukturen*, ed. Fuchs and Mottekat, 1962).

Günther, Johann Christian, 1695–1723

Born at Striegau where his father practised medicine, Günther studied medicine at Frankfurt/Oder and Wittenberg, but led a wild life of carousals and pranks. Already known as a gifted poet, he failed to be appointed Court Poet at Dresden owing to an irresponsible satirical outburst. His unruly and disordered temperament prevented him from finding any settled employment, and meagre earnings did not rescue him from the poverty in which he died. In his lyrical poetry, despite modish Baroque rhetorical flourishes, there are elements of genuine individuality and personal feeling.

Works:

Sämtl. Werke, ed. Krämer, 6 vols, 1930–7, reprinted 1964.
Gedichte (DNL 38, DD (17)6).

Studies:

W. Krämer, *Das Leben des schlesischen Dichters J.C.G.*, 1950.
H. Dahlke, *J.C.G. Seine dichterische Entwicklung*, 1960.
E. F. E. Schrembs (*see under* Gryphius).

Happel, Eberhard Werner, 1647–1690

Born in Hessen, where his father was a needy clergyman, Happel had to break off his studies at Marburg when his father was removed from his living. Thenceforth he led a difficult and restless life, sometimes as a tutor, and doing odd literary jobs in Hamburg. He turned out a number of far-fetched adventure-novels in the courtly-galant mode, which he filled with often dubious historical, geographical and ethnographical information (*Der Africanische Tarnolast*, 1689—written when he was nineteen— *Der Asiatische Onogambo*, 1673, etc.). His translation of Huet's *Traité de l'origine des Romans* of 1670 was included by A. C. Rotth in his *Deutsche Poesie* of 1688. By far Happel's best work is *Der academische Roman* (1690), a satire of student manners.

Studies:

T. Schuwirth, *E.W.H. diss*. Marburg 1908.
G. Lock, *Der höfisch-galante Roman des 17 J. bei E.W.H.*, 1939.

Harsdörffer, Georg Philipp, 1607–58

Harsdöffer was born of a wealthy patrician Protestant family in Nürnberg, owners of considerable estates. He studied in Altdorf, and travelled for five years in France and Italy. From 1632 he settled in Nürnberg where he filled important positions, being a member of the Kleiner Rat from 1655. He joined whole-heartedly in the literary reform-movements, carrying on a correspondence with Ludwig von Anhalt, and being admitted to the Fruchtbringende Gesellschaft in 1642 ('Der Spielende'). With Klaj, his protégé, he founded the Pegnesischer Blumenorden in 1644, and was its first president ('Oberhirt'). He translated Italian and Spanish pastorals, Catholic works of devotion by Novarini and St Theresa, and political-moral works by Du Refuge and the English anti-parliamentarian Joseph Hall. He himself composed numerous pastorals, in mixed prose and verse, and other poetry, and the text of a religious opera (*Seelewig*). He composed a Poetics, the *Poetischer Trichter*, and in his voluminous *Frauenzimmer-Gesprechspiele* he gave an idealized example of thedis cussions of a cultured company, the themes including poetry and the arts, history and geography, mathematics and science, all made palatable for the ladies. Riddles, too, play their part in elegantly sharpening the wits: Harsdörffer published a collection of riddles in 1650, most of them having a moral pointe (reprinted 1964). Much of Harsdörffer's work betrays the dilettante, and he much encouraged the practice of poetry as a social adornment; the excessive and precious decoration of the Nürnberg school became a byword. But he was an intelligent and able man, and his attempts to popularize science and culture are worthy of respect. Some of his religious poems show genuine feeling.

Works:

Frauenzimmer-Gesprechspiele, 8 vols, 1641–9.
Poetischer Trichter . . . 3 parts, 1647–48–53.
Pegnesisches Schaefergedicht, 1644—with Birken and Klaj—(DN 8).
  Pastorals of Harsdörffer's are also contained in Birken's
  Pegnesis, 1673–9.
Seelewig, 1644 (DL *Barockdrama* 5).
Fried- und Freuden-Schall, 1649.
Nathan und Jothan, das ist Geistliche und Weltliche Lehrgedichte . . .
  Samt einer Zugabe . . . *begreiffend hundert vierzeilig Rähtsel*,
  1650–1.
Schauplatz jämmerlicher Mordgeschichte, 1652 (reprinted 1964).

Studies:

J. Tittmann, *Die Nürnberger Dichterschule*, 1847.
T. Bischoff, *G.P.H.*, 1894 (*Festschrift zur 250 Jubelfeier des Pegnes. Blumenordens*).
A. Krapp, *Die ästhetischen Tendenzen Harsdörffers*, 1903.
G. A. Narziss, *Studien zu den Frauenzimmer-Gesprechspielen H.'s*, 1928.
W. Kayser, *Die Klangmalerei bei H.*, 1932 (Pal 179).
E. Kühne, *Emblematik und Allegorie in H.'s Frauenzimmer-gesprächsp.*, diss. Wien 1933.

Hofmannswaldau, Christian Hofman von, 1617–79

Born of an ennobled patrician legal family of Breslau, he studied at Leyden and travelled in England, France, and Italy. He held high office in Breslau, becoming an Imperial Councillor and president of the City Council; he often represented the city in negotiations with the emperor, and had many friends among the landed nobility. He was the dominant figure in Breslau cultural life, and his translations from the Italian and his own poetry established the bombastic and ornate style of the so-called Second Silesian School, best illustrated in his *Helden-Briefe*, imaginary verse-epistles exchanged between famous lovers of history and legend.

Works:

Deutsche Übersetzungen und Gedichte, 1679 (DNL 36).
Herrn von H. und andrer Deutschen auserlesene Gedichte, ed. B. Neukirch, 7 parts 1695–1727 (Parts 1 and 2 Nd Neue Folge 16).

Studies:

R. Ibel, *H. von H.*, 1928 (Germ. Stud. 59).
H. Geibel, *Der Einfluss Marinos auf H. von H.*, 1938.
E. Rotermund, *C.H. von H.*, 1963.

Hutten, Ulrich von, 1488–1523

Born near Fulda, the son of an imperial knight, Hutten was destined for the church, but fled from the monastery school. At Erfurt he joined the circle of Humanists round Mutianus. From 1509 he travelled restlessly in Germany and Italy, studying and seeking patronage, and embroiled in feuds. He joined the band of Reuchlin's supporters against theological obscurantism, and was responsible for the most brilliant and virulent parts of the *Epistolae obscurorum virorum* (1515). His opposition to the papacy led him to translate into German (1517) the Humanist Valla's work proving that Rome's claim to pre-eminence over all other churches was based on a forged document (the 'gift of Constantine'). His *Epistola* (1518) to Pirckheimer is a proud statement of his personality, his faith in knowledge, his joy in living in great times. He fearlessly took sides with Luther, and in the *Dialogi* of 1520, which he issued in German in 1521, bitterly attacked the power, wealth, and cynicism of the Church hierarchy, calling on the Germans to shake off the Italian yoke, particularly appealing to the imperial knights to take the lead. He joined Franz von Sickingen's revolt in 1523, but was forced to flee, and found no refuge till he died, diseased and in poverty, on Ufenau in the lake of Zürich.

Works:

Opera, ed. Böcking, 7 vols, 1859.
Deutsche Schriften, ed. Szamatolski, 1891.
Clag und Vormanung, 1520; *Gespräch büchlin*, 1521; *Beklagunge der Freistette deutscher nation*, 1522 (DNL 17).
Epistolae obscurorum virorum, 1515, ed. with an English translation by Stokes, 1964[2]; in German translation, *Briefe der Dunkelmänner*, ed. Amelung, 1965.

Studies:

P. Kalkoff, *U. von H. und die Reformation*, 1920.
P. Kalkoff, *Huttens Vagantenzeit und Untergang*, 1525.
F. Walser, *Die politische Entwicklung U. von H.'s*, 1928.
H. Holborn, *U. von H. and the German Reformation*, 1937.

Klaj, Johann, 1616–56

Born at Meissen, Klaj studied theology at Wittenberg where his poetical tastes were formed by Buchner. He went to Nürnberg in 1644 and entered into close relationship with Harsdörffer, founding with him the Pegnesischer Blumenorden and issuing a joint volume of pastorals. In 1647 he became a teacher at the grammar school there, in 1651 pastor at Kitzingen. In many of his poetical works Klaj appears as an ornate and precious formalist, and plays extravagantly with metres and words, especially so in the many pastorals he wrote under Harsdörffer's influence. Adulation of the mighty and linguistic conceits characterize the masques and poems he wrote for the Peace Celebrations at Nürnberg 1649–50. But at times, and especially in his religious poetry, a simpler language and a musical cadence are evident. His most ambitious works are the series of religious oratorios he wrote for declamation in church, accompanied by instruments and chorus. Using all the devices of rhetoric and a great variety of metres, he tries dramatically to evoke all the emotions connected with Christ's Passion, Resurrection, and Ascension. Klaj also declaimed in church a lyrical drama on Herod, and a versified Poetics.

Works:

Pegnesisches Schaefer Gedicht in den Berinorgischen Gefilden (with Harsdörffer), 1644 (DN 8).

Schwedisches Fried- und Freudenmahl, 1649.
Engel und Drachenstreit, 1650.
Freudengedichte, 1650.
Weyhnacht-Liedt, 1644 (DL *Barocklyrik* 2).
Höllen- und Himmelfahrt Jesu Christi, 1644.
Aufferstehung Jesu Christi, 1644.
Herodes der Kindsmörder, 1645.
Der Leidende Christus, 1645 (selections from these, DL *Barocklyrik* 2).
Die seligmachende Geburt Jesu, 1650 (DL *Barockdrama* 6).
Redeoratorien, 1644–50, and *Lobrede der Teutschen Poeterey*, 1645 (DN 4).
(The last six titles have been edited by Wiedemann, *Redeoratorien*, 1965).

Studies:

A. Franz, *J.K.*, 1908.

Krüger, Bartholomäus, 1540?–after 1580

Krüger was born in Brandenburg of a Protestant family. He became organist and town clerk at Trebbin; little is known of his life. His *Spiel von Anfang und Ende der Welt* (DD *Schauspiele* 2) is a late survival of the mystery play. *Hans Clawerts Werckliche Historien* of 1587 is a collection of tales in the Eulenspiegel manner, woven round a practical joker who lived in the neighbourhood (Nd 33).

Kuhlmann, Quirinus, 1651–89

The son of an artisan, Kuhlmann was born in Breslau and studied law in Jena. Visions that came to him in severe illness convinced him that he was to be the prophet of a new world, the 'Jesusmonarchie', and he turned from learning to devote himself to preaching a gospel of Christian brotherhood which was opposed to established churches and challenged secular authority. He created circles of adherents, particularly in tolerant Holland where several of his works were published. He travelled to Constantinople to convert the Sultan and barely escaped with his life. A similar call took him to Moscow, but denounced there by the

German Lutheran and Reformed leaders, he was arraigned by the Russian Patriarch and burned to death. His first volume of religious poetry, *Himmlische Libes-Küsse*, owing much to the imagery of the Song of Solomon, is overladen with imagery and conceits in the late Baroque manner. In *Der Kühl-Psalter*, one of the strangest books of the seventeenth century, he sought to 'Davidisiren' instead of 'petrarcisiren'; the strange combinations of images and highly personal use of words betray a mind over-wrought with religious exaltation and yet are at times obscurely and mysteriously expressive.

Works:

Ausgewählte Dichtungen, 1923.
Himmlische Libes-Küsse, 1671.
Der Kühl-Psalter, 3 vols, 1684–6 (Nd neue Folge 3 and 4).

Studies:

J. H. Scholte, 'Q.K. als Dichter des Hochbarock' (*Festschr. für Walzel*, 1924).
J. Hoffmeister, 'Q.K.', 1930 (*Euphorion*, 31).
L. Forster, 'Zu den Quellen des Kühlpsalters', 1958 (*Euphorion*, 52).
W. Dietze, *Q.K., Ketzer und Poet*, 1963.

Lauremberg, Johann, 1590–1658

The son of a professor of medicine at Rostock, Lauremberg studied at Rostock and travelled in Holland, England, France, and Italy. After a period as professor of poetry at Rostock, he became professor of mathematics in Denmark where he remained till his death. He was a man of wide learning, and published works on mathematics, geography, and the ancient Greeks. In early life, apart from Latin verses, he composed German poetry and two comedies (1635) in the Baroque style. In his late satires, his most important work, he puts off modish trappings, and with easy good humour satirizes high-falutin foreign fashions and reproves the pretensions and artifice of Opitzian poetry. His own homely style links up with the sixteenth century, and he champions the expressive idiom of Low German.

Works:

Veer Schertz Gedichte, 1652 (LV 58, Nd 16–17).

Studies:

H. Weimer, *L.'s Scherzgedichte, diss.* Marburg 1899.
C. F. Bayerschmidt, 'The Low German of L.'s Scherzgedichte',
 1946 (*Germanic Review*, 21).

Logau, Friedrich von, 1604–55

Born in Silesia of an aristocratic Lutheran family, Logau in-
herited an estate completely devastated by Wallenstein's troops,
and was plagued by poverty throughout his life. He held minor
posts at the petty courts of Brieg and Liegnitz, and his resentment
over his subservience was exacerbated by financial and domestic
worries. He is the sharpest and most polished epigrammatist of
the seventeenth century. The rhyming epigram was established as
a genre by Opitz, Zincgref and their successors, but Logau, influenced by John Owen and the Roman epigrammatists, turned
it into a much sharper weapon of social satire. His language is
simple and direct, provincial in some respects, but neatly pointed
and antithetical. Though he was admitted to the Fruchtbringende Gesellschaft, he was isolated in his time—he himself called
his verses 'spinsters'—and was appreciated only after Lessing and
Ramler published a selection of his *Sinngedichte* in 1759.

Works:

Zwei hundert Teutscher Reimen-Sprüche, 1638.
Deutscher Sinn-Getichte Drey Tausend, 1654—pseud. Salomon von
 Golau (LV 113; DNL 28; DD (17) 3).

Studies:

P. Hempel, *Die Kunst Fr. von L's*, 1917 (Pal 130).
J. Baumeister, *Der Gedankengehalt der Epigramme Fr. von L.'s, diss.*
 Erlangen 1922.
S. H. Moore, 'A neglected poet—Fr. von L.', 1949–50
 (GLL new series 3).

Lohenstein, Daniel Casper von, 1635–83

Like his patron Hofmannswaldau, Lohenstein came of an ennobled Protestant patrician family of Breslau, and after extensive study and travels occupied high office in the administration of the city. He was a precocious child, and his first play, *Ibrahim Bassa*, closely modelled on Gryphius, was performed at his school when he was fifteen. During the course of his short and busy life he wrote much, mostly religious, poetry, a long novel, and many tragedies, all performed at the Elisabeth Gymnasium. His style was extremely florid and bombastic. His poems are marked by the sensational realism with which he described physical suffering, decomposition, and death. His novel *Arminius*, the apotheosis of Hermann as a modern absolutist prince, builds up a series of climaxes, but is turgid with pedantic information. His tragedies, which centre in the glory and precariousness of earthly power, show a peculiar interest in violent and wayward passions; he favoured oriental and barbaric settings that gave the opportunity for outlandish and sensational horrors, for which in learned notes he provides the authorities. The Prefaces to *Ibrahim Bassa*, *Cleopatra*, and *Ibrahim Sultan* contain his views on tragedy. Lohenstein took the artifice of Baroque to its extreme, and his bombast and sensationalism provoked even in the seventeenth century a return to the less pretentious style of Opitz.

Works:

Türkische Trauerspiele; *Römische Trauerspiele*; *Afrikanische Trauerspiele*, ed. Just (LV 292–3–4).
Ibrahim Bassa, 1653.
Cleopatra, 1661 (DNL 36; Reclam).
Ibrahim Sultan, 1673.
Sophonisbe, 1680 (DL *Barockdrama* 1).
Poetische Schriften, 2 vols. 1680.
Grossmüthiger Feldherr Arminius oder Herrmann, 1689–90. Reprint 1968 (shortened DNL 37).

Studies:

K. G. Just, *Die Trauerspiele L.'s*, 1961.
G. E. P. Gillespie, *L.'s Historical Tragedies*, 1965.
F. Schaufelberger, *Das Tragische in L.'s Trauerspielen*, 1945.

W. Martin, *Der Stil in den Dramen L.'s*, diss. Leipzig 1927.

M. O. Katz, *Zur Weltanschauung D.C. von L.'s*, diss. Breslau 1933.

L. Laporte, *L.'s Arminius*, 1927 (Germ. Stud. 48).

M. Wehrli, *Das barocke Geschichtsbild in L.'s Arminius*, 1938.

H. Jakob, *L.'s Romanprosa*, diss. Berlin 1949.

H. Müller, *Studien über die Lyrik D.C. von L.'s*, diss. Greifswald 1921.

Luther, Martin, 1483–1546

Born at Eisleben, the son of a miner, Luther studied at Erfurt with the intention of becoming a lawyer. In 1505 he became a novice of the Augustinian Order, in 1507 a priest. He was sent to Wittenberg to complete his theological studies, and at the same time took a prominent part in disputes within his Order over the reform of discipline, visiting Rome 1510, and soon occupying a post of responsibility. From 1512 he remained in Wittenberg, lecturing in the university and preaching; tortured by the consciousness of sin, he began in this period to doubt the efficacy of exercises and penances, and sided with the Humanists in their attacks on the dogmatism and superstition within the Church. His first open attack on papal practice and doctrine occurred with his protest against the Indulgence (1517), and in the ensuing conflict with the ecclesiastical powers he came to challenge the authority of pope, canon law, and even the ecumenical councils, asserting that the only true authority was the Holy Scripture; he addressed himself to his compatriots in German, and through the printing press his pamphlets reached Germans in all countries and of all ranks. His able and courageous comportment won widespread support, not least because he appeared as a champion of Germany against a papacy that seemed to be a foreign power. By 1520, often in violent polemical terms, he established the principles of his evangelical doctrine, and, asserting that the Church is the community of all believers, called on the secular authorities to carry out its reform. Summoned to the Imperial Diet in 1521, he refused to recant, and was placed under the ban of the Empire. Sheltered by his prince, the Elector of Saxony, he began his German translation of the New Testament with the object of making Holy Scripture accessible to all believers.

In his absence, adherents in Wittenberg began to carry out

reforms, abandoning the monasteries and their vows of celibacy, abolishing the mass and other sacraments he had declared unwarranted by Holy Scripture. Alarmed at the confusion and turmoil, Luther returned to Wittenberg to restore order. He violently attacked sectarians who claimed divine inspiration, all who sought to reform the secular order on religious principle, all who denied the need for authority in church and state. Thus he established his church as a state-church, defined the training and duties of the clergy, prescribed the form of church services, and with the help of able lieutenants like Melanchthon laid the basis of a new orthodoxy. His horror of anarchy and his violent temperament led him to call for the ruthless destruction of the rebellious peasantry in 1525, and he was implacable to dissidents like Sebastian Franck and to the Anabaptists. At the same time, within an authoritarian framework, he enlarged and deepened the participation of the lay believer in religious observance, and infused a religious spirit into personal and family life.

Luther's polemical writings show a vigour and variety of expression unparalleled in German; his works of edification and exegesis, combining the homely with the exalted, are vivid and eloquent. His hymns are mighty confessions of faith. His translation of the Bible, which he repeatedly revised, is a magnificent work of literature, brilliant in its rhythms as well as in its imagery, exalted and simple. His *Sendbrief vom Dollmetschen* in which he justifies his use of the common speech of his countrymen is a brilliant exposition of his principles of translation. As a writer Luther stands far above all his contemporaries and successors and did not find an equal till Goethe, who acknowledged a great debt to him and in his early works drew upon his expressions.

Works:

Werke, Kritische Gesamtausgabe, 62 vols, 1883–1948.
Briefwechsel, 11 vols, 1930–48.
Werke in Auswahl, ed. Clemen, 4 vols, 1950.
Deutsche Schriften, ed. Goldschneider, 1927 (modernized spelling).
Ausgewählte dt. Schriften, ed. Volz, 1955.
Die Bibel, final revision, 1545.
An den Christlichen Adel . . ., 1520 (DNL 15, DL *Reformation* 1).
Von der Freyheyt eines Christen menschen, 1520 (DNL 15, DL *Reformation* 1).

Vom Eelichen Leben, 1522 (DNL 15, DL *Reformation* 1).

Von weltlicher uberkeyt, 1523.

An die Radherrn . . . das sie Christliche schulen auffrichten und hallten sollen, 1524 (DNL 15, DL *Reformation* 1).

Von Kauffshandlung und Wucher, 1524.

Ermanunge zum fride auff die zwelf artikel der Bawrschafft, and Widder die reubischen und moerdisschen rotten der andern Bawren, 1525.

Ein Sendbrief vom Dolmetschen, 1530, ed. Amburger-Stuart, 1940 (DL *Reformation* 1).

Studies:

J. Köstlin and G. Kawerau, *M.L.* 2 vols, 1903⁵.

R. H. Bainton, *Here I stand* (*M.L.*), 1951.

A. E. Berger, *L. und die dt. Kultur,* 1919.

H. Böhmer, *L.,* translated Potter, 1930.

H. Bornkamm, *L. im Spiegel der dt. Geistesgeschichte,* 1955.

H. Bornkamm, 'L. als Schriftsteller' (*Festschr. für Böckmann* 1964).

W. Walter, *Luthers deutsche Bibel,* 1917.

C. Franke, *Grundzüge der Schriftsprache L.'s,* 3 vols, 1913–22, reprint 1967.

Macropedius (*Langveldt, Georg*), *1475?–1558*

A fellow-countryman of Gnaphaeus, Macropedius composed a vast number of plays in Latin that were performed in schools. His *Asotus,* based on Gnaphaeus's *Acolastus,* develops the domestic interest; other Biblical plays show skilful characterization (*Susanna,* 1540, *Josephus,* 1544). His most successful play was *Hecastus,* in which the Everyman theme is infused with evangelical tendencies. His satirical comedies (*Rebelles,* 1535 and *Aluta,* 1535) show a gift for comic characterization.

Works:

Omnes fabulae comicae, 2 vols, 1552.

Hecastus, 1538, ed. Bolte in *Drei Schauspiele vom sterbenden Menschen,* 1927 (LV 269–70).

Rebelles, Aluta, 1535 (LLD 13).

Studies:

K. Goedeke, *Everyman, Homulus, und Hecastus,* 1865.

D. Jacoby, *G.M.,* Programm Berlin 1866.

Manuel, Niklaus (Deutsch), 1484–1530

Born in Bern, Manuel was the illegitimate son of Emmanuel Aleman, the Germanized form of whose name he later used. He was a man of great ability and energy. For some time an officer of Swiss mercenaries, he was later a leading statesman of Bern in the troubled period in which this then powerful state joined in the evangelical reform movement. He was a gifted painter, showing in his work (signed NMD) the influence of the Renaissance. He began to write only in 1522 when he wrote two Fastnachtspiele for production in Bern, evangelical in purpose and strongly critical of the papacy: *Vom Bapst und siner priesterschafft* is an imaginative and brilliant invective. *Der Ablass Kraemer* (1525) is a skilfully composed satire of an indulgence-seller. His later playlets lack the passion and concentration of the earlier.

Works:

Schriften, ed. Baechtold, 1878 (ed. Fetter, 1917).
Underscheid zwischen dem Bapst und Christum, 1522 (DD *Schauspiele* 1).
Vom Bapst und siner priesterschafft, 1522 (DL *Reformation* 5).
Der Ablass Kraemer, 1525, with his own woodcuts (DL 22).
Barbali, 1526.
Krankheit der Messe, 1528.
Elsli Tragdenknaben, 1530.

Studies:

B. Haendcke, *M. als Künstler*, 1889.
R. Lössel, *Das Verhältnis des P. Gengenbach und N.M. zum dt. Fastnachtspiel*, 1900.
L. Stumm, *N.M.D. als bildender Künstler*, 1925.
C. Grüneisen, *N.M.*, 1937.

Maximilian I, Kaiser, 1459–1519

The Emperor Maximilian was a warm patron of German scholars and artists, and himself planned and in part carried out two allegorical epics for which magnificent illustrations were provided by leading artists of the time like Hans Burgkmaier and Hans Schäufelein. *Teuerdank*, published in 1517, is an allegory of the education and trials of Maximilian himself; the text, in very wooden Knittelvers, is mainly by his secretary Melchior Pfinzing. It was remodelled in 1553 by Burkhard Waldis, and was often reprinted. *Weisskunig*, the text of which is by Marx Treitzsauerwein, remained in manuscript and was not published till 1775. Both works are reprinted DNL 19; *Teuerdank* also DD 10.

Melanchthon, Philipp (*Schwarzerd*), *1497–1560*

A great-nephew of Reuchlin, Melanchthon was born near Karlsruhe, the son of a smith. He studied at Heidelberg and Tübingen, lectured on Aristotle and the Classics, and became famed for his scholarship. He was appointed professor of Greek at Wittenberg in 1518 and published a Greek grammar. He became one of Luther's most able and reliable collaborators, taking especial responsibility for the new organization of schools and universities; to him is largely due the emphasis on a thorough training in the classics. To him also is due the systematic formulation of Lutheran theology. There were often small differences of opinion between Luther and Melanchthon, for he was a more pliable, scholastic, and rational man, but Luther often entrusted him with important missions, and the Augsburg Confession of 1530, which remained a basic statement of Lutheran belief, is largely Melanchthon's work. He was one of Luther's closest collaborators in the translation of the Bible. His influence was so great that he was called the 'Praeceptor Germaniae'. Almost all his writing is in Latin.

Works:

Kritische Ausgabe, 28 vols, 1834–60.
Supplementa, 6 vols, 1910–27.

Studies:

K. Hartfelder, *M. als Praeceptor Germaniae*, 1889.
G. Ellinger, *P.M.*, 1902.

Morhof, Daniel Georg, *1631–91*

Born at Wismar, the son of a notary, Morhof studied at Rostock and became professor of poetry there in 1660, moving to Kiel in 1665. He was a man of immense learning in all fields, and this indiscriminate knowledge earned him great prestige in his time—

he travelled in England and was elected a Fellow of the Royal Society. He wrote poems in Baroque style and composed a work on German language and poetry which gives a remarkably full account of the early history of German as well as a systematic analysis of the principles of grammar, metrics, etc. A typical scholar's autobiography is contained in *D.G. Morhofii Dissertationes*, 1699.

Works:

Teutsche Gedichte, 1682.
Unterricht von der Teutschen Sprache und Poesie, 1682.
Polyhistor, 1682, extended in later editions.

Studies:

M. Eymer, *M. und sein Polyhistor*, 1893.
M. Kern, *D.G.M.*, 1928.

Moscherosch, Johann Michael, 1601–69

Born in Baden, the son of a Protestant official, Moscherosch studied law, and travelled in France. He held at different times administrative posts in Strassburg and the Alsatian region, and was much respected for his practical ability and learning. Several times he was plundered by soldiers. He served under Catholic and Protestant authorities, under town-councils and princes, and was several times forced to move by religious and political enemies. Leaving Strassburg in 1656, he served as Privy Councillor in Hanau and finally under the Elector of Mainz. Apart from his many learned publications, he wrote satires directed against the linguistic extravagances of his day, and against disorders in society and morality from which he himself suffered. A gift of characterization, linking him with the older Alsatian satire of Brant, Murner and Fischart, makes these satires lively; of the greatest importance, and vivid through its narrative form, is the description of the banditry in the armies in his *Gesichte Philanders* (the section entitled 'Soldatenleben'), which influenced Grimmelshausen. His style is a curious mixture of the older plebeian language and the conceits of the Baroque. He was admitted to the Fruchtbringende Gesellschaft as 'Der Träumende'—his most important work is in the form of a series of visions based on the *Visiones* of Quevedo.

Works:

Gesichte Philanders von Sittewald, 1642 (in part DNL 32).
Der Unartige teutsche Sprachverderber, 1643.
Insomnis Cura Parentum, 1643 (Nd 108–9).

Studies:

W. Hinze, *M. und seine dt. Vorbilder in der Satire*, diss. Rostock 1903.
J. Cellarius, *Die politischen Anschauungen J.M.M.'s*, diss. Frankfurt 1925.
K. G. Knight, *J.M.M.*, diss Cambridge 1950–1.
C. von Faber du Faur, 'J.M.M. der Geängstigte', 1957 (*Euphorion*, 51).

Münzer, Thomas, *1490–1525*

Born at Stolberg, Münzer entered the Church and became an adherent of Luther's after meeting him at the Leipzig Disputation 1519. In 1520 he became a parish priest at Zwickau where he met among the poor weavers remnants of the Hussites, and began to preach the imminent coming of a new world in which secular and spiritual authority would fall away. Forced to flee from Zwickau, then from Prague, he became in 1521 a preacher at Allstedt (Mansfeld) where he reformed the services in the spirit of Luther's doctrine, but went much further in calling for a return to the simple brotherhood of primitive Christianity and attacking in violent terms the wealthy and mighty and those in authority in Church and state. The revolts of peasants in 1524 led to sharper measures on the part of the authorities, urged on by Luther, and Münzer again had to flee, and after a brief stay at Mühlhausen, was ejected once more. Now linking up with the peasants whose revolts had become a war, in several pamphlets he violently attacked Luther's support of the established order, calling him a 'Fürstenknecht', 'Doktor Lügner' 'das sanftlebende Fleisch zu Wittenberg'. He returned to Mühlhausen in 1525 and there set up an 'Ewiger Rat' which drew up a plan for the reorganization of the town on the Gospel principle of equality and the sharing of property. After the defeat of the peasant army at Frankenhausen, May 1525, Mühlhausen surrendered, Münzer was taken prisoner and executed. Münzer is the outstanding spokesman of the poor and oppressed to whom Luther's message seemed to be a prophecy of a new world, a 'fifth monarchy' in which secular and ecclesiastical authority would be swept away and replaced by a communistic brotherhood living in the spirit of Christ. His pamphlets show in their extravagant invective and exaltation his reckless idealism; he is one of the outstanding revolutionaries of German history.

Works:

Werke, ed. Brandt, 1932.
Briefwechsel, ed. Böhmer and Kirn, 1931.

Studies:

H. Böhmer, *Studien zu T.M.*, 1922.
A. Meusel, *T.M. und seine Zeit* (with documents), ed. Kamnitzer, 1952.
E. Bloch, *T.M. als Theologe der Revolution*, 1960².

Murner, Thomas, 1475–1537

Born in Alsace, Murner was brought up in Strassburg where his father was an official of the town council. He entered the Franciscan Order, and pursued his studies at several universities in Germany and in Paris. He held responsible positions in his Order at Strassburg and in other places and lectured on Roman Law at Freiburg and Trier; but his contentious spirit involved him in repeated conflicts with civic and ecclesiastical authorities, and he struck roots nowhere and in no community. His respect for truth led him to attack the anti-French prejudice of Wimpfeling's *Germania*; in verse satires such as *Die Narrenbeschwörung* he attacked priests and laymen who used their position and wealth for their selfish purposes; he showed his sympathy with the Humanists in the Reuchlin controversy, and attacked the Swiss Dominicans for burning presumed heretics; he translated into German the Institutions of Roman Law, in order to loosen, as he thought, the hold of lawyers and judges over the common man. In his criticism of abuses in the Church he seems to anticipate Luther, but he resolutely defended the papacy and canon law against Luther and wrote a famous anti-Lutheran invective *Von dem Grossen Lutherischen Narren* (1522)—though it was characteristic of him that he translated into German Luther's *De captivitate Babylonica* together with Henry VIII's refutation so that Germans might know the texts and judge for themselves. He became a notorious butt for the evangelical writers, and was severely handled by Hans Sachs, Gengenbach, and Niklaus Manuel among others. Soon after his return to Strassburg in 1519 the city adopted the reform and dissolved his monastery; his house was plundered by the mob. He found a refuge in Luzern, but since he continued with his anti-evangelical polemics was again forced to flee, spending his last years in obscurity in his native village. Murner's best writing is to be found in the series of verse satires that he wrote before the issues of the Reformation gave a poisoned virulence to his pen. In these he gives vivid sketches of the manners and mode of thinking of his times, sharper than Brant upon whose *Narren-schiff* he modelled his works, but not without humour. His language, often imaged and pithy, is full of the idiom of the common man.

Works:

Deutsche Schriften, ed. Schultz and others, 9 vols, 1926–31.
Die Narrenbeschwörung, 1512 (DNL 17, Nd 119–24).
Schelmenzunfft, 1512 (facsimile ed. Müller, 1926; DNL 17, Nd 85).
An den grossmächtigsten und durchlauchtigsten Adel deutscher Nation, 1520 (Nd 153).
Von dem Grossen Lutherischen Narren, 1522 (DNL 17, DL *Reformation* 3).

Studies:

G. Kawerau, *T.M. und die dt. Reformation*, 1891.
J. Lefftz, *Die volkstümlichen Stilelemente in M.'s Satiren*, 1915.
P. Merker, *Murner-Studien*, 1917.
P. Scherrer, *M.'s Verhältnis zum Humanismus*, diss. München 1929.

Naogeorgus, Thomas (Kirchmayer), 1508?–63

Born at Straubing, Naogeorgus studied at several universities and became an excellent classical scholar. He joined the Lutheran Church, and held various livings in Saxony, but his leanings towards Zwinglianism and the violence with which he expressed his views, in pamphlets and plays, brought severe conflict with the authorities, which he evaded by flight. He then held various livings in South Germany, but provoking continual strife through his attacks on other theologians and civil authorities, was often in great distress. He wrote several plays in Latin verse. The first, *Pammachius*, is one of the most violent and effective anti-papist documents; the second, *Mercator*, gives the Everyman theme a Lutheran slant. Both these were published in Saxony; his later Biblical plays, *Hamanus* (1543), *Hieremius* (1551), and *Judas Iscariotes* (1552), belong to the milder, more conventional type of school drama. Amongst his many translations are those of seven tragedies by Sophocles into Latin.

Works:

Tragoedia nova Pammachius, 1538 (LLD 3, DL *Reformation* 5; in a contemporary German translation DNL 22).
Mercator, 1540 (LV 269–70).

Studies:

L. Theobald, *Das Leben und Wirken des Tendenzdramatikers T.N.*, 1908.
F. Wiener, *N. im England der Reformationszeit*, diss. Berlin 1907.

Neukirch, Benjamin, 1665–1729

Born in Silesia, of a Protestant family, Neukirch studied law and history at Frankfurt/Oder and Leipzig; he lectured on poetry and eloquence at Frankfurt. Patronized by Canitz, he held various tutorial posts in Berlin, and later taught at the Ritterakademie there; ultimately he settled as tutor and 'Hofrat' at Ansbach. He was, like Canitz, an admirer of the contemporary French culture, and advocated the principles of French classicism. His own verse is, however, florid and 'galant' in the style of the Second Silesian School. His most important work was the collection of late Baroque poems enlarged in many volumes from 1695 onwards, and he published Lohenstein's *Arminius*; Gottsched published a selection of his poems.

Works:

Gedichte (DNL 39).
Galante Briefe und Gedichte, 1695.
Herrn von Hofmannswaldau und andrer Deutschen auserlesene Gedichte,

7 parts, 1695–1727. The volume issued in 1725 contains Neukirch's 'Vorrede von der deutschen Poesie'. (Parts 1 and 2 Nd neue Folge 1 and 16).

Studies:

W. Dorn, *B.N.*, 1897 (Lit. Forschungen ed. Schick and Waldberg, 4).

A. Hübscher, 'Die Dichter der Neukirchschen Sammlung', 1923–5 (*Euphorion*, 24, 26).

Neumark, Georg, 1621–81

Born at Langensalza, Neumark studied at Königsberg and became archival secretary and librarian at Weimar where he stayed till his death. He was admitted to the Fruchtbringende Gesellschaft ('Der Sprossende') and in 1650 became its 'Ertzschreinhalter'—in 1668 he published its first history. He was also a member of the Pegnesischer Blumenorden. He translated 'galant' and precious French novels by Gerzan and La Calprenède, composed poetry and pastorals, and reduced the Poetics of Schottel, Harsdörffer, and Titz to the form of a students' primer.

Works:

Betrübt-verliebter doch endlich hoch-erfreuter Hirte Filamon, 1648.
Poetisch- und Musikalisches Lustwäldchen, 1651.
Fortgepflantzter Musikalisch-Poetischer Lustwald, 1657.
Poetische Tafeln oder Gründliche Anweisung zur Teutschen Verskunst, 1667.
Der Neu-Sprossende Teutsche Palmbaum oder Ausführlicher Bericht von der Hochlöblichen Fruchtbringenden Gesellschaft Aufstieg . . . 1668.

Studies:

G. Claussnitzer, *G.N.*, diss. Leipzig 1924.

Omeis, Magnus Daniel, 1646–1708

Omeis was born in Nürnberg where his father was a Lutheran clergyman. After studying theology and classics, he travelled widely as a tutor. From 1674 professor of eloquence, poetry and ethics at Altdorf, he remained closely in touch with Nürnberg life, and enjoyed great prestige there. He became a member of the Pegnesischer Blumenorden in 1667, and was its 'Oberhirt' from 1697; his wife, a poetess, was also a member. His many learned and philosophical writings show the learning of his times at its most indiscriminate, pedantic, and orthodox; among other things he demonstrated that the Bible was the source of the Greek divinities. His own poetical work, florid and precious in the Nürnberg style, is emphatically religious and moral in intention. His Poetics of 1704 is a compilation intended for the use of students and ladies.

Works:

Gründliche Anleitung zur Teutschen accuraten Reim- und Dicht-Kunst,
    1704.
Teutsche Mythologie (appended to the above).
Geistliche Gedicht- und Lieder-Blumen, 1706.

Studies:

J. Tittmann, *Die Nürnberger Dichterschule,* 1847.

Opitz, Martin, 1597–1639

A Lutheran by upbringing, Opitz was the son of a butcher, a town councillor of Bunzlau. A brilliant classical scholar, while still a schoolboy at Beuthen, at the age of seventeen, he composed his *Aristarchus* in which, following the example of Ronsard and Du Bellay, he boldly called on his countrymen to create a German poetry equal to that of the Ancients. He studied for a while at Frankfurt/Oder and Heidelberg, visited Holland and France, and came into touch with leading scholars and poets; a tutorship took him to Leyden where he met Heinsius whose principles and verse influenced him greatly. Returning to Silesia, where he became a Calvinist (1621), he courted the patronage of princes, and spent some time in Siebenbürgen as professor—here he wrote his idyll *Zlatna.* Returning to Germany, he travelled extensively in search of a patron; in 1624 his friend Zincgref published Opitz's *Teutsche Poemata,* and because of its imperfections Opitz rapidly wrote his *Buch von der deutschen Poeterey* and published a revised edition of his poems. These works established Opitz as the leader of the new school of poetry and many other works followed in which, building on Italian and French forms, he created examples of the tragedy, pastoral, novel, the new metrical verse, the new poetical language. He met Ludwig von Anhalt in 1625, but was admitted to the Fruchtbringende Gesellschaft (as 'Der Gekrönte') only after he had been crowned Laureatus (1625) and ennobled (1627) by the emperor; his relations with Ludwig always remained cool, and the great success of his literary work in no way depended on the somewhat grudging approval of Ludwig.

In 1626 Opitz became secretary to the Catholic Burggraf von Dohna, the energetic representative of the imperial power, who was engaged in constant military and diplomatic conflict with the Protestant estates and cities of Silesia; Opitz was engaged in diplomatic missions in his service, and on grounds of expedience at this time (1629) translated a book of Catholic propaganda, though his co-religionists, including his father, were persecuted and forced into exile by imperial policy. He visited many courts; the opera text *Dafne*, music by Heinrich Schütz, was written for a princely wedding in Dresden, the *Schäfferey von der Nimpfen Hercynie* was a tribute to another lord. He visited Paris, and there came into touch with men advocating a tolerant, pacifistic, non-confessional Christianity, and translated Grotius's *Von der Warheit der Christlichen Religion* (1631). With the death of von Dohna, Opitz became the diplomatic agent of Protestant princes in Silesia, and now could publish his elegiac epic on the War, the *Trostgedichte*, which he had begun in 1621. In this period he had close contact with the Swedes, to whom the Silesian Estates looked for help in their struggle against the Catholic emperor. Their defeat led him to take service with the King of Poland as whose diplomatic agent he lived in Danzig until he died there of the plague. He continued writing till his death, the most important works of his later years being the religious lyrical play *Judith* (1635), his translation of the Psalms (1637), and his edition of the medieval *Annolied* (1638).

Opitz is the real founder of Baroque poetry and enjoyed immense prestige throughout the century; even Gottsched praised him. His works show a virtuose skill, but lack personal feeling; indeed a large part of his work consists of translations through which he aimed at providing models. His ready allegiance to different princes betrays a weakness of conviction, but he was less obsequious than many of his contemporaries, and seems genuinely to have deplored confessional dogma and strife.

Works:

Teutsche Poemata, 1624 (enlarged and revised 1625 and 1629), together with *Aristarchus. Sive de contemptu linguae Teutonicae*, 1617 (Nd 189–92).
Buch von der deutschen Poeterey, 1624 (Nd 1, Nd neue Folge 8).
Zlatna, 1623 (DNL 27, DD (17) 1).
Die Trojanerinnen, 1625 (DL *Barockdrama* 1).
Dafne, 1627 (DNL 27, DD (17) 1).
Schäfferey von der Nimpfen Hercynie, 1630 (DNL 27, DD (17) 1).
Trostgedichte in Widerwertigkeit des Krieges, 1633 (DNL 27, DD (17) 1).
Judith, 1635 (*Judithdramen*, ed. Sommerfeld, and DNL 27).
Geistliche Poemata, 1638 (ed. Trunz, 1965) (DN 1).
Weltliche Poemata, 1644 (DN 2 and 3).

Studies:

M. Szyrocki, *M.O.*, 1956 (contains a full bibliography of Opitz's works and of secondary literature).
F. Gundolf, *M.O.*, 1923.
M. Max, *M.O. als geistlicher Dichter*, 1931.
J. B. Birrer, *Die Beurteilung von M.O. in der dt. Litgesch.*, diss. Freiburg 1940.

Paracelsus (Hohenheim, Theophrastus Bombastus von), 1493?–1541

Little is known of Paracelsus's life. He was born at Einsiedeln, where his father was a doctor. He studied, and became a doctor of medicine at Ferrara. For some time at Strassburg, he became in 1527 professor at Basel where he knew Erasmus. Involved in much controversy, he travelled widely over central Europe practising his art; he died at Salzburg. Popular legend attributed to him magical powers. As a doctor he ridiculed traditional theory and cures and tried to study nature and carry out experiments; but his own theory is arbitrary and his practice close to that of the alchemists. His many works range over many areas of knowledge, and are a strange medley of luminous and confused opinion. Underlying them all is a mystical conception that God is evident in nature and human reason, and it is associated with an anti-worldly and evangelical veneration for the poor and simple. The works of Paracelsus were studied in many communities which sought a religion beyond the Confessions, and influenced the speculations of mystics and theosophists like Kepler and Jakob Böhme. Several of them were written in a German that, often obscure and difficult to understand, is also often vigorously plebeian and expressive.

Works:

Sämtliche Werke in neudeutscher Übersetzung, ed. Aschner, 4 vols, 1926–32.

Studies:

W. E. Peuckert, *T.P.*, 1941.
E. Metzke, *P.'s Anschauung von der Welt und vom menschlichen Leben*, 1943.

Peutinger, Conrad, *1465–1547*

Born of a patrician family of Augsburg, Peutinger became in 1497 town-clerk there and confidential counsellor to the emperor from 1500. He travelled in Italy, Hungary, England, and the Netherlands, and showed a lively interest in Humanistic scholarship. He himself collected historical materials, and used original documents for his biographical accounts of the emperors of Rome and the German emperors (*Liber Augustalis* and *De caesaribus*). His house was a genial meeting-place for the Augsburg Humanists, and he was a patron of artists like Hans Holbein the elder and Hans Burgkmaier; he headed the Augsburg 'sodalitas' founded by Celtis in 1500. His Table Talk shows his wide interest in contemporary events, in sea-voyages and discoveries as well as theology and learning.

Works:

Sermones conviviales, 1506.
Briefwechsel, ed. König, 1923.

Studies:

A. Buff, *Augsburg in der Renaissancezeit*, 1893.
H. Lutz, *C.P. Beiträge zu einer politischen Biographie*, diss. München 1953.

Pirckheimer, Willibald, 1470–1530

A member of a patrician Nürnberg family, Pirckheimer lived 1488–95 in Italy and later played an active part in city politics as a member of the council, a military leader, and a diplomat. He became a patron of the arts and sciences, and was active as a collector and editor of literary and historical documents. He joined other Humanists in support of Reuchlin, and his letters show his friendship and sympathy with men like Hutten; he was a friend and patron of Dürer and wrote a moving elegy in Latin on his death. He never broke with the Catholic Church, although he was sympathetic to the Lutheran movement and was probably part-author of *Eccius dedolatus*, a satire directed against Luther's opponent Eck.

Works:

Opera, ed. Reicke, 1907.
Apologia seu podagrae, 1522 (DL *Humanismus und Renaissance* 2).
Eccius dedolatus, 1520 (DL *Reformation* 2).
Briefwechsel, ed Reimann and Reicke, 2 vols, 1940, 1956.

Studies:

W. E. Peuckert, 'W.P.' (*in Die grosse Wende*, 1948).
E. Reicke, *W.P., Leben, Familie, Persönlichkeit*, 1930.

Probst, Peter, 15?–after 1569

We know little of Probst's life. He lived in Nürnberg and held minor posts in the city administration; from 1544–66 he was active as a Meistersinger and writer of Fastnachtspiele. His plays show the influence of Hans Sachs, but are coarser, while the moralizing is more pedantic. They are reprinted Nd 219–21. The most useful study is:

C. Grönlund, *Studien zu P.P., mit einer Neuausgabe des Textes der Lieder und Sprüche*, 1945 (Lunder German. Forschungen, 17).

Pufendorf, Samuel, 1632–94

Born at Chemnitz, Pufendorf studied at Leipzig and Jena, then in Holland and Denmark. In 1661 he became professor of law at

Heidelberg, went to Lund in 1670 and became in 1677 court historiographer and secretary of state in Sweden. In 1686 he was appointed court historiographer and privy counsellor at Berlin, being ennobled in 1693. He wrote valuable histories of Charles Gustavus of Sweden and the Great Elector, but his main work was in the field of political theory in which he is the first German writer to assert the autonomy of the secular state, particularly in respect to emperor and church. An adherent of absolutism, he defined also the 'natural law' which the ruler must observe and which includes freedom of conscience. He was thus the founder of the Aufklärung theory of state.

Works:

De statu imperii Germanici, 1667 (ed. Salomon, 1910).
Gründlicher Bericht von dem Zustande des Heiligen Römischen Reichs Teutscher Nation (the German translation of the above, ed. Bresslau, 1870).
De jure naturae et gentium, 1672 (ed. Mascovius, 2 vols, 1759, reissued 1965).
Briefe an Thomasius, ed. Gigas, 1897.

Studies:

H. Rödding, *P. als Historiker und Politiker*, 1912.
E. Wolf, *Grotius, Pufendorf, Thomasius*, 1927.

Queintz (Gueintz), Christian, 1592–1650

Queintz was one of the many scholars associated with Ludwig von Anhalt in the reform of German grammar, style, and orthography. Born at Guben, his father a Lutheran pastor, he was appointed professor of law at Wittenberg in 1619; from 1627–50 he was headmaster of the Gymnasium at Halle. Ludwig von Anhalt employed him as advisor on educational reforms. At Ludwig's request he wrote a German 'Sprachlehre' which was much discussed in the leading circle of the Fruchtbringende Gesellschaft before its publication in 1641, and he invented a German form for many Latin grammatical terms. He was admitted to the Fruchtbringende Gesellschaft as 'Der Ordnende'. He also wrote a German 'Rechtschreibung' and a number of treatises on the classics, theology, and law.

Works:

Deutscher Sprachlicher Entwurf, 1641.
Deutsche Rechtschreibung, 1645.

Rachel, Joachim, 1618–69

Born in Dithmarschen, the son of a Lutheran pastor, Rachel studied at Rostock and Dorpat. He became a headmaster at schools in Holstein and Schleswig where among other reforms he introduced the study of German poetics into the curriculum. In his *Satires,* which are strongly influenced by the Roman satirists, he criticizes the extravagance of the later Baroque, and the sobriety of his attitude and his style links him both with Opitz and with the early Aufklärung.

Works:

Teutsche Satyrische Gedichte, 1664, to which two further satires, Der Freund and Der Poet, were added in 1667 (Nd 200–2). The two later satires have been edited by Lindquist, 1920.

Studies:

B. Berends, *Zu den Satiren des J.R., diss.* Leipzig 1897.
A. Leitzmann, *Zu J.R.'s Satiren,* 1928 (Beiträge zur Gesch. der dt. Sprache und Lit., 52).

Rebhun, Paul, 1505?–46

Of Austrian birth, Rebhun studied in Wittenberg where he became intimate with Luther and Melanchthon. He remained in Saxony, first as a schoolmaster, then as a pastor. He wrote in German several plays for production at school, all on Biblical subjects, all showing a classical structure; his *Susanna* is outstanding for the metrical regularity and variety of the verse, and is the first play in which iambics and trochaics are consciously employed.

Works:

Geistliches Spiel von der gottfürchtigen und keuschen Frauen Susannen, 1535 (LV 49, DNL 22, DD *Schauspiele* 1).
Hochzeitsspiel auf die Hochzeit von Kana, 1538 (LV 49).

Studies:

R. Pilger, *Die Dramatisierungen der Susanna im 16 J.*, 1879.

Regiomontanus (Müller, Johann), 1436–77

Born at Königsberg in Franken, Regiomontanus studied in Italy and Vienna, and in 1471 settled at Nürnberg. He is the creator of modern trigonometry and composed a table of the planets. He built the first astronomical observatory in Germany, and also set up a mechanical laboratory and a printing press. His cooperation with craftsmen and printers and his mathematical and technological enquiries illustrate an important aspect of Humanism. *See* H. Drewing, *Vier Gestalten aus dem Zeitalter des Humanismus*, 1946.

Rettenbacher, Simon, 1634–1706

Born at Salzburg, Rettenbacher studied in Italy and entered the Order of St Benedict in 1661. After teaching at Kremsmünster he became a professor at Salzburg. He wrote a number of theological, pedagogical and historical works, but is now remembered only for his plays, most of which were written for production in the university theatre at Salzburg. Their subjects were taken, in the main, from the more romantic, legendary ancient world though they also included medieval legend (*Demetrius, Perseus, Ulysses, Osiris, Rosimunda*). All written in Latin, they illustrate the height of the Benedictine school drama, melodramatic, colourful, rhetorical, and pious; they were produced with the lavish scenery and effects of the Benedictine tradition.

Works:

Dramata selecta, 1683.
Demetrius, 1672 (DL *Barockdrama* 2).

Reuchlin, Johannes, 1455–1522

Born at Pforzheim, Reuchlin studied in Germany and France, and then held various legal posts, being from 1502–13 one of the judges of the Swabian League. Later he was professor of Hebrew and Greek at Ingolstadt and Tübingen. His Latin comedies, *Sergius* (1496) and *Henno* (1497)—the latter an adaptation of the

French farce of *Maître Pathelin*—satirize the ignorance of priests and the rapacity of lawyers. When a converted Jew, Pfefferkorn, seeking with the emperor's support powers to confiscate the sacred books of the Jews, came into conflict with German civil authorities, Reuchlin, known as a Hebrew scholar (*Rudimenta hebraica*, 1506) was asked for a judicial opinion. In a truly Humanistic spirit Reuchlin resisted the pressure from Pfefferkorn and the Theological Faculties and defended the purity of doctrine of much of the Hebrew teaching, notably of the Talmud. A violent controversy arose, and Reuchlin's *Augenspiegel* (1511), in which he both defended the Jewish books and attacked the theologians, was repeatedly banned by ecclesiastical authorities and by the emperor. In 1514 this book, together with the Talmud that it defended, was condemned to be burnt by the Theological Faculty at Paris. However, after Reuchlin had appealed to the Pope, the whole controversy was shelved and died away. Reuchlin's example mobilized all the German Humanists in defence of learning and truth, and many of them expressed their support in the *Epistolae clarorum virorum* of 1514; the ostensible riposte, the *Epistolae obscurorum virorum* of 1515, was a scathing parody of the ignorant theologians, written probably by Crotus Rubianus and Hutten. The moral victory went to the Humanists, and this rallying of forces encouraged some of the Reuchlin party—Luther, Melanchthon, Hutten, Vadian—to proceed to the great challenge that issued in the Reformation.

Reuchlin himself, however, opposed the radicalism of Luther's reform of doctrine and church, and remained faithful to the Catholic church. In his later years, following Pico della Mirandola, he became involved in mystical theosophical speculations, in particular trying to interpret the mysteries of the Hebrew *Cabbala* in terms of Christian doctrine (*De arte Cabbalistica*, 1517).

Works:

Komödien, ed. Holstein, 1888.
Henno (together with the German translation by Hans Sachs), ed. Preisendanz, 1922.
Briefwechsel, ed. Geiger, 1876 (LV 126).

Studies:

L. Geiger, *J.R.*, 1871.

H. Holstein, *R.'s Komödien*, 1888.
W. E. Peuckert, 'J.R.' (in *Pansophie*, 1956[2]).

Reuter, Christian, 1665–1712?

The son of a well-to-do Protestant peasant near Halle, Reuter studied at Leipzig where he passed much of his time in carousals. As a student he published gay satirical comedies about his landlady to whom he gave the name 'Frau Schlampampe', and a parody of the heroic novel about her son 'Schelmuffsky'. In trouble with the university authorities because of these lampoons, he was relegated in 1699. Engaged as secretary to an aristocratic chamberlain at Leipzig, another farce, *Ehrenfried*, involved him in further scandals, and he left Leipzig. He seems to have tried his luck in Berlin, and there published a text for an oratorio, *Passions-Gedanken* (1708), but then his trace is lost. His rather grotesque and disrespectful satire indicates the beginnings of the breakdown of Baroque dignity and pose.

Works:

Werke, ed. Witkowski, 2 vols, 1916.
Die ehrliche Frau zu Plissine, 1695 (DL *Barockdrama* 4).
Der ehrlichen Frau Schlampampe Krankheit und Tod, 1696 (Nd 90–1 contains both these plays).
Letztes Denck- und Ehren-Mal, 1697 (also concerns Schlampampe).
Schelmuffskys Warhafftige . . . Reisebeschreibung, 1696 (Nd 57–9).
Graf Ehrenfried, 1700 (Nd neue Folge 2).
Passions-Gedancken, 1708 (DL *Barockdrama* 6).

Studies:

F. J. Schneider, *C.R.*, 1936.
E. Gehmlich, *C.R., der Dichter des Schelmuffsky*, 1891.
K. Tober, *C.R.'s Schelmuffsky*, diss. Münster 1952.
F. J. Schneider, 'C.R.'s Komödien und die Bühne', 1937 (*Ztschr. f. dt. Phil.* 62).

Rhenanus, Beatus (Bild), 1485–1547

Born at Rheinau in Alsace, Rhenanus studied at Paris and became an excellent classical scholar. He spent his later life in Alsace, and in Basel belonged to the circle round Erasmus. He edited works of Roman and Greek writers, and also of the Fathers of the Church. He shared the historical interests of the Humanists, but is distinguished by his scrupulous concern for the authenticity of documents and his recognition of the Germanic roots of the names given in Tacitus. His *Rerum germanicarum libri tres* (1531) describes the condition of Germany in Roman times, the 'Völker-wanderung', and the history of the Franks and other Germanic peoples up to the Middle Ages; in it the laws of the Germanic tribes are examined. Like Erasmus, Rhenanus expressed at times sharp criticism of the practices of the Church, but remained distant from the Reformation. In his earlier life he studied Aristotle and strove to reconcile his teachings with Christianity; after 1518 he devoted himself to the study of Plato, and joined in the neo-Platonic theosophical speculations that occupied many of the Italian and German humanists in their search for a metaphysical system that would embrace and justify the Christian faith. Rhenanus's *Briefwechsel* has been edited by Horawitz and Hartfelder, 1886.

Rist, Johann, 1607–67

Born near Hamburg, Rist's father was a Lutheran clergyman, as he and his brothers were to become. He studied at Rostock, probably also at Leyden and Leipzig, and in 1635 became pastor at Wedel near Hamburg where he remained till his death. During the Thirty Years War his house was plundered by the armies, and at times soldiers were quartered on him; in several of his allegorical plays a genuine longing for peace is expressed, while in comic interludes he satirizes the soldiery. He wrote much lyrical verse in the Opitzian style, delighting in variety of image and metre, though refraining from the extravagances of Zesen (also of Hamburg), whom he ridiculed in *Das Friedejauchtzende Deutschland*. Of his many hymns, one or two ('O Ewigkeit, du Donnerwort') have remained in the hymnals. He enjoyed great prestige as a clergyman and a poet, though he was attacked for writing secular, parcularly love poetry, which in fact he solemnly abjured in 1638. He founded in 1656 the 'Elbschwanenorden' and published *Monatsgespräche*, after the model of Harsdörffer's *Frauenzimmergesprechspiele*, as examples of cultured and improving discourse.

He was crowned laureate in 1645, was admitted to the Frucht-bringende Gesellschaft in 1647 (as 'Der Rüstige'—one of its two clerical members), and was also a member of the Pegnesischer Blumenorden.

Works:

Irenaromachia, 1630 (DL *Barockdrama* 6).
Perseus, 1634 (comic interlude in DL *Barockdrama* 4).
Das Friedewünschende Teutschland, 1647 (DD (17) 15 contains this and selections from other works).
Das Friedejauchtzende Deutschland, 1653.
Musa teutonica, 1634.
Poetischer Lust-Garte, 1638.
Des Dafnis aus Cymbrien Galathee, 1642.
Des edlen Dafnis aus Cymbrien Besungene Florabella, 1652.
Himlische Lieder, 3 vols, 1641, 1642, 1651.
Rettung der Edlen Teutsch n Hauptsprache, 1642.
Monatsgespräche, 1663.

Studies:

T. Hausen, *J.R. und seine Zeit*, 1872.
O. Kern, *J.R. als weltlicher Lyriker*, 1919.
A. Jericke, *J.R.'s Monatsgespräche*, Berlin/Leipzig 1928.
O. Heims, *J.R. als Dramatiker*, diss. Marburg 1929.

Sachs, Hans, 1494–1576

The son of a Nürnberg tailor, Sachs learnt the cobbler's trade, and after travelling as a journeyman to Austria and the Nether-lands, settled in Nürnberg as a master-shoemaker. He became a man of substance, a house-owner, and was able to devote much time to literature. He eagerly joined in the Lutheran reform movement, writing a famous poem 'Die Wittembergisch Nachti-gall' in 1523, and composing a number of prose dialogues in which he skilfully argues the evangelical case—the *Disputation zwischen einem Chorherren und Schuchmacher*, 1524 (DL *Reformation* 2), became famous, and was also influential in English translation. After the publication of a violent anti-papistic work in 1527, he was ordered by the Town Council to refrain from publishing, and his subsequent work, though often satirical of contemporary manners, is good-humoured and non-polemical. He was a skilful versifier, excelling in narrative. He became the leader of the Nürnberg Meistersinger, drawing up the rules of composition and of meetings, inventing new melodies, and enlarging the subject matter; his work, passed round in manuscript, became exemplary elsewhere too. His verse 'Schwänke' and fables show his narrative skill and humour at their best and bear witness to the width of his indiscriminate reading. He brought the Fastnachtspiel to its height, composing many hundreds, and drawing on material from the Bible, from romances, from German translations of Boccaccio and medieval tales, from fable and anecdotal literature, from the school drama, etc. The spiritual range is limited, but he catches with humour and insight the manners and ways of thought of the common burgher and peasant of his time. He tried his hand too at larger plays, tragedies and histories, but he was neither able to compose a large action nor to grapple with great emotion or deep moral problems. Sachs was proud of his literary craft, and his Fastnachtspiele are not only more skilful in composition and literary quality than those of his predecessors or successors, but they are also remarkably free from the obscenity traditionally associated with these plays. He himself also played a leading part in their production. Sachs's verse is, throughout, the Knittelvers, which did not lend itself to subtleties of emotional or moral expression; but his *Summa all meiner gedicht* of 1567, written when he thought he was dying, is a moving confession of his literary aims.

Works:

Werke (LV 102 ff.; reissued, 26 vols, 1964).
Lieder, Spruchgedichte, Dramatische Gedichte (DD *Sachs* 1, 2, 3).
Sämtliche Fastnachtspiele (Nd 26–7; 31–2; 39–40; 42–3; 51–2; 60–1; 63–4).
Sämtliche Fabeln und Schwänke (Nd 110–7; 126–34; 164–9; 193–9; 207–11; 231–5).
Selections in DNL 20–1.
Dialoge des H.S., ed. Zoozmann, 1904.
Das Gemerkbüchlein (Nd 149–52).
   There are many editions of Fastnachtspiele and Schwänke in modernized spelling, e.g. Reclam. Sachs himself published his works in 5 folio vols, 1557–79.

Studies:

R. Genée, *H.S. und seine Zeit*, 1894.
H. V. Wendler, *H.S. Einführung in Leben und Werk*, 1953.
G. W. Kawerau, *H.S. und die Reformation*, 1889.
W. Sommer, *Die Metrik des H.S.*, 1882.
L. Pfannmüller, 'Zur Auffassung des H.S. Verses' (*Beiträge zur Gesch. der dt. Sprache und Lit.*, 43).
A. Zion, *Stoffe und Motive bei H.S. in seinen Fabeln und Schwänken*, diss. Würzburg 1924.
E. Geiger, *Der Meistergesang des H.S.*, 1956.
E. Geiger, *H.S. als Dichter in seinen Fastnachtspielen*, 1904.
E. Edert, *Dialog und Fastnachtspiel bei H.S.*, diss. Kiel 1903.
J. Münch, *Die sozialen Anschauungen des H.S. in seinen Fastnachtspielen*, diss. Erlangen 1936.
M. Herrmann, *Die Bühne des H.S.*, 1923.

Salat, Hans, 1498–1561

Born in Switzerland, Salat, a rope-maker and surgeon by trade, after several years as a mercenary in France took part in the two Kappel campaigns against the Zwinglians, and settled in Luzern where he became clerk at the law-courts. In several historical works he championed the Catholic cause against the Zwinglian reform, writing also two crudely exultant poems on Zwingli's death in 1531–32. He was one of the first Catholics to adopt the school drama, using the same themes as the Protestants, but turning the moral in a Catholic direction (*Judith*, 1534, and *Der verlorne Sohn*, 1537). He also directed the great Easter (Passion) Play performed at Luzern in 1538. In 1540 he lost his post and his unruly temperament drove him again to take service with mercenaries; further misfortunes as a schoolmaster followed, and his trace is lost after 1552.

Studies:

J. Bächtold, *H.S.*, 1876.
D. Cuoni, *H.S.*, Luzern 1938.

Schirmer, David, 1623?–85?

Born in Saxony, the son of a Lutheran pastor, Schirmer was a pupil of Queintz at Halle and studied at Leipzig, then at Wittenberg under Buchner. In 1650 he went to Dresden where a few years later he became librarian. He wrote much verse to suit court taste, smooth, frivolous, and sometimes graceful. *Poetische Rosengepüsche* (1657–8) is characteristic. Like other poets in the Saxon regions (Stieler, Beer) he rarely falls into the ostentation and bombast of the Silesian school or the over-ornamentation of the Nürnberg tradition.

Schottel, Justus Georgius, 1612–76

Born at Einbeck in Hanover, the son of a Lutheran pastor, Schottel studied theology at Leipzig and Wittenberg where he came under Buchner's influence, and law at Leyden where he met the admired Heinsius. He became tutor to the young Anton Ulrich of Braunschweig and then a Consistorial Councillor at Wolfenbüttel, where he remained till his death. He was admitted to the Fruchtbringende Gesellschaft ('Der Suchende') and took a zealous part in the discussions on German grammar, orthography, and metrics; his *Teutsche Haubt Sprache* is one of the most systematic attempts to reconcile (and correct) the vagaries of the spoken language with the 'laws' of grammar, and it enjoyed great esteem. Though in general following Opitz, he was still Latinist enough to cling to the idea of quantity as determining metrical accentuation. He wrote secular poems in the Opitzian style, religious poetry of pompous gravity, and an allegorical masque, *Friedens Sieg*, that was performed at the Braunschweig court in 1642. Schottel is perhaps the most impressive of the scholars who championed the dignity of the German language, and his own style is vigorous and weighty; like Queintz he created a number of important German equivalents of foreign words that have remained in the language (such as 'Abhandlung', 'Darstellung', 'gebundene Rede', 'Lustspiel', 'Mundart', 'Wörterbuch').

Works:

Teutsche Sprachkunst, 1641.
Teutsche Vers- oder Reim-Kunst, 1645.
Ausführliche Arbeit von der Teutschen Haubt Sprache, 1663.
Fruchtbringender Lustgarte, 1647.
Neu erfundenes Freuden-Spiel genanndt Friedens Sieg, 1648 (Nd 175).
Eigentliche und Sonderbare Vorstellung Des Jüngsten Tages, 1668.

Studies:

F. E. Koldewey, *J.G.S.*, 1899.
F. Gundolf, 'J.G.S.' (*Festschrift für Panzer*, 1930).

Schupp, Johann Balthasar, 1610–61

Schupp was born at Giessen where his father was a citizen of substance. He studied philosophy and theology at Marburg, in Prussia and Poland, and at Rostock, several times forced to evade the warring armies. Appointed professor and preacher at Marburg, he was officially warned against discussing the issues of the war. In 1645 he lost all his possessions at the storming of Marburg. In 1646 he became court preacher and counsellor at Hessen-Darmstadt, and in 1649 he was called to Hamburg as Hauptpastor, an office he held to his death. He was a popular preacher and writer, a stout Lutheran, vigorous in his refutation of Papists and Calvinists, but stressing good works and Christian behaviour more than orthodoxy. His popularity as a preacher, the exuberant and often burlesque style he adopted in his sermons as in his published work, raised the ire of his fellow pastors, and he was frequently involved in controversies with them. His polemical pamphlets, though over-burdened with learning, are witty and not without fantasy, and rank among the best prose satires of the seventeenth century. In some respects his style goes back to the sixteenth century, and in the Preface to his *Morgen- und Abendlieder* (1655–62) he attacks Opitzian artifice.

Works:

Schrifften, 1663.
Lehrreiche Schrifften, 1677.
Streitschriften (Nd 222–4, 225–6).
Ineptus orator, 1640 (translated by B. Kindermann as '*Der ungeschickte Redner*').
Der Freund in der Not, 1657 (Nd 9).
Corinna, 1660 (Nd 228–9).

Studies:

T. Bischoff, *J.B.S.*, 1890.
C. Vogt, 'J.B.S.' (*Euphorion*, 16, 17, 18, 21, 1909–10–11–14).
H. E. Wichert, *J.B.S. and the Baroque satire in Germany*, 1952.

Silesius, Angelus (Scheffler, Johann), 1624–77

Scheffler was the son of a prosperous Lutheran merchant who settled in Breslau. He studied medicine at Strassburg and Leyden, and in Amsterdam met the Silesian Abraham von Franckenberg who introduced him to the works of Jakob Böhme and the thought of other Silesian mystics. After taking his doctorate in Padua he became in 1649 physician to the Duke of Württemberg-Oels, and entered into intimate relations with the circle of Daniel von Czepko. His first book of poetry containing translations from Catholic mystics brought him into conflict with Lutheran orthodoxy, and in 1653 he joined the Catholic church, taking holy orders in 1661. For some years he joined zealously in the intensive Catholic campaign for the subjugation and re-conversion of the Protestants in Silesia. His profound and paradoxical mystical verse, *Der Cherubinische Wandersmann*, first published in 1656, is in its antithetical brevity the most brilliant expression of Silesian mysticism, and owes much to the sectarian Protestant tradition. *Heilige Seelenlust*, first published in the following year, is in its verse-forms and imagery closer to the ecstasy and rapture of Catholic religious verse.

Works:

Sämtliche poetische Werke, ed. Held, 3 vols, 1952³.
Der Cherubinische Wandersmann, 1674–5 (Nd 135–8).
Heilige Seelenlust, 1675 (Nd 177–81).

Studies:

G. Ellinger, *A.S., Ein Lebensbild*, 1927.
J. Flitch, *A.S.*, 1932.
B. von Wiese, 'Die Antithetik in den Alexandrinern des A.S.', 1928 (*Euphorion*, 29).
R. Neuwinger, *Die dt. Mystik unter besonderer Berücksichtigung des 'Cherub. Wandersmanns'*, diss. Leipzig 1937.
E. Spörri, *Der 'Cherub. Wandersmann' als Kunstwerk*, 1947.
E. Meier-Lefhalm, *Das Verhältnis von mystischer Innerlichkeit und rhetorischer Dichtung bei A.S.*, diss Heidelberg 1958.

Spee, Friedrich von, 1591–1635

Spee, born at Donauwörth of a noble family in the service of the
Elector of Cologne, entered the Society of Jesus in 1611 and was
ordained priest in 1622. He worked first as teacher and preacher
in districts recently regained by the Counter-Reformation from
Protestantism, and wrote during this period his religious poems,
in which he adapts pastoral motifs to express the soul's love for
Christ. In 1632 he wrote his *Guldenes Tugendbuch*, a book of religious exercises closely related to those of Ignatius Loyola and
François de Sales. The sometimes excessive sweetness of these
works, which were not published till after his death, is belied by
his *Cautio criminalis*, the boldest attack on the persecution of
alleged witches in this whole period. At a time when the belief in
witchcraft was sweeping Europe, and when many hundreds of
victims were burnt in Germany, Spee was appointed as chaplain
to the condemned—it is uncertain whether at Würzburg or
Paderborn. His experience taught him that many of the victims
were innocent, but a rule of his Order prohibited him from any
action that might offend ecclesiastical or secular authorities.
Criticism of the judicial procedures, particularly the extortion of
confessions, had however been voiced by other Jesuits (Cusan and
Tanner), and Spee proceeded in 1641 to publish his protest
anonymously in Protestant Rinteln. While not doubting the
existence of witchcraft, Spee stated that hardly any of those found
guilty were in fact guilty. He gives a damning description of the
procedures of examination, the extortion of confessions and incriminations by torture, and claims that such methods would result in condemnations whether the victims were guilty or not. At
the same time he sharply criticized prison conditions and proposed reforms. *Cautio criminalis*, one of the noblest and most
humane documents of the seventeenth century, was translated
into German in 1649, but though many Germans must secretly
have sympathized with it, it was not till Thomasius's *De crimine
magiae* (1701) that another German spoke so decisively—this time,
however, to dismiss witchcraft as an evil superstition.

Works:

Cautio criminalis, 1631.

GL—I

Trutz Nachtigall, oder Geistlich-Poetisch Lust-Wäldlein, 1649 (Nd 292–301, DD (17) 13).
Guldenes Tugendbuch, 1649.

Studies:

H. Zwetslot, *F.S. und die Hexenprozesse,* 1954.
A. Becker, *Die Sprache F. von S.'s,* 1912.
E. Jacobsen, *Die Metamorphose der Liebe in F.S.'s Trutznachtigall,* 1954.
E. Rosenfeld, *Neue Studien zur Lyrik von F.S.,* 1963.

Stieler, Caspar, 1632–1707

Born at Erfurt of a Lutheran family, Stieler studied at several universities, campaigned as a soldier for a while, and after completing his studies became a secretary at various small courts in Thüringen. In his early lively years he wrote, in the Opitzian tradition, love poetry which has an exceptional directness, musicality and imaginativeness. Published under a pseudonym, it was for long ascribed to Jakob Schwieger, but Stieler's authorship was established by Köster. He also wrote allegorical masques for performance at the Rudolstadt court. Later he abjured secular poetry, and composed a book of devotions, and primers on grammar and style. He was admitted to the Fruchtbringende Gesellschaft in its period of decline ('der Spate').

Works:

Die Geharnschte Venus, 1660 (Nd 74–5, ascribed to Schwieger).
Der bussfertige Sünder, 1679.
Der Allzeitfertige Secretarius, 1680.
Der Teutschen Sprache Stammbaum und Fortwuchs, 1691.
Dichtkunst. Eine ungedruckte Poetik Stielers, ed. Bolte (Sitzungsber. der Preuss. Akad. der Wiss., 1926).

Studies:

A. Köster, *Der Dichter der Geharnschten Venus,* 1897.
C. Höfer, *Die Rudolstädter Festspiele aus den Jahren 1665–7 und ihre Dichter,* 1904.

Thomasius, Christian, 1655–1728

Born at Leipzig, the son of a professor of philosophy, Thomasius studied law there and at Frankfurt/Oder before becoming a professor at Leipzig. From 1687 he lectured in German, the first professor to do so. A bold and outspoken critic of dogma and established opinions, he issued in 1688–9 his *Monatsgespräche*, the first literary journal in German, in which he castigated the prejudices and charlatanry of academic pedants. The hostility of his colleagues forced him to leave in 1690; he found refuge in Berlin and was appointed Rektor of the new university of Halle where he stayed till his death. Thomasius lectured and wrote upon many subjects—philosophy, religion, morals, political science, literature. In all he shows a robust common sense, a strong feeling for the practical and moral purposes of study, and a combative self-confidence. He stood in close relations with Pufendorf and the movement of rational enlightenment spreading throughout Europe, and his refutation of the belief in witchcraft, *De crimine magiae* (1701), is one of the decisive works of the early Aufklärung. An opponent of Baroque ornamentation and bombast, he used and advocated a robust and vigorous prose. He was in the early years at Halle much influenced by A. H. Franke's pietism, but later abjured its puritanical and anti-intellectual devoutness. Thomasius is one of the principal founders of the Aufklärung, which was to centre from that time in Saxony and Prussia; his transient alliance with the pietists was symptomatic of the tenuous association of pietism and rationalism in the struggle against dogmatic orthodoxy.

Works:

Kleine dt. Schriften, ed. Opel, 1894.
Gedanken über allerhand Bücher, 1688–90.
Selections from the following are to be found in DL *Aufklärung* 1:
Einleitung zur Vernunftlehre, 1691; *Ausübung der Sittenlehre*, 1696; *Kurtze Lehrsätze von dem Laster der Zauberei*, 1703 (translation of *De crimine magiae*); *Politische Klugheit*, 1705; *Höchstnötige Cautelen für einen Studiosus juris*, 1713 ('Von dem Studio der Poesie').

Studies:

W. Becker, *C.T. Leben und Lebenswerk*, 1931.

E. Wolf, *Grotius, Pufendorf, Thomasius*, 1927.
L. Neiner, *C.T. und seine Beziehungen zum Pietismus, diss.* Heidelberg 1928.
J. Kirchner, 'Deutschlands erste Literaturztschr., Die Monatsgespräche C.T.'s,' 1960 (*Welt und Wort*, 15).

Tscherning, Andreas, 1611–59

Born at Bunzlau, a fellow-citizen of Opitz, Tscherning was the son of an artisan. After studying, he held various tutorial posts, and from 1644 was professor of poetry at Rostock where he remained till his death. He was a zealous disciple of Opitz, and published Latin and German poetry in the Opitzian manner. His poetics, *Unvorgreiffliches Bedencken* . . ., is little more than an exposition of Opitz's principles, and contains a repertoire of metaphors and expressions suitable for poetry. His *Sprüche Alis* (1641) is the first German translation from Arabic.

Works:

Deutscher Getichte Früling, 1642.
Vortrab des Sommers deutscher Gedichte, 1655.
Unvorgreiffliches Bedencken über etliche missbräuche in der deutschen Schreib- und Sprach-Kunst, insonderheit der edlen Poeterey, 1658.

Studies:

H. H. Borcherdt, *A.T. als deutscher Lyriker*, 1911.

Waldis, Burkard, 1495?–1556

Born in Hessen, Waldis joined the Franciscan order, and in 1522 entered the service of the Archbishop of Riga. Engaged in the bitter disputes that arose when the city adopted the evangelical reform, he joined the Lutherans in 1525, abandoned his vows and became a pewterer. Travelling widely in Germany, he established close connections with the German Lutherans, and in the ensuing troubled years played a prominent part in the political and religious struggles of Riga with local feudal lords and the Teutonic Order, by which he was imprisoned in 1536. Freed in 1540, he studied theology in Wittenberg, and in 1544 became pastor in Hessen. In 1527 he wrote, as a Fastnachtspiel, his *Prodigal Son*, a play with an explicit Lutheran moral that anticipates the Protestant school-drama. He also wrote religious polemical verse and evangelical hymns, and a rhymed version of the Psalms. Late in life he published a versified *Aesop* in which, with considerable literary skill, he transfers the original to German soil.

Works:

De parabell vam vorlorn Szohn, 1527 (DNL 22, DL *Reformation* 5).
Esopus, Gantz neu gemacht, 1548, ed. Kurz, 3 vols, 1862 (DD 16–7, DNL 19, DL *Reformation* 4).

Studies:

G. Milchsack, *B.W.* 1881.
H. Lindemann, *Studien zur Persönlichkeit des B.W.*, *diss.* Jena 1922.

Weckherlin, Georg Rudolf, 1584–1653

Weckherlin was born at Stuttgart of an evangelical family; his father was a high official in the service of the Duke of Württemberg. He studied classics and law at Tübingen, and travelled with diplomatic missions in Germany, France and England. Appointed a secretary to the Duke in 1615, he was in London from 1620, and from 1625 to 1641 was a diplomatic advisor to the English court. From 1644–9 he was a Parliamentary secretary and personal adviser to the King, but though he seems to have sympathized with Parliament was replaced as secretary by Milton. Throughout this busy diplomatic life he composed much verse, odes, epigrams, eclogues, and court masques. With Theobald Hock he was one of the first scholars to adopt, before Opitz, the themes and forms of the French and Italian Renaissance and to write a scanned verse, but his verse is often clumsy because he did not, until his late poems, base his metre on the natural stress of German. His odes and political verse (often directed against the emperor and the pope) have sometimes a vigorous movement, but like his religious verse, are often congested and turgid. He published his collected works in 1648.

Works:

Gedichte (LV 199–200, 245, reprint 1968; DD (17) 5).
Das erste Buch Oden und Gesänge, 1618—a second vol. 1619.
Geistliche und Weltliche Gedichte, 1641.

Studies:

H. Gaitanides, *G.R.W.*, *Stilanalyse*, diss. München 1936.
L. W. Forster, *G.R.W.* *Zur Kenntnis seines Lebens in England*, 1944.
H. Lentz, *Zum Verhältnis von Versiktus und Wortakzent im Verstakt G.R.W.'s*, 1966.

Weigel, Valentin, *1533–88*

Born at Naundorf in Saxony, Weigel studied theology and became a Lutheran pastor in Saxony. He shared the pietistic mysticism of Sebastian Franck and Kaspar von Schwenkfeld, seeking a renewal of religious life in a loving self-identification with Christ, and combining this with theosophical ideas like those of Paracelsus, asserting the spiritual identity of all Creation as the expression of God. His works were not published till after his death, but his manuscripts were passed round secretly and influenced many people, particularly Jakob Böhme.

Works:

Nosce te ipsum, 1615.
Der güldene Griff, 1616.

Studies:

H. Maier, *Der mystische Spiritualismus V.W.'s*, 1926.
W. Zeller, *Die Schriften V.W.'s*, 1940.

Weise, Christian, *1642–1708*

Weise was born at Zittau where his father, a Lutheran, was schoolmaster. He studied at Leipzig, was a secretary and tutor in aristocratic houses, professor of poetry at the Weissenfels Gymnasium, and from 1678 till he retired headmaster of the prosperous Zittau Gymnasium. He was famed as a teacher of German and of that practical sagacity then known as 'politics'. He was a voluminous writer, composing treatises of moral and religious edification, practical instruction, etc., in addition to a great quantity of verse, plays, and novels. His verse, mostly religious and moral in character, is sober, pious, and humble, discarding the extravagance of the Baroque though still preserving some of its forms. The prose of his novels is in general plain and practical; they instruct his readers to live soberly according to their station, and satirize all foppery and pretence. For his school he provided each year (with few exceptions) three plays for performance, a Biblical play, a historical play, and a comedy. His object was to give useful didactic instruction and training in deportment and speech; in the historical plays he shows some understanding of political matters, with a marked deference to established authority, and in the comic parts and in his comedies he satirizes with observant realism the foibles of everyday. His dramatic form is very loose, and closer to the popular drama of his times than to high Baroque tragedy; *Der Niederländische Bauer* and *Die Böse Catharina* are both based on a Wanderbühne version of *The Taming of the Shrew*. Despite his deference to the aristocracy, Weise's concern for the realities of burgher life and his practical, moralistic sobriety mark the beginnings of the Aufklärung.

Works:

Der grünenden Jugend überflüssige Gedancken, 1668 (Nd 242–5).
Der grünenden Jugend nothwendige Gedancken, 1675.
Curiöse Gedancken von deutschen Versen, 1691–2–3.
Der politische Näscher, 1678.
Reiffe Gedancken, 1682.
Die drei ärgsten Erznarren, 1673 (Nd 12–14).
Masaniello, 1683 (Nd 216–8).
Die Unvergnügte Seele, 1688, and *Vom Verfolgten Lateiner*, 1696 (DL *Aufklärung* I).
Die Böse Catharina, 1693? (DNL 39).
Der Bäurische Machiavellus, 1696 (DNL 39).
Der Niederländische Bauer, 1700 (DL *Barockdrama* 4).
Von Verfertigung der Komödien und ihrem Nutzen, 1708 (DL *Aufklärung* I).

Studies:

J. Beinert, *C.W.'s Romane in ihrem Verhältnis zu Grimmelshausen und Moscherosch*, 1907.
W. Eggert, *C.W. und seine Bühne*, 1935.
H. Schauer, *C.W.'s biblische Dramen*, diss. Leipzig 1921.
H. Haxel, *Studien zu den Lustspielen C.W.'s*, 1932.
A. Hess, *W.'s historische Dramen und ihre Quellen*, 1893.

M. Zarneckow, *C.W.'s Politica Christiana und der Pietismus*, diss. Leipzig 1924.
K. Schaefer, *Das Gesellschaftsbild in den dichterischen Werken C.W.'s*, diss. Berlin 1960.

Wickram, Jörg, 1505–62?

Wickram was the illegitimate son of a wealthy burgher of Colmar. He had little education and probably was at first an artisan, for he founded a Meistersingerschule there in 1549. He read voraciously and acquired such literary skill that he was appointed town clerk at Burkheim where he died. He wrote Meisterlieder and a 'Tabulatur' on the Nürnberg model, several satirical Fastnachtspiele (*Das Narrengiessen*, 1538), and biblical school plays on the Prodigal Son (1540) and Tobias (1550). His collection of prose anecdotes, *Das Rollwagenbüchlein*, was one of the most popular of such collections. He versified an older translation of Ovid's *Metamorphoses*, and also wrote romances, *Ritter Galmy* (1539) and *Der Goldtfaden* (1557). His most remarkable tale is *Der Jungen Knaben Spiegel* (1554), the story of the rise of a hardworking boy to success, that can be reckoned the first German novel. The prose of this novel, as of his later *Von Guten und Boesen Nachbaurn* (1556), is often clumsily didactic, but at times fresh and realistic.

Works:

Werke, 8 vols (LV 222–3–9, 230–2–6–7, 241).
Das Rollwagenbüchlein, 1555 (DNL 24, also Reclam).
Der Jungen Knaben Spiegel, 1554.
Von Guten und Boesen Nachbaurn, 1556 (selections from this and the preceding item in DL *Volks- und Schwankbücher* 7).

Studies:

G. Fauth, *J.W.*, 1916.
W. Scherer, *Die Anfänge des dt. Prosaromans*, 1877.
G. Jacke, *J.W. Analyse seiner Prosaromane*, diss. Tübingen 1954.
M. Mencelin-Roeser, *Studien zum Prosastil J.W.'s*, diss. Basel 1955.
K. Stöcker, *Die Lebenslehre im Prosawerk J.W.'s*, diss. München 1956.

Wimpfeling, Jakob, 1450–1528

Born at Schlettstadt, Wimpfeling studied at Freiburg, Erfurt and Heidelberg, and took holy orders. He taught at Heidelberg, was Domprediger at Speyer from 1494–8, professor of poetry at Heidelberg 1498–1500. Later he lived in Strassburg where he sought to reorganize the school on humanist lines and to awaken patriotic feeling. His *Germania* (1501) shows an extravagant patriotism, with a strong anti-French bias, and provoked the criticism of Thomas Murner. He also wrote patriotic poetry, and was a stout adherent of the emperor Maximilian. In a Latin dialogue, *Stylpho* (1480—printed in 1494) he satirized the ignorance of the clergy. Wimpfeling published a number of learned works, among them editions of Augustine and Bonaventura. Despite his criticism of the clergy, he defended the cult of the Virgin and remained faithful to the Catholic church.

Works:

Germania, 1501, ed. (with Murner's reply), Schmidt, 1875—translated into German by Martin, 1885.
Pädagogische Schriften, trans. and ed. Freundgen, 1892.
Stylpho, ed. Holstein 1892.

Studies:

J. Knepper, *J.W.*, 1892.
E. von Börries, *W. und Murner im Kampf um die ältere Gesch. des Elsasses*, 1926.

Zesen, Philipp, 1619–89

Zesen came from a line of Lutheran pastors, was born near Dessau, and went to school at Halle where, under Queintz's influence, he began to occupy himself with the new poetry. He studied at Wittenberg under Buchner, and also at Leyden. He went to live at Hamburg where in 1643 he formed the 'Teutschgesinnte Genossenschaft', but stayed frequently in Holland where he spent the years from 1655–67. He stayed in 1647 in Cöthen with Ludwig von Anhalt, and was admitted to the Fruchtbringende Gesellschaft in 1649 ('Der Wohlsetzende'); he also entertained intimate relations with the Nürnberg poets. He was ennobled in 1653. He had no settled position. Occasionally engaging in trade, in the main he lived on his pen and on patronage, undertaking various small private missions for the nobility; a man of extravagantly courtly manners, he was a great favourite with the ladies. In later life he was oppressed by poverty. He was one of the most virtuose and productive writers of the Baroque, and in addition to many translations wrote much verse, several novels, and works on poetry, grammar, and orthography. His verse is distinguished by its complex and mixed metres, and by a plethora of images; it, like his prose, takes imagery to the extreme of preciosity, replacing words like 'Fenster' and 'Handschuh' by stilted circumlocutions (he translated a novel of Mlle de Scudéry). At the same time, he invented some German words that have remained ('Augenblick', 'Bücherei', 'Sinngedicht'). In his effort to make spelling conform to speech, he created an orthography of his own, and his obstinacy in this and other respects led to conflict with Ludwig von Anhalt. His views were often repudiated in the later part of the century, notably by A. D. H. Habichthorst in *Wohlbegründete Bedenkschrift über die Zesische sonderbahre Ahrt Hochdeutsch zu schreiben*, 1685. Yet he was one of the most skilful prose-writers of the century, creating complex sentences that, if overburdened by conceits, are balanced and pointed. His *Adriatische Rosemund* is one of the few elegant novels of the time that have a personal reference and a contemporary theme, and is the first German sentimental novel. The problem of religious tolerance with which it is concerned shows the serious side of a man who usually seems merely a virtuose player with words; Zesen also translated works by Comenius and others advocating religious tolerance. His own religious verse, that includes a translation of the Song of Solomon, luxuriates in high-falutin imagery. He published a popular book of devotions for ladies, and invented harmless equivalents for the names of the classical gods. His two late novels, *Assenat* and *Simson*, are on Biblical themes.

Works:

Poetischer Rosenwälder Vorschmack, 1642.
Dichterische Jugend-Flammen, 1651.
Gekreuzigter Liebsflammen . . . Vorschmack, 1653.
Geistliche Wohl-Lust oder Hohes Lied, 1657.
Dichterisches Rosen- und Liljentahl, 1670.

Die Adriatische Rosemund, 1645 (Nd 160–3).
Assenat, 1670.
Simson, 1672.
Deutscher Helikon, 1640 (enlarged 1649 and 1656).
Hoochdeutsche Spraach-übung, 1643.

Studies:

K. Dissel, *P. von Z. und die Deutschgesinnte Genossenschaft*, 1890.
R. Ibel, *Die Lyrik P. von Z.'s*, diss. Würzburg 1922.
A. Gramsch, *Zesens Lyrik*, 1923.
H. Körnchen, *Zesens Romane*, 1912 (Pal 115).
W. Beyersdorf, *Studien zu Z.'s biblischen Romanen*, 1928.
H. Obermann, *Studien über Z.'s Romane*, diss. Göttingen 1934.
P. Baumgarten, *Die Gestaltung des Seelischen in Z.'s Romanen*, diss. Zürich 1942.
W. Kettler, *Z. und die barocke Empfindsamkeit*, diss. Wien 1948.
J. H. Scholte, 'Z.'s Adriatische Rosemund', 1949 (DVLG 23).

Zigler und Kliphausen, Heinrich Anselm von, 1663–96

Of an aristocratic Silesian family, Zigler studied at Frankfurt/ Oder, but lived a retired life on the family estate in Oberlausitz. He wrote histories, but is remembered only for his novel *Die Asiatische Banise*, a romance of heroism and love, full of sensational incidents, slaughter, and superhuman constancy. The novel was immensely popular, was dramatized on the Wanderbühne, and was republished up to 1766. Zigler's *Helden-Liebe*, in the style of Hofmannswaldau's *Heldenbriefe*, contains imaginary exchanges between Biblical lovers.

Works:

Die Asiatische Banise oder Das blutig, doch muthige Pegu, 1689, ed. Pfeiffer-Belli, 1965 (DNL 37).
Helden-Liebe der Schrifft des alten Testaments, 1691.

Studies:

M. Pistorius, *H.A. von Z., sein Leben und seine Werke*, diss. Jena 1928.
E. Schön, *Der Stil von Z.'s Asiatische Banise*, diss. Greifswald 1933.
W. Pfeiffer-Belli, *Die asiatische Banise*, 1940 (Germ. Stud. 220).
E. Schwarz, *Der schauspielerische Stil des dt. Hochbarock* (*Die asiatische Banise*), diss. Mainz 1956.

Zincgref, Julius Wilhelm, 1591–1635

Zincgref was born at Heidelberg where he studied law. After travels in France he settled in Heidelberg and wrote moral-satirical works that are akin to Fischart's. More modern was his *Emblematum Ethico-Politicorum Centuria* (1619), a commentary on a collection of emblems engraved by Merian that made the emblem a German literary genre. Driven by the war from Heidelberg, he went to Strassburg, and here met Opitz whose leadership he immediately acknowledged. In 1624 he published *Martini Opicii Teutsche Poemata und Aristarchus*, the first decisive manifesto and exemplar of the new poetry, though Opitz was vexed that, in addition to many inaccuracies, it contained early verse of his that did not conform to his new metrical principles. Together with this volume Zincgref published *Mehr auserlesener geticht anderer Teutscher Pöeten* containing poems of the new type by himself, Melissus, Weckherlin, Lingelsheim, and others. Some of Zincgref's own poems, like some of Opitz's, are based on French melodies; some betray folksong influence. In 1626 Zincgref published his *Teutsche Apophthegmata*, a collection of epigrams that contributed greatly to the establishment of the pointed Baroque epigram. (*See* R. Graupner, *J.W.Z. und seine Apophthegmata, diss.* Leipzig 1922). The *Auserlesene Gedichte deutscher Poeten* is reprinted Nd 15.

Zwingli, Huldrich, 1484–1531

The son of a Toggenburg peasant, Zwingli studied at Vienna and Basel. He became a priest in Glarus, then a chaplain to Swiss mercenary troops in Italy—he was later to oppose the enlistment of the Swiss as mercenaries. In 1516, when a priest at Einsiedeln, he met Erasmus, and under his influence began to study the original texts of the New Testament and the Fathers of the Church. His sermons show evangelical leanings before 1517, and when Luther's writings began to appear at Basel, he became one of his most zealous champions. In 1519 he became preacher in Zürich, and in 1523 persuaded the town council to reform the church. In this republic, Zwingli's reform took a more radical and democratic form than Luther's; church government was placed in the hands of the community, ministers were appointed by their parishioners, church property was used for communal and charitable purposes. Theologically, too, Zwingli differed from Luther, in particular asserting a more rational interpretation of the Eucharist as a symbol and memorial. When, at the Marburg 'Religionsgespräch' of 1529, the two Reform parties met, they were unable to reconcile their theological and organizational differences; from this time there were two recognized Protestant Churches, the Lutheran and the Reformed. Other Swiss cities adopted Zwingli's reform, and there was armed conflict between the Catholic and the Reformed cantons; Zwingli, who accompanied the Reformed troops as a chaplain, was killed at Kappel in 1531.

Zwingli's doctrines won adherents in Germany, particularly in the south-west. Much of his doctrine was taken over and systematized by Calvin in Geneva, and after 1555 Calvinism was adopted by a number of German cities and states, notably by Hessen and the Palatinate. The hostility between Lutherans and Calvinists became often as bitter as that between them and the Catholics. Zwingli left no such literary legacy as Luther.

Works:

Hauptschriften, ed. Blanke, Farner, and Pfister, 3 vols, 1941–7.
Sozialpolitische Schriften, ed. Muralt and Farner, 1934.
Von Freiheit der Speisen, 1522 (Nd 173).

Studies:

R. Staehelin, *Ulrich Z., sein Leben und Wirken*, 2 vols, 1895–7.
O. Farner, *Z.*, 2 vols, 1946.

GERMAN PAINTING*
by Hannah Priebsch Closs

I

WE frequently encounter, when reading criticisms of German art by non-German writers, a tendency to decry it as formless, or to deplore its insistence on illustrative rather than aesthetic elements. Such criticism is in reality based upon a comparison which requires the art of Central Europe to conform to certain aesthetic principles the outcome of a *Weltanschauung* very different from the German. The pagan sensuousness of the Italians, the logical genius of the French enable these peoples to create an art of serene harmony, of exquisite lucidity. They find it easier to reconcile imaginative emotion and reality than the German, whose very consciousness of this conflict seems often the primary urge to artistic creation, manifesting itself in violent contrasts of unrestrained fancy and ruthless realism. A passion for psychological penetration may sometimes result in a lack of subtlety, but with its suggestion of superficial description the term 'illustration' ignores the greatest quality of German art—its extraordinary force of expression. Moreover, the accusation 'formlessness', with its insinuation of literal transcription, fails to recognize the German artist's power to compel the object to his will, according to no fixed standard of beauty but to the necessity of individual truth.

Yet to recognize in the art of Central Europe only a tendency towards boundless subjective expression is to ignore forces that constitute as important a part of its genius as this predilection towards the 'Gothic' and Romantic. For from time to time, in the conflict between spirit and matter, a sudden longing for clarification and harmony awakens in the German that 'yearning for the south' of which Georg Dehio with his great insight into the art of his country speaks. But northern classicism thus born is,

* The General Editor thanks Messrs Methuen for kind permission to reprint with slight alterations from *Germany: a Companion to German Studies*, 1955, revised edition, J. Bithell.

through its very function of discipline and restraint, far removed from that of the Apolline south, and a true understanding of either can only be won through the realization of their divergent ideals.

When, with the foundation of the Holy Roman Empire, art was incorporated in the machinery of the State as a symbol of imperial and theocratic authority, Central Europe turned to the south. For neither the involved linearity characteristic of Germanic decorative art and the manuscripts of the Irish monks in Britain and St Gall, nor the Merovingian illuminations with their symbols of bird and fish were suited to the grandiose dogmatic art dreamed of by Charlemagne. What these lacked—monumental representation of the human form—the Carolingians found in late Classic and Byzantine art which provided them with a prototype both for the painting of manuscripts and for fresco in church and palace. Of the latter only inscriptions, 'tituli', remain. That the German monks who copied the foreign designs aimed at classicism in any real sense, that they were aware of the true significance of three-dimensional form in relation to space, is scarcely credible, as indeed the rude and summary manner in which these problems were treated proves. The name Carolingian Renaissance, which is often applied to this period (750–918), can therefore only be justified in as far as it denotes a decided attempt to create, like the south, an art that concerns itself with the material world.

Under the Saxon and Ottonian kings (919–1024) illuminative art continues as in the *Codex Egberti* on similar lines. But simultaneously the expressive decorative line beloved of Germanic art reasserts itself against the illusionistic form and impressionistic technique of the late Classic. Charged with an almost electric vitality it hastens over the page, causing draperies to twist and coil or straighten to tongues of flame and rectangular shapes rigid as metal (*Evangelist Markus* Munich lat. 4454). Three-dimensional form is negated. But a sense for monumentality of design gives the wild gesticulation and distortion of the figures an intensity which often amounts to apocalyptic frenzy (*Evangelienbuch Otto III*). Expression rather than representation is the key-note of this art, a tortured subjectivity, a reaction against reality in favour of the transcendental. The anthropomorphic interest of the south has here been subordinated to an anaturalistic decorative ideal.

Iconographically these anti-materialistic tendencies are reflected in a frequent recurrence of the theme of the Last Judgment (the *Weltuntergangsmotiv* beloved of German literature), not only in manuscripts but on frescoes in the churches of this period.

Amongst the monastic schools of painting, Treves, Echternach, Regensburg, Reichenau, the last was exceptionally productive in both branches of this art. In the church of St Georg, Oberzell, may be traced the remains of a *Last Judgment* of about the year 1000, a supreme example of the Ottonian style with its negation of three-dimensional form and the division of the picture-plane into three parallel strips of brown, green, and blue. A strict monu-mentality helps to create an atmosphere of suspense in the long file of apostles turned towards the enthroned Christ, the *terribilis vultus* from whom the dread decree is about to fall. Then in a wall-painting at Burgfelden, probably of the second half of the eleventh century, we are confronted with the chaos of demolition, and again expressive power of line gives dramatic force to the on-slaught of trump-blowing angel and pitch-forked devil.

This fresco falls under the period known as Romanesque, in which, with the development of building, painting was soon faced with a new problem—namely, its relation to the vault. In the Klosterkirche Prüfening, near Regensburg, towards the middle of the twelfth century, the tectonic design of the vault is still ignored by the painter, though the arrangement of the hieratic figures on the walls shows a fine sensibility to the noble rhythm of the archi-tecture. But in Schwarzrheindorf (1151–57) and in the chapter-house of Brauweiler church the painted scenes are divided to fit the caps, and colour is no longer applied in parallel strips but concentrically, the figures cutting the borders.

The majestic figures that loom isolated or in rows from the walls of twelfth-century German churches ornament also the glass-painting of this period. But in both cases a second style is met with in which descriptive scenes or single figures of compara-tively small dimensions are enclosed within medallions, producing a rich jewel-like effect. Influences from France may be traced, but their origin might also be ascribed to a development from Ottonian illuminations of the school of Regensburg. A supreme example of the medallion style is to be found in the painted wooden ceiling of St Michael, Hildesheim (1186?–1200), in which the figures of Adam and Eve show an astounding comprehension of the human form. Simultaneously the totally anaturalistic treatment of the draperies with their writhing zigzag folds is characteristic of a mannerism of the time. The almost baroque intensification of these lightning lines with their negation of volume approaches the bizarre in the Frankenberg Kirche, Goslar. In a painting of the vault of Sta Maria zur Höhe, Soest (1220–30) it becomes the direct expression of the transcendental. Defying the limitations of measurable space, it quickens the Byzantine monumentality where the angelic choir stand ranged around the Madonna with wings upspread like tongues of flame —*sub specie aeternitatis*.

In the meantime a tendency towards a certain naturalism began to manifest itself, a love of description. Musicians and jongleurs enliven the feast of Herod, the heroes of the Old Testament appear wearing the armour and costumes of contemporary knights (Brauweiler). In the *Hortus deliciarum*, pen-and-ink drawings which Herrad, Abbess of Klosterhohenburg (Alsace), prepared for the delight and edification of her nuns, scenes from everyday life intersperse a complex treatise of theology and science. Thinner draperies, following a softer flow of line, suggest vaguely the contours of the body (Schwarzrheindorf).

Crossing the threshold of the 'Gothic' period, art awakens to a long-lost sensuousness. The purgatorial terror and apocalyptic vision of Ottonian and Romanesque times are exchanged for a dream of Paradise that finds its way earthward. Christ is no longer the dread majesty but the friend of the supplicator. The terrible countenance of the angels has grown tender that they may laugh and weep with the Madonna—herself no more the regal bearer of the sceptred prince, but the mother absorbed in her child. The artist has rediscovered the beauty of the earth, not, like the Greeks, as an end in itself, but as a mirror of the spirit of God. Under the influence of chivalry, man and woman seek to give their lives a new dignity by aspiring towards the ideal of *zuht* and *mâze* (the Aristotelian Μεσότης, the Ciceronian *temperantia modesta*). No Neo-classicism or Renaissance, perhaps, appears so Greek as the unconscious Hellenism of thirteenth-century sculpture, except that the Gothic dream of harmonious perfection was permeated by a dogmatic tendency that insists on the subjective and symbolic value of representation, regarding it as an incentive to spiritual contemplation and activity. In reality, the corporeal beauty of early Gothic sculpture is little more than an illusion, for the thirteenth-century artist interested himself less in the anatomy of the body than in the draperies which rise and fall independently of movement in the limbs beneath. Nor are the painted figures confined to a real limit of space, but, moving against a formal background of gold or diaper work, cut the decorated border, oblivious of the boundaries of the finite.

Thus German art turns once more towards 'die Welt des schönen Scheins', curbing its passion for emotional expression, this time under the guidance of France—yet here, as in her literature, bending foreign influences to a need of her own. It is significant that in German thirteenth-century art idealism is permeated by an individuality, a dramatic sense that often causes French art, aesthetically more subtle, more sensitive though it be, to appear by comparison representative and conformable to type. As yet sculpture in its attendance upon architecture was the most expressive medium of medieval artistic thought, so that we must seek here rather than in painting characteristics peculiarly German. In the prophetic grandeur of the *Elizabeth of the Visitation* and in the immense spiritual control which renders more deeply significant the physical beauty of the *Knight* (Bamberg Cathedral) we become aware of qualities which almost foreshadow the art of Dürer. Painting during the thirteenth and early fourteenth centuries held a humbler place and remained, above all, essentially medieval and Gothic. In the form of fresco it enjoyed comparative importance in the churches of the Rhine, where interrelations with England have been traced. A particularly fine example of fourteenth-century wall-painting is found on the choir walls of the Klosterkirche Wienhausen, near Celle, in the province of Hanover, where figures in medallions are encompassed by a rich ornamentation of leafy tendrils. But fresco was forced to yield the power it had exercised on the Romanesque basilica, for, with the development of Gothic architecture, the walls were reduced to a minimum and the vast spaces between the skeleton of pier and tracery were spanned by painted glass. Sometimes, as in the *Three Kings Window* of Cologne Cathedral, slender Gothic figures rise against a diaper background crowned by fantastic architectural motifs, gleaming in golden-yellow and silver-grey. Later, vague attempts at perspective and modelling with half shadows make themselves evident. In its various branches, painting conforms to the idealistic manner described above. But when the artist's vision, rejecting abstraction for the illusion of physical beauty, turned earthward, the first seeds of medieval naturalism were unconsciously sown. Curiosity was gradually aroused for the manifold wonders of nature—a parallel to the conception of Thomas Aquinas, who tells us 'God rejoiceth in the beauty of all things'. The new interest manifests itself not only in an unlimited range of subject-matter, which includes countless illustrations to medieval romance and Minnelied, as for instance the illuminated Minnesinger manuscripts (Manesse Codex of Heidelberg) and Wolfram von Eschenbach's *Parzival* and *Willehalm* (Munich), or the great tapestries recounting the tale of *Tristan and Isôt* in Wienhausen, near Celle (1300–25). Of far greater consequence than the increase in motifs are the first signs of a systematic observation of nature which seeks to clarify the chaos of appearances. As early as the fourteenth century a panel in the museum at Erfurt representing *The Birth of Christ* shows an attempt on the part of the artist to bring the architectural motif (still more or less a fantastic piece of decoration) into direct plastic relation with the figures. It is significant that the development of naturalism goes hand in hand with the emancipation of painting from its bondage to monumental decoration, the panels of the fine altar (which gradually attains considerable importance) affording an excellent background for actual pictures. Naturalistic tendencies received a great stimulus in influences brought by way of Avignon from Italy, where Giotto and the Sienese school had achieved triumphs in elucidating relations of volume and space. Thus Bohemia, under the patronage of Charles IV, who even invited Italian artists such as Tommaso da Modena to his court, became a prominent artistic centre of the fourteenth century. The majesty of the *Glatzer Madonna* (Berlin Kaiser Friedrich-Museum, fourteenth century) is no longer due to linear rhythm, but to a new understanding of volume, whilst an increased interest in reality is seen in *The Birth of Christ* (Hohenfurth Stiftsgalerie), an actual shed being introduced into a landscape. Influences from the school of Prague were manifest in Bavaria and in the art of Meister Bertram of Hamburg. But soon the attention of German artists was directed towards the west, to Burgundy, where Italian form had been more thoroughly comprehended and absorbed. The alien iconographical schemes adopted by Bohemia were here dispensed with, whilst the structural truths underlying them provided the Burgundians with the means of clothing religious scenes naturalistically according to their own environment.

Amongst the artists whom Philip the Bold entrusted with the decoration of the Carthusian Monastery at Dijon was a certain Hermann de Coulogne, probably identical with Hermann Wynrich von Wesel, to whom must now be ascribed many of the works of the Cologne school of the fourteenth century formerly attributed to Meister Wilhelm. In spite of its contact with Burgundy, this German school, which during the earlier part of the century had favoured the delicately decorated and brilliantly coloured English manner, continued to produce a style deeply transfused with Gothic idealism. A lyric mood almost mystic in its simple piety pervades these paintings, which later aroused such enthusiasm among the nineteenth-century romanticists. Sometimes a tendency towards effeminacy is combined with power of expression, and *Die heilige Veronika* (Munich, Pinakothek, early fifteenth century) shows an emotional depth that raises it to an outstanding place in German art. Burgundian influences are more marked in the works of the Westphalian Konrad von Soest. In his *Crucifixion* at Nieder-Wildungen (1404) naturalism triumphs in the rendering of fashionable dress which enlivens the picture with rich contrast. But the bodies with their lack of plasticity, their spidery limbs, have a tapestry-like effect, and it is still the *linear* rhythm that predominates.

In Meister Franke of Hamburg, probably synonymous with Heuselin of Strassburg, we meet with an artist of true creative power. His strangely naïve fancy and dramatic expression are very German. In *altar panels* (in the Hamburger Kunsthalle) he was able, without the help of complex linear perspective, to produce an effect of depth in space rarely known at this time. The night hangs like a curtain spangled with stars where Mary kneels whitely radiant amidst the lonely wooded landscape, but the mantle with which the angels encircle her forms a cavern of living shadow. Archaic streamers with inscriptions flutter through the air, yet they grow small with the distance, and the face of God piercing the darkness is dimmed by fleeting clouds.

In the middle-Rhine district a worldly chivalric art is reflected in the joyous picture of the *Paradiesgärtlein* (c. 1420). The Madonna sits amidst the flowers and trees of a fair pleasaunce surrounded by her saintly company, who, clad in sumptuous robes, make music and converse. It seems more than probable that, as with a great deal of medieval art, we are here faced with Eastern influences which recall, even iconographically, Persian art and, more remotely, a vision of the Mazdaian paradise.

Courtly ideals manifest themselves in frescoes that decorate many a castle chamber of the period, more especially in the Tyrol, where influences from the south mingle wth others from north and west. Here in the castle of Runkelstein, near Bozen (Bolzano), the walls abound with scenes from the medieval romances of *Tristan and Isôt*, and *Garel*. Courtiers join with ladies in the swinging rhythm of the dance beneath orchard trees; or in the Adler Turm at Trent the artist's vision roams over meadow, hill, and stream accompanying knight and lady, peasant and labourer as they pursue the tasks or pastimes meted out to the various seasons. Again one is reminded of Persian miniatures.

In Swabia Lukas Moser, enjoying the patronage of the art-loving lords who foregathered at the Council of Constance, became acquainted with the ideals of Burgundian art, and was thus enabled to play an important part in furthering the development of German fifteenth-century naturalism. In the *Tiefenbronner Altar* of 1431 several incidents are combined to form a continuous narrative, so producing the effect of a unified panorama, whilst delight in descriptive detail is rendered artistic by an appreciation of texture and atmosphere which manifests itself especially in a sensibility to the beauty of rippling expanses of water beneath the light.

During the fifteenth century the altar rises to a supreme position in German art. A great winged structure, its decoration was entrusted solely either to the hands of the painter or else employed also the art of the sculptor in wood which, enclosed in the middle shrine, becomes visible when the painted wings are opened on feast-days. And now painting really begins to vie with sculpture, permeating naturalism with a monumentality and a power of expression which hitherto only statuary had known. No longer tempered by the chivalric ideal of 'diu mâze' the art that thrived under the burghers of the fifteenth century was impelled by a real German lust for individuality to a violent and often brutal realism, whilst passion for subjectivity finds release in overwrought fantasy. These tendencies, rising to a climax towards the end of the century, contribute with similar traits shown in architecture to the development of a late Gothic style that triumphs over foreign influences as a supreme expression of German feeling.

II

Prominent amongst German-speaking painters of the early fifteenth century, Konrad Witz, of Basel (1390/1400–1446/47), inspired by the master of Flémalle, dedicates himself to solving the problems of plastic form. A distinct aesthetic vision, a fine sense of selection dominate his interest in actuality, so that his paintings show a unity lacking in much art of the period. Witz sees the world in terms of volume. In the *Heiligspiegelaltar* (Basel) his stocky figures—carved they seem out of blocks of wood— advance with plodding stride or stand gesticulating like automatons. Every trace of the swinging rhythm of early Gothic has departed. Divining almost instinctively the laws of gravity and corporeal structure which were to become a science with the Renaissance, he conceives space as cubically measurable, achieving this effect not only by intersections but by light and shade and the use of reflection and cast shadow. Delicate tones are incorporated in his strong, rich colouring. In the landscape background of his *Fischzug Petri* (1444, Geneva Museum) these qualities enable him to realize in nature a beauty more deep than the fleeting impression. Yet, for all his interest in physical truth, the German love of the anaturalistic expressive line remains. In the *St Katharine and St Magdalene* (Strassburg) the draperies are filled with an abstract momentum. Fold piles itself upon fold, but the flowing curves of earlier Gothic are frozen to jagged crystalline formations. Similar tendencies are found at this time in the art of Bavaria and Nuremberg, which remains for the most part crude and primitive and suffers from overcrowding, though some paintings, in particular those of Hans Multscher and the Meister des Tucheraltars often possess dramatic feeling.

A very different spirit pervades the paintings of Stephan Lochner (+1451), who, leaving the Lake of Constance for the Lower Rhine, gave the traditional idealism and effeminacy of Cologne painting a new monumentality. The lucidity of design, the broad rhythm of light and shade that blends the figures to a harmonious unity, creating an illusion of space, fill the *Adoration* in Cologne Cathedral and the *Presentation in the Temple* (1447, Darmstadt) with a serene harmony.

During the second half of the fifteenth century the interest of German artists, directed towards the schools of Rogier van der Weyden and Dierick Bouts, enjoys an interlude of comparative ease. The thick-set figures of Witz and his followers are replaced by slender graceful types robed in thinner draperies, their livelier movement filling the wide landscape with a variety of detail and contrast. Thus in the *St George* (Lüneburg) of Hindrik Funhof of Hamburg the tessellated hall is open to the country-side, which abounds with incidents of secondary interest, whilst legendary content is subordinated to contemporary anecdote. In the *Crucifixion* (Munich, Pinakothek) of Hans Pleydenwurff (1420–72) of Nuremberg the scene is expanded beyond the crowd foregathered at the foot of the cross, and the white road by which these people must have come winds its way amongst hills towards the turrets and timbered houses of the little town. Or in the *Master of the Life of the Virgin Mary* an earnest matter-of-fact feeling and a predilection for green reminiscent of Bouts is allied to the delicate gleam of paint traditional in the Cologne school.

The last decades of the fifteenth century witness the division of German painting into countless local schools. In some, the lust for expression, lately suppressed by the happier Netherlandish naturalism, breaks forth with redoubled violence, revelling in anguished and chaotic form. The Bavarian and Franconian schools, particularly that of Dürer's master, Michael Wolgemut (1434–1519), tend towards what may be termed a baroque Gothic. To what tangled complexity it may lead the *Crucifixion* (Munich, Nationalmuseum) of Jan Pollack bears witness, whilst the power and dignity of an unknown Bavarian master's *Holy Trinity* (in Blutenburg) proves the grand possibilities of this style.

Italy, too, was at this time experiencing her baroque naturalism, and in the Tyrol the boundaries of north and south dissolve. The work of Michael Pacher (+1498) has much of the rock-hewn force of Mantegna. But the figures are more attenuated, the angularity of the draperies that throw up sharp edges of light reflects the style of the wood-carver, in which art this master equally excelled. Since Witz no German painter had so rejoiced in the glory of volume achieved by a scientific study of linear perspective which recognizes in space a factor as important as the human form. Theoretical knowledge helped Pacher to heighten the dramatic significance of a scene. Space is used as an emotional medium. In the *Cleansing of the Temple* (from the altar of St Wolfgang in Tyrol) the vast receding aisle seems indeed swept clean by the irate figure of Christ. The dynamic force with which the angel in the *Baptism* (ibid.) pierces the air was scarce seen again before the days of Tintoretto, whilst the group of pitchers in the *Wedding Feast at Cana* (ibid.) seem to hold a double miracle—suggesting almost twentieth-century cubism. And neither before nor since has an artist penetrated the depths of animal instinct as here in the *Adoration* (ibid.), where the light touching the haunches of the ox, the muzzle, the horns makes one slowly aware of the great beast which looms lost in dumb wonder from out the shadows of the stable whilst angels circle on bright wings above.

Marx Reichlich, another Tyrolese artist, concentrating his interest upon light, uses a strange chiaroscuro as emotional element, whilst Rueland Frueauf of Salzburg and his son (who seems sometimes to foreshadow the fairy-tale art of Schwind) incline to a quieter style practised in Swabia under Hans Schuchlin and Bartholomäus Seitblom. In strongest contrast to the violent passion of Bavarian late fifteenth-century art stands the gentle beauty of Martin Schongauer's painting (1445–91), which, inspired though it be by Rogier van der Weyden, became impregnated through the artist's personality with a spirit essentially German. In the exquisite *Maria im Rosenhag* (1473, Colmar) a supreme sense of form enables him to transfuse northern delight in detail with spiritual depth. A simple scene—Mary and the Child seated before a garden fence where birds perch amongst rose-briars and wild strawberries grow at the Madonna's feet. But the great swinging draperies with their impenetrable chasms of gloom rise sheer as rock, enclosing in their dark pyramid the bright surfaces of naked flesh, the melodious interchange of contrasted rhythm in the limbs, whilst above, two angels bearing a gigantic cross darken the sunlit air.

In his engravings Schongauer abandons himself to the decorative vagaries beloved of the late Gothic. But the very irrationality of design, the negation of organic construction, tends in the *Flight into Egypt* to render the playful work of the angels more convincing where the tree bends beneath their weightlessness. Those unaccustomed to German form may not realize perhaps that the design to which *Christ on the Mount of Olives* is subordinated has more than an ornamental value. The outline which, provided by the figure of Christ, may be traced again in the group combining the rock and the apostles, and once more in the silhouette of the tree, is based on no aesthetic norm of symmetry, but on an emotional motif born of the picture's spiritual content, the motif of supplication. In the *Carrying of the Cross* an ever-swelling rhythm manifests itself as a sequence of intricately studied detail and incident, even as the late Gothic church, abandoning itself to the dynamic energy of space, demands simultaneously the elaboration of each part. But no harmonious composition of well-proportioned figures could have rendered so convincing the tumultuous clamour and ruthless pressure of the mob, nor the weariness of the interminable climb up the hill. Those who have once realized the power of German art to translate emotion into immediate design will scarcely speak of formlessness and illustration. They will understand also why the graphic arts with their double possibility of detailed characterization and absolute expression rose to a supreme independence in Central Europe, whilst in Italy they remained as studies from nature and compositional schemes for the most part subservient to the monumental arts.

III

But Gothic art had run its course and betrays even in Schongauer a tendency to fall into decadence or effeminacy, and once again German art stood in dire need of that will to clearer vision and more objective thought which reasserts itself from time to time as a curb to subjective emotion. In the renaissance of the classic ideal in Italy it discovered a means of salvation, and simultaneously a new danger. That it did not share the doom of Netherlandish Romanism, and sink into slavish subjection to an alien form, is primarily due to the individuality of Albrecht Dürer (1471–1528). Knowledge gained in two journeys to Italy urged him to no repudiation of national tradition but spurred on an inherent longing for a regeneration of German art. And indeed the name Reformation might lead to fewer misunderstandings of early sixteenth-century art in Central Europe than the designation Renaissance with its suggestion of Italian classic form. Even now the ideal of perfect beauty, of an aesthetic norm, proved less interesting to the German than the old quest of individual truth. Only a new comprehension of the laws of anatomical structure and monumental design enable him to express his aims with greater conviction than before. The acute thoroughness with which Dürer applied himself to the study of those problems which seemed so easily solved in Italy is characteristically northern. His own words, 'die Schönheit herausreissen aus der Natur', betray an attitude towards nature different from that which seeks to build up ideally proportioned landscapes. Dürer's very knowledge of the structure and growth of tree and plant help him to render them overwhelmingly individual.

In the *St Michael*, from the woodcut series of the Apocalypse, an understanding of movement gives the furious onslaught of the Archangel a dramatic vigour hitherto unknown. Yet Dürer, as his engraving and painting of *Adam and Eve* betray, was lured also to seek the norm of corporeal beauty. But characteristically his interest in the aesthetic problem is imbued with the semi-ethical aim of recovering that original beauty which man was forced to relinquish at his Fall. The idealistic Christ-like *Self-portrait* in Munich has a vertical tension, a realism in the nervous fingers utterly remote from the worldly self-assurance of Raphael's *gran' signori*. In the engraving *Knight, Death and the Devil*, a formal problem that Donatello, Verrocchio, and Leonardo had loved, the relation of horse to rider in an equestrian group is permeated in Dürer's case with a symbolic meaning—the *miles Christianus* who rides on his way undaunted by the grim perils that beset his path. Or again in the woodcut *Christ's Farewell to His Mother*, a motif of antithesis—complex movement versus simple rest—is used as a direct emotional element. The figure of Jesus, whose calm resolution is expressed in strict finality of design and noble swing of draperies, affords a poignant contrast to the broken body of Mary, in whose robe the anaturalistic Gothic line writhes as though quickened by the anguish of her soul. The classic ideal of balance between vertical and horizontal plays a primary part in the design of the renowned engraving *Melancholia*. But simultaneously the sudden diagonal of the ladder, the menacing poise of the crystalline block, the ponderous pose of the woman herself change calm to an atmosphere of oppressiveness and paralysing gloom.

Expressive form is used by Dürer to render even the simplest intimate scene. Thus an almost classic design, in which lucidity of plastic form is intensified by brilliant light, creates an atmosphere of serenity where *St Jerome* sits in his study surrounded by his beasts. Or the crisp lines of the woodcut fill many a scene from the *Life of the Virgin Mary* with the hum of household activity.

Not always are expression and form transfused to a perfect unity. Dürer's great improvements on the technique of the woodcut enabled him to produce an illusion of plasticity that lent itself to the creation of a more formal representative style, and we may sometimes regret the loss of unrestrained imaginative force that distinguished his earlier works. This tendency is especially evident in his paintings. But where monumentality is the direct means of intensifying emotion Dürer's work in this branch of art can stand side by side with that of the Italians. The *portraits* of his later years, which in their magnificently controlled form seem to reflect the iron character of the men who stood on the threshold of the Reformation, the *Rosenkranzmadonna*, with its atmosphere of mingled joy and gravity, the panels with the *Four Apostles* where the suppressed rage in the countenance of St Paul seems echoed in tumultuous dissonances locked within the precipices of his mantle —all these are emblems of what this art, which sacrifices sensual beauty to expressive power, may achieve—the will of German classicism made manifest.

That passion for unrestrained imaginative emotion, which in Dürer's case is curbed by a tendency towards scientific objectivity and moral discipline, breaks forth as a flood of subjectivity in the painting of his contemporary Matthias Grünewald (c. 1480–1528). Neither before nor since was the *Crucifixion* portrayed with so overwhelming a truth as on the tremendous panels of the Isenheimer Altar in Colmar. Yet reality as perceived by the eye or the laws of reason is utterly ignored. The scourged body that looms gigantic from the impenetrable darkness of night bears proportionally no relation to the remaining figures. Its size is symbol, is fulfilment of the prophecy proclaimed by the hand of the Baptist—'Illum oportet crescere me autem minui'. The infinite linearity in the folds of the Magdalene's robe defies all possibility. But no plastic form could have rendered so convincing this utter abandonment to grief—a supreme contrast to the white rigidity of the other Mary who, in her agony, seems frozen to stone.

Grünewald beheld in the theme of the *Resurrection* (ibid.) not, like most Italians and even Dürer, an opportunity for anatomic corporeal representation, but a chance for dramatically supernatural expression—the annihilating force of the miracle. A broad treatment of paint, very different from Dürer's linear plasticity, adds to the passionate quality of his style, and the changing surfaces of brilliant colour follow the process of transubstantiation as the figure of Christ soaring upwards is dissolved in blinding light. As to Jörg Ratgeb's presentation of the same subject-matter in the Herrenberg altar (commissioned in 1517), see A. Burkhard's monograph 1965, Cambridge, Mass. U.S.A. For Grünewald light has more than a rational significance. As a magic element it can fill the earth with ecstatic vision. In the *Christmas* (ibid.) the angel's music seems light made audible—we can understand the conception of the nineteenth-century romanticists, 'ich höre das Licht'. It is the substance of which the heavenly beings are born who, swept downward upon the fiery flood like leaves on the wind. bear the news to the amazed shepherds. Blue mountain, lake, and stream, the roses of that strange landscape are transfused with its glory, where the Madonna sits unaware of the miracle wrapt in contemplation of her Child.

In the background of this picture, and still more in that of *St Paul and St Anthony in the Desert* (ibid.) we may study Grünewald's attitude towards nature—a strange pantheistic conception in which bird and beast, rock and plant, seem to lose their individual existence, and, intertwined to a pattern almost Chinese, merge in the infinite rhythm of being. Here, and in some small engraving or tinted sketch of Dürer's—*Christmas* or the *Madonna amongst many Animals*—, the landscape or architectural environment begins to assert its importance over the figures, a natural development of northern art which was never bound to the anthropomorphic conceptions of the south. But these, and yet more the romantic landscapes of Albrecht Altdorfer (1480?–1538), Wolf Huber (c. 1490–1553), and the School of the Danube reflect a conception of nature far removed from the objective naturalism that had flourished beneath the influence of the Netherlands. The ruins and grottoes, the primeval trees trailing long strands of moss which form a background to incidents from the Old Testament or to legends of the saints provide the principal emotional element in the picture, awakening a particular

Stimmung. In Altdorfer's *Birth of the Virgin Mary* (Munich, Pinakothek) the vast spaces of vault and aisle with their intricate intersections and play of light and shadow defying the clear construction and perspective beloved of the Italian are the means of
filling a quaint *genre*-scene with an atmosphere of heavenly fes-
tivity. Here the figurative motif of the circling garland of angels is
still used to accentuate the dynamic quality of space, but in the
Birth of Christ (Vienna) the figures seem inwoven in the snow-
bound darkness of the winter night by countless threads of light
cast from the divine radiance above. The white war-horse that
bears the black-mailed knight in his *St George* (Munich) scarce
treads the tangled undergrowth of the wood but hangs as though
suspended before the impenetrable wall of foliage that rises sheer
as a chasm to the edge of the picture frame—a forest perilous,
opening as through a rift in the rock to the blue distance. No
organic construction, no clear relation of volume and space is
here, even the trunks of the trees have no plasticity, and the
minute figures are but a point of light accentuating the oppressive
density of the leaves. So Altdorfer foreshadows the nineteenth-
century romanticists, beholding a landscape neither as a monumental composition nor as a foil to the actions of human beings,
but as a fragment of the infinite in which man sees reflected his
own mood. These tendencies, allied to a wild fantasy, find a perfect medium of expression in woodcut and chiaroscuro drawing
in which curling white lines and dark shadows cover tinted paper
with calligraphic swiftness, subordinating figure and environment
to a single rhythm. The same technique gives the figures of
Witches and *Death* beloved of Hans Baldung Grien (1480?-1565)
a terrible intensity. In his paintings strangely fantastic conceptions and mannerisms are rendered exquisite by a delicate Gothic
ideal of beauty and a rare sensitiveness to colour and texture.
Unforgettable are the white body of the woman, the pearl-grey
snake against the mossy darkness of trees in the *Allegory of Wisdom*
(1529, Munich, Pinakothek), or the blue velvet that gleams
jewel-like from the darkness of the *Birth of Christ* (Frankfurt), a
perfect foil to the bemused face and the long Gothic hands bathed
in that extraordinary concentration of light. In the *High Altar of
Freiburg Cathedral* (1513-17) Baldung revels in the complexities of
late Gothic design both in the composition of the paintings and in
labyrinthine entanglement of decorative wood-carving. But

passionate abandonment to movement was never rendered so expressive as in the master's woodcut of the *Ascension,* where the body of Christ, whirled by cherubs through the clouds, arouses a sense of immeasurable dynamic space.

Heavenly and profane elements intermingle with charming incongruity in the art of Lukas Cranach (1472–1553). But the naïve sensuality of the allegories in which he delights have little in common with the sublime detachment of the classic. These Venuses, Dianas, and Graces are porcelain-like figures with tripping feet and piquant gestures. These lemon groves and glades of laurel open on German meadows and pine-woods. Cranach lacks an understanding for monumental structure. Nature is for him an earthly *Paradise* (Kunsthistorisches Museum, Vienna), that holds a thousand infinitesimal wonders for the artist to discover. Master of gleaming surfaces, he models the figures of his maidens in tones of mother-of-pearl and bluish shadows, draping them with diaphanous veils. Watching animal life, he discovers the sleek beauty of fur and hide. He rejoices in the coolness of marble, the spring's crystal, the translucency of tranquil water, the gleaming pebble, the jewel-like flower. His woodcuts with their impetuous line strike a graver note, as also the portraits of those earnest pioneers of the Reformation who were his friends.

How inadequately the name renaissance fits German art of the sixteenth century may well be felt in reviewing the work of these painters. Each of them may betray at times a tendency to succumb to foreign influence, but classic form in the Italian sense is far more evident in the lesser artists of this period, in the last works of Hans Holbein the Elder, in Kulmback, Schäufelein, and Burgkmair, where, unassimilated, it at times produces a cold and barren atmosphere. But a continuous reassertion of old traditions, evident in the engravings and woodcuts of Beham, and especially in the passionate and graphic art of Urs Graf, and in the manneristic fantasies of Niklaus Manuel Deutsch and Hans Leu, saves German art from falling into dead formalism.

In Hans Holbein the Younger (1497–1543) a will to simplification of form, born of an inner necessity, manifests itself in the astounding objectivity of such portraits as *Robert Cheseman* (The Hague), where the austerity of design is heightened by the severe background with its inscription in antiqua. So sure is his sense of form that his German love of characteristic detail results, as in the

Ambassadors Jean de Diuteville and Georges de Selva (London National Gallery), in no loss of unity, whilst the warm glow of his colour renders hard construction sensuously palpable in the portrait of his *Wife and Children*. In the *Madonna with the Burgomaster Jakob Meyer* (Darmstadt), Holbein was able to build a formal composition with an ease Dürer had struggled in vain to achieve. The cartoons for the wall-paintings in the Basler Rathaus (1530) show a monumentality akin to Raphael's permeated by northern vigour. Yet in this objective mind lived also an urge for freer dramatic expression, and in his decorative designs for the *Haus zum Tanz* and the *Londoner Stahlhof* fancy runs riot in music, revel, and dance, whilst in the woodcut series of the *Totentanz* it abandons itself to the grim rhythm of death.

Thus during the first decades of the sixteenth century, German art alone was worthy, by its very independence, to stand beside the High Renaissance of Italy. In the succeeding period, Central Europe, like the other countries, fell beneath the sway of the so-called 'decadence'. Yet here again earlier German mannerism, visible in the last works of Cranach and Baldung Grien, has a *raffinement* very different from the lifeless schematism of much painting of the Italian Late Renaissance, and the artificial movements of these tightly modelled figures, whose enamel-like flesh gleams with ribbons and jewels, is subordinate to a linear rhythm that suggests the name Gothic rococo. Later German painting under Tobias Stimmer, Christoph Schwarz, Johann Rottenhammer and others sinks to the level of an eclecticism common to the rest of Europe. But it is significant that where mannerism was understood not as mere formalism, but as a reaction against representation and the pagan sensuality of the Renaissance, Italian artists, Pontormo and even Tintoretto, turn to Germany to find in Dürer's rendering of Christ before Pontius Pilate motifs of psychological interest. Nor must it be forgotten that Germany had long before produced her El Greco in Matthias Grünewald.

The long years of comparative sterility that followed the German Renaissance were shadowed by the Thirty Years War. And where the northern countries once more gave birth to a great era of painting, the field of activity had changed to the Netherlands. Yet a true understanding of the art of Rubens and Rembrandt is impossible unless we recognize therein the legacy of Dürer and Holbein, of Grünewald and Altdorfer, the Germanic spirit that, once more transfusing foreign ideals with its own feeling, produced a seventeenth-century art very different from that of the south. However, the immediate incentive, the development of Italian baroque, cannot be negated, and amongst the mediators between southern and northern art tribute must be paid to the German Adam Elsheimer (1578–1610). Consorting in Rome with the circle of Annibale Carracci, he played an important part in the development of the ideal landscape of the seventeenth century in which the artist, breaking with the anthropomorphic conceptions of the Renaissance, seeks to attain unity between man and the cosmos. Central Europe had dreamed of some such idea long before; but, whereas Altdorfer abandons himself to a vague romantic dream of infinity, the baroque painter strives by a formal process of subordination to bring all parts into relation with the whole. Colour and light, freed from their dependence on the plastic object, become primary elements in design. A partiality for unbroken colour prevents Elsheimer from achieving altogether the baroque ideal, but his tree landscapes with their diagonal division of the picture-plane foreshadow Claude Lorraine; night-scenes such as the *Flight into Egypt* (Munich and Vienna), with their dimly lit figures merged in the vast expanse of nature, suggest the art of Rembrandt, whilst his compositions of interiors were adopted by Adriaen Brouwer and other exponents of Netherland genre.

Towards the end of the seventeenth and during the eighteenth centuries the art of Central Europe experienced a resurrection, not in painting, which under the historian of art Joachim Sandrart and others remained the slave of eclecticism, but in music and architecture. In the southern German territories, under the influence of the Counter Reformation, the tremendous dream of the baroque found its consummation in church and palace. In Central Europe alone, where the late Gothic had wrestled against finite plasticity, was the architect able to abandon himself utterly to the inebriation of space. Whilst in Rome the interior decorations of Andrea Pozzo and the virtuosi of false perspectives still betray vestiges of plastic isolation of form, those of the Brothers Asam, their pupil Matthäus Günther, Johann Zick, and Franz Anton Maulpertsch emulate rather the rococo of Tiepolo, who himself worked in Germany. Confronted by this worldly-mystic art, born of the spirit of St Ignatius of Loyola and St Teresa, of the ecstatic sublimation of the sensual, the senses reel, unable to distinguish between earth and heaven. Here every rational boundary is dissolved; architecture, sculpture, and painting flow to one inseparable harmony; and space is audible as music.

(to be continued in following volume)

INDEX

Personal names and the more important German place-names